DESIGNERS

Marie Wallin • Kaffe Fassett • Martin Storey
Erika Knight • Sarah Dallas • Brandon Mably
Grace Melville • Lisa Richardson • Amanda Crawford
Jennie Atkinson • Sarah Hatton

INCLUDES 46 DESIGNS

ROWAN

EDITOR'S LETTER

The collections this season from the Rowan team have a certain tranquillity and calmness about them. The last year has been challenging for most of us on both a national and global level and it is therefore even more uplifting than ever to escape into the world of fantasy through the layers of imagination displayed in the new Rowan magazine. Even though the colours used in the magazine are of a pale and pastel hue we have introduced some bright and vibrant new shades as highlights to the existing palettes

There are as always three stories. Two of the stories are shot in Mallorca using the backdrop of Deia and Sineu's ancient cobbled streets and elegant sandstone buildings. You can almost feel the heat and atmosphere of those long forgotten summer days. The third story was shot very simply in a studio to launch the first of our essential collections. I believe it showcases all the key shapes and textures on trend, styled in a more accessible way in naturals, white and creams. This will hopefully allow your own creativity to be set free and for you to create your own colour combinations.

My personal favourites this season have to be the 'Unwind Wrap' by Kaffe, I love the way he has used the Summer Tweed and Kidsilk Haze together in this simple striped design. Also 'Wonder' the long cardigan by Martin Storey is such a timeless piece in terms of its versatility, it would not look out of place at either a formal wedding or on an alfresco stroll.

Within the magazine there is an interesting article about 'Make Do and Mend'. How attitudes have changed to handy work and its place in society. There is also a fantastic article showcasing the talent at the Royal College of Art. The students were set a challenge to approach sustainability in a more conceptual way and create a capsule range of hand knitted or crocheted garments which reflect their own personal view of sustainability. Judging by the results, they have really risen to the challenge and have created some very individual statements. Finally and following on from last season we have asked the master textile artist himself Kaffe Fassett to create art pieces and homeware from his knitted designs. I believe these art pieces either framed or made into cushions and throws would make wonderful heirloom pieces for all to enjoy from generation to generation.

As always I do hope that all of you will find a design or an idea in our magazine that will truly inspire you and that you will enjoy knitting, wearing or having around your home.

Kate Buller

Kate Buller
Rowan Brand Manager

ON THE COVER
Foxtail by Martin Storey
Photographer Peter Christian Christensen
Stylist Marie Wallin
Hair & Make-up Carol Morley (One Photographic)
Model Beth Brown (Premier Model Management)

Rowan Brand Manager Kate Buller
Rowan Head Designer Marie Wallin
Design Room Manager David MacLeod
Publications Co-ordinator Paul Calvert
Rowan Junior Designer Grace Melville
Graphic Designer James Knapton
Pattern Co-ordinator Lisa Richardson
Yarn & Photoshoot Co-ordinator Ann Hinchliffe
Garment Co-ordinator Gemma Saxon
Knitting Co-ordinator Andrea McHugh
Garment finishing Lisa Parnaby & Pauline Ellis

Rowan Magazine Design Layout Simon Wagstaff

Sales Manager Emma Mychajlowskyj
Consumer Manager Emma Wood

With special thanks to the following handknitters:
Wendy Stevens, Helen Ardley, Jenny Cooper, Joan Broadbent, Andrea McHugh, Ros Miller, Audrey Kidd, Elizabeth Jones, Marjorie Pickering, Ella Taylor, Clare Landi, Helen Dawson, Diane Armstrong, Cynthia Noble, Pauline Ellis, Ann Banks, Janet Oakey, Paula Dukes, Honey Ingram, Susan Grimes, Elsie Eland, Teresa Gogay, Margaret Morris, Elizabeth Jones, Jean Fletcher, Sandra Richardson, Jean Goslin, Wendy Shipman, Jyoti More, Lorrainne Hearn, Yvonne Rawlinson, Marie Wallin, Sandra Taylor, Judith Chamberlain, Janet Mann, Jane Duffy

First published in Great Britain in 2010 by Rowan Yarns Ltd.
Green Lane Mill,
Holmfirth,
West Yorkshire,
England,
HD9 2DX
E-mail: mag49@knitrowan.com

British Library Cataloguing in Publication Data
Rowan Yarns.
Rowan Knitting & Crochet Magazine Number 49
ISSN 2045-340X

Copyright Rowan 2010
Printed in the UK by Hague
Reprographics by Gloss Solutions

CONTENTS

ROWAN

illusion

Inspired by the ghostly atmospheres
of fragile, time worn Mediterranean
hill top villages, ILLUSION is a very
feminine, delicate collection of exquisite
knits. The collection combines fine
antique lace, crochet and ethereal
openwork with the soft colouring of
powdered neutrals and spectral greys.

FANTASY
Purelife Organic Cotton 4 ply
Marie Wallin
🧶 147

ILLUSION WRAP
Purelife Organic Cotton 4 ply
Marie Wallin
150

ALLURE
Purelife Organic Cotton 4 ply
Lisa Richardson
106

WONDER
Fine Milk Cotton
Martin Storey
108

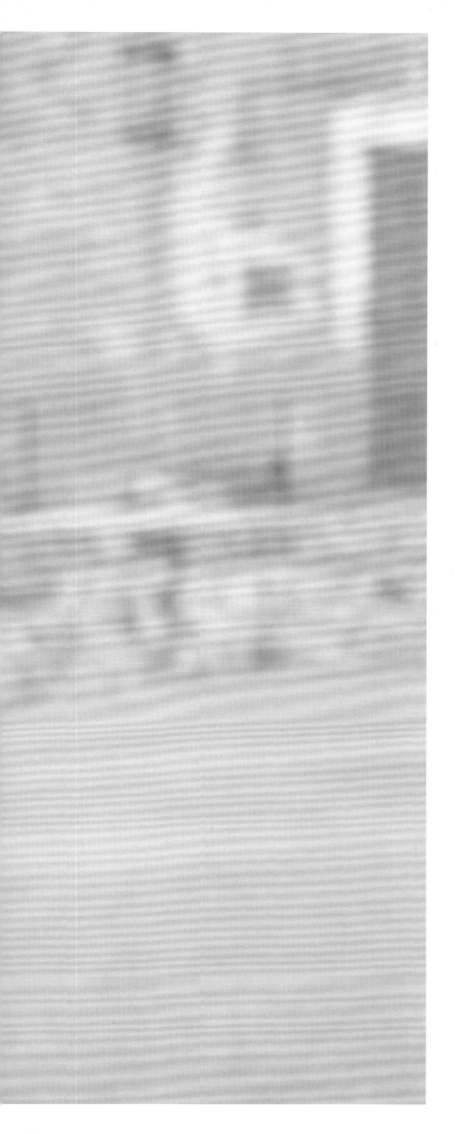

DAYDREAM
Purelife Organic Cotton 4 ply
Marie Wallin
🧶 101

BEWITCH
Fine Milk Cotton
Grace Melville

111

Photographer: Sheila Rock. **Styling:** Marie Wallin. **Hair & Make Up:** Carol Morley (One Photographic). **Art Direction:** Marie Wallin.
Model: Bronte (Select Model Management). **Location:** Deia and Sineu, Mallorca. Many thanks to Cem and Olaf from Watson Production, Palma de Mallorca.

Rowan design awards
sustainability

Words by Dr Margy Cockburn. Photography by Peter Christian Christensen

Sustainability – 'stain', 'taint', 'bliss' and 'sun' all lurk in that word somewhere, and that pretty much covers the range of reactions from London's Royal College of Art Fashion & Textile students who rose to Rowan's Award 2010 challenge to 'approach sustainability in a more conceptual way and create a capsule range of hand-knitted or crochet garments which reflect your own personal view of sustainability.'

Some dwelt on the things under threat from our mindless assumption that natural resources can be endlessly tapped, cheap labour unthinkingly exploited and waste products unceremoniously dumped. Some were determined to be part of the solution to balancing human needs with what the world can provide, by checking they source materials only from companies with ethical production methods (and Rowan's Purelife range is leading the way there!). Others eschewed the whole idea of 'fast' fashion in favour of an heirloom approach and making beautiful things that last. Given the UK alone, buys 2 million tonnes of textiles each year, most of which ends up in landfill, that's a fair place to start.

One, recognising that consumers, who use millions of gallons of water, oceans of detergent and megawatts of electricity in laundering their clothes, are also a big part of the problem, came up with a design that practically cuts out washing!

Read on…

Using Rowan Purelife Organic Cotton DK, 4 ply and Revive the students have designed five very special garments incorporating very different techniques such as Tunisian Crochet, Slip Stitching and Dip Dyeing.

Purelife Organic Cotton DK & 4 ply

Maria Kamper

Royal College of Art - MA Fashion Knitwear (Womenswear).

Maria has very clear ideas on the ethics of production: "I am very focussed on using natural fibres that are developed under good, honest circumstances, using a natural approach. It's really important that we are aware of how polluting the textile industry is and we all take steps, even small ones, to change the situation. One of the most important issues is to protect the people who work in the industry – the dyers in Morocco and India, or the knitters in China."

And, a woman of her word, she went straight into her kitchen and started experimenting with the colours that can be achieved using beetroot and onions. "I think you should just try dyeing with the things you have in your house - I wonder if coffee would work..!" Recognising what happens to garments in the hands of the owner can be quite as environmentally damaging as the processes involved in production – we use megawatts of

energy, oceans of water and gallons of detergent in caring for our garments - Maria had the perfect solution: "I think things can look more beautiful the dirtier they are, they develop a sort of patina. I will design things so, if they get a bit worn-looking, then you can just turn them inside out or over-dye them again."

Maria's designs are inspired by a tribal feel and play on contrast - chunky knit to very fine, open work that reveals a bit of skin underneath; close-fitting garments worn under a much looser, less constructed top-garment; flat knits livened up with textured fringing. And all laundry shy!

Purelife Revive and Purelife Organic Cotton DK & 4 ply

Catherine Tremellen

Royal College of Art - MA Textiles.

Catherine's take on the theme was to immerse herself in one of the natural environments under threat from our profligacy. She headed off to the rain forest. Well… Kew Gardens, the closest London has to offer. She prowled through the glass houses, navigated the aerial walkways and found her inspiration in the forms and colours around her – lush blue-green hues; lacy shadows cast by light filtering through the canopy; the delicacy of fern fronds.

Armed with a pile of photographs she set out to test her conviction that 'you can do absolutely anything with hand knitting". And succeeded! Using an intricate mix of structured stitches and crochet, Catherine somehow managed to knit dappled sunlight and achieve a camouflage effect with a delicacy a million miles from anything military.

"Fashion is seen as being about consumption, the opposite of sustainability, but it doesn't have to be throw-away. People are becoming interested in how things are made and where they come from, so they can check the processes involved aren't environmentally damaging. Maybe we should have a picture of the farmer/grower on each garment to connect people with where the materials come from?" That might be some time coming but, if you get your hands on a design by Catherine Tremellen, you certainly won't be in a hurry to throw it away!

Lucy Faulke

Royal College of Art – MA Textiles.

Lucy knew exactly where to go to get some answers on how to be more sustainable. "Insects are doing it right!" she declared and, while explaining that termite mounds can teach you all you need to know about natural air ventilation, produced a sketch book full of dragonflies, wing details and insect dwellings, reflecting perfectly her twin interests – the natural world and architectural structures.

She then put a couple of honeycombs on the table, knitted, of course: "I used cord, made with a 'Knitting Nancy', and supported with metal rings. I did try using recycled elastic bands but they didn't hold the shape well enough."

Some wonderfully fine pieces of lacy knit followed: "I've used hair-pin lace, Tunisian crochet and Solomon knots. I really like to construct things using a mix of knots and loops and I've learnt some new techniques for this project." She then left the insect world for a moment and recognised the impracticality of going out wearing only . . . a wing!

"This" she declared, indicating a sample of very intricate and open crochet, "could be a bit daring; you might have to wear it over a body stocking."

Her fascination with how structures are formed then displayed itself in some elegant columnar designs evoking an African Goddess/tribal feel. "I don't want the current interest in sustainability to be a fad. We've got to really buy into its importance and always make informed choices on the materials we use in our designs."

Guided by that principle, focussing on the world of insects and accepting an eclectic approach to technique, Lucy is likely to provide some inspiration all her own.

Purelife Organic Cotton DK & 4 ply

Victoria Hill

Royal College of Art – MA Fashion Knitwear (Womenswear).

Victoria leapt straight into what people will be wearing in the future – it turned out to be a sort of stylishly revamped version of the bag-lady!

"I was attracted to the whole idea of different lifestyles - how people might become very local and self-sufficient or might be continually moving around, the modern version of the traveller. So I started thinking of nomads, gypsies, and the patterns they use. I tried to put those patterns into 3-D relief by using different stitches together so the garment would end up like a big sampler.

Then I thought how important it would be to take everything with you, so I came up with the idea of pockets. Loads of pockets - pockets within pockets, hidden pockets, pockets that could work as hoods. And then I liked the idea of adorning yourself with things you might need on the journey – ropes and lanyards, bits of leather, things you found on the way. And I would want all these bits to be an integral part of the garment, not just added on to it as an afterthought. Then I experimented with macramé – the bigger it got the more I liked it. And that could be used to develop pockets on top of pockets to store even more things!

You could experiment with a plain yoke and some lacy bits on the main body - sort of reworking the apron but for a 'housewife' that travels around and wants functionality and elegance married together." And sustainability built in!

Purelife Organic Cotton DK

30

Purelife Organic Cotton DK,
Handknit Cotton, Kidsilk Haze

Hannah Taylor

Royal College of Art - MA Fashion Knitwear
(Menswear).

Hannah sat down and immediately the table
was full of lengths of I-cord in pinks and
purples; a selection of tassels and chunky,
textured knits; a sketch book that started with a
volcano in full flow, cantered past over-sized
tropical forests and ended with a wheelie bin
stuffed to the gunnels and, sitting engagingly to
one side, a small, knitted, panda with huge blue
eyes. She blamed it all on her Dad!

"I thought of sustainability, then recycling, then
the fact that my Dad just won't do it and still
insist on throwing everything in one bin. So I
decided we needed some eco warriors to get
people to recycle. That made me think of

Robin Hood, which led to the forests where
he lived, then to jungles and the animals
endangered by the size of our carbon footprint,
the emissions of an erupting volcano which
outstrips 100-fold anything we do, global
warming that will result in global cooling, and
how that means, although this project was
aimed at Spring/Summer designs, that could
end up meaning Autumn/Winter ones. (There
was, in truth, quite a lot in between but space
and the speed of my short-hand intervened!)

Hannah's entire romp through the topic of
sustainability – what we have to sustain, why
we need to sustain it and how we can do so –

is deliberately done with her tongue very
firmly in her cheek. "I think it's good to have a
bit of a sense of humour because that can draw
attention to things!"

And attention she will get. Her knits are
oversized, 3-D, with chunked-up patterns; entire
knitted gardens are incorporated (using pom-
poms for trees); balaclavas appear in the guise of
animal faces; dreadlocks hang from the balaclavas;
solar panels are incorporated into the garment to
provide an adjustable microclimate and a collection
of soft animals peep out of the melee. She lets her
wit run wild and her designs both ask the
question and provide clues to some answers.

summer essentials

is a collection of the key shapes
and textures on trend, designed
into more simple, easy to wear styles
that will compliment the season's
ESSENTIAL looks. Photographed
in the neutral colours of white,
cream, pale grey and stone, this
collection is a blank canvas on which
to play with colour.

THE
OPEN
TEXTURE
TOP

GENTIAN
Siena 4 ply
Grace Melville
123

THE
LADDER
STITCH
TUNIC

CLEAVERS
Lenpur™ Linen
Erika Knight
124

CICELY
Cotton Glacé
Grace Melville
127

THE
LITTLE
STRIPE
CARDIGAN

LOBELIA
Cotton Glacé
Sarah Dallas
🧶134

THE
SIMPLE
TEE

TEASEL
Lenpur™ Linen
Sarah Hatton
104

HONESTY
Siena 4 ply
Marie Wallin
🧶 133

THE
CUT
AWAY
SLEEVE

HELLEBORE
Cotton Glacé
Martin Storey
113

THE
LOOSE
KNIT
TUNIC

CAMPION
Siena 4 ply
Marie Wallin
119

THE BANDEAU WRAP

CHARITY
Siena 4 ply
Marie Wallin
🧶125

BALSAM
Lenpur™ Linen
Lisa Richardson
🧶120

PIMPERNEL
Kidsilk Haze
Martin Storey
🧶 117

THE
MESH
HANKERCHIEF

Photographer:
Peter Christian Christensen.
Styling: Marie Wallin.
Hair & Make Up:
Carol Morley (One Photographic).
Art Direction: Marie Wallin.
Model:
Beth Brown
(Premier Model Management).

GHOST
Siena 4 ply
Amanda Crawford
🧶 105

at home
with kaffe

Photography by Moy Williams.

Due to the popularity of the 'Kaffe's Summer House' feature in Magazine 47, we decided to ask Kaffe to create another collection of homeware designed in his own unique and inimitable style. Knitted exclusively in Purelife Revive and Rowan Cotton Glacé and photographed at a beautiful converted water mill in Wiltshire, this striking collection of cushions, art pieces and a throw will add plenty of drama, interest and style to any interior.

Left
Jumping Jack Cushion knitted in Cotton Glacé

Right
Triangle Squares Cushion knitted in Purelife Revive and Cotton Glacé

Left
Bubbles Art knitted in Purelife Revive

Below
Polka Dot Patches Art knitted in Purelife
Revive and Cotton Glacé

Heatwave Throw
knitted in
Purelife Revive
and Cotton Glacé

58

Above
Scully Stripe Art knitted
in Purelife Revive and
Cotton Glacé

Right
Heatwave Throw,
Jumping Jack Cushion
and Triangle Squares
Cushion

make do and mend

Words by Dr Kate Davies

Knitting is an investment both of time and money. And as every knitter knows, this investment has a payoff: there is nothing like the satisfaction of completing a beautiful hand-made sweater. But who wants to see their investment unravel or fall prey to the ravages of moths? Knitters generally take the long view, and want to create a well-finished garment, which, with proper care, and the occasional darn, might see several years of wear. Attitudes to the 'plain work' of thrifty knitting have shifted dramatically over time.

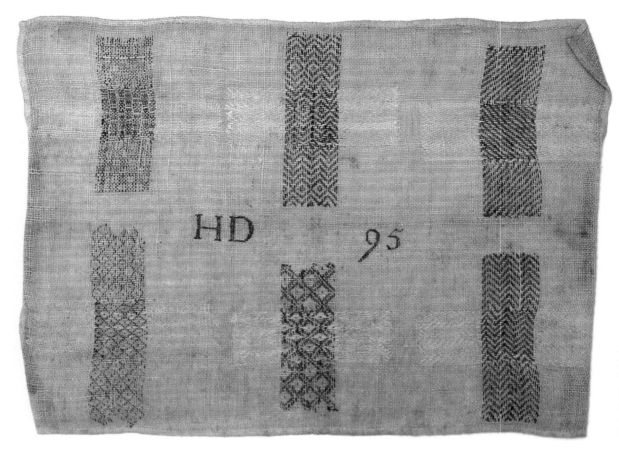

Left
Damask Darning sampler by 'HD' (1795). Reproduced from Carol Humprey's quaker school girl samplers (Needleprint, 2006), © Ackworth School Estates.

Three hundred years ago, textiles were precious things. An ordinary suit of clothes might be an individual's most expensive possession; a woollen coat would be expected to last through five or more winters, and knitted stockings were routinely darned, unravelled, and remade. Court accounts of eighteenth-century thefts reveal that textiles were identified by their mended areas. In this era, darns and patches were like birthmarks, lending clothes distinct personalities.

But if a darn was a garment's identity card, it might also be regarded as a badge of poverty. In the early 1800s, Benjamin Shaw of Dent recalled, with some exasperation, his wife's attitude to plain work: "instead of mending the children's clothes, she bought new ones. Her common saying was that she did not wish to appear poor." As an aspirant married woman, Mrs Shaw felt that mending was beneath her, and her attitude is echoed in nineteenth-century fiction. Though adept with their needles, Jane Austen's heroines are only ever depicted embroidering: plain work was seen as the business of women with few social expectations. Alongside learning to read and write, the girls of Ackworth School in Yorkshire (who came from Quaker families "not in affluence") were taught to darn and knit—activities from which they might later expect to derive an income. By today's standards, the Ackworth girls were exceptionally skilled needlewomen, and evidence that plain work is not plain at all can be

seen in their beautiful darning samplers, preserved in the school archives.

It is notable that the first knitting manuals do not include instructions for plain work. While Jane Gaugain's Lady's Assistant (1847) might teach a woman of upper rank to make an elaborate lace layette, or a bag shaped like a pineapple, she would be none the wiser about how to darn or knit a stocking. But signs of change were appearing too: in Louisa May Alcott's Little Women (1869), only Amy is well-versed in the fashionable and decorative art of crochet, while the other three March sisters all perform needlework of the determinedly plain variety. When Jo offers to teach Laurie to knit socks for soldiers, she reminds us how plain work takes on a new significance in wartime.

This was, of course, especially true of Britain during the Second World War. Mass-produced clothing and textiles were no longer readily available, and like other consumer goods, wool was subject to strict rationing. It became the norm to unravel a sweater to make a new garment; to patch or re-knit a threadbare elbow; to carefully darn the heels and toes of socks; and to put knitwear that had worn beyond use to other household purposes. Regardless of her class, during the 1940s, every woman who was handy with her needles found that she had to be resourceful. In fact, the very necessity of thrift meant that knitting took an unusually creative turn. It is no coincidence that what is often referred to as knitting's "golden age"—a time of innovative design and new techniques—was also the era of mending and making do. The ornamental designs of the Victorians disappeared, and rather than seeing plain work as an unpleasant chore, knitting manuals began to describe it as an opportunity for invention. Pattern books, such as Margaret Koster and Jane Murray's Knitting for All Illustrated (1945) devoted large sections to the creative business of make do and mend.

Taking eleven "disreputable and deplorably unattractive ancient woollen garments" Koster and Murray devised several ingenious ways of remaking them into "smart" and "attractive" sweaters and accessories. They fashioned socks out of jerseys, formed pixie-hoods from felted vests, and showed how to reinforce their recycled garments to prevent further wear and tear. Moss stitch and cables were condemned as an "extravagant" use of wool, while lace was celebrated as an occasion for economy rather than ornament. Because of the small amounts of

wool expended, Murray and Koster were particularly keen on drop-stitch patterns, and described how to make "a charming, filmy and gossamer-like," bedjacket which held the additional benefit of being "perfectly practical" while being "produced almost out of nothing."

One of the most notable things about the 1940s attitude to plain work is that it seems to be a source of fun rather than grim moralising. "It remains to you," counselled Koster and Murray, "to use a little of your own imagination, and you'll burst forth looking radiant in a creation contrived from two pairs of father's old socks, an old beret and a ball of string." This good-humoured tone also characterised official State directives on wartime thrift, from the publicity surrounding utility clothing to the Government's famous make do and mend campaign.

Four years into the war, the Ministry of Information declared that "the necessity for repairing and replacing well-worn clothes is bringing out all the inventive qualities of British women." To further encourage this

inventiveness, the Board of Trade created "Mrs Sew and Sew"—the thrifty spirit of make do and mend personified. Mrs Sew and Sew dispensed her advice to the nation through newspapers, magazines, and several well-produced pamphlets. She revealed the best methods of "deft darning;" taught women how to make "slippers for the whole family" out of rug-wool and twine; and cheerfully instructed them to "Make War On Moths!" Dressmaking classes were established in village halls; swap shops and clothing exchanges specialised in supplying outgrown clothes to children; and women formed ad-hoc associations to pool sewing machines, knitting needles, and other equipment.

Noreen Powers was taught to mend as a child in the 1940s. Sitting by the fireside, she joined the other women of her family in darning socks and patching sweaters. Noreen enjoyed—and still enjoys—plain work, and recalls that while her mother's repairs were a little on the lumpy side, hers were always smooth and neat. Many years later, Noreen passed on the family skills, teaching

Believe it or not, this was made from the sad remains of a cardigan photographed on page 270. A contrast front panel was introduced to make up for the wool which had to be wasted in the unpicking.

Above
Image from 'Knitting for All Illustrated' by Margaret Murray & Jane Koster (Odhams Press, 1945).

Right
'Make do and Mend' – dressmaking workshop in wartime London (1943), © Imperial War Museum.

Above
Darning a pair of socks (2010),
Kate Davies.

her daughter-in-law, Mandy, to darn. Now a knitwear designer and teacher herself, Mandy says that "having learnt from Noreen, who did the mending because there wouldn't otherwise have been socks to wear, I feel a sense of duty to teach others how to do it."

Today, in a world of cheap, throwaway textiles, the plain work of darning can be an occasion for reflection. Inspired by a repeatedly mended sweater she had inherited from her uncle Roly, artist Celia Pym began an ongoing project she calls The Catalogue of Holes. Members of the public bring items to be repaired, and Pym documents each garment's signs of wear and tear, before mending, and restoring them to their owners. Her work returns us to that eighteenth-century sense of darn as birthmark, as the visible repairs become integral to each garment's identity. Pym's thoughtful mending reveals how an aesthetic of use can carry its own quiet beauty.

Much has been made of recent trends in sewing and knitting as symptoms of an exigent economic climate, but perhaps they should rather be seen as signs of a broader cultural change. Anyone who has made the choice to knit a sweater, rather than buy one ready-made, knows that it is not about saving money in the short term. But although knitting isn't necessarily a cheap activity, it can certainly be thrifty. For thrift is not necessarily about denial, but involves spending wisely, and then taking the time to value and care for what you have bought. If slow food is all about appreciating the processes of cooking, then, in the understanding it prompts about the production and design of clothing, hand-knitting could be seen as slow fashion. While a mass produced garment might be thoughtlessly bought and instantaneously discarded, knitting unfolds slowly, laboriously, over time. Each garment becomes a personal document of the places and the moments of its making; each worn-out sleeve, each darned heel, records the shape of a body and its distinctive signs of use. And looking after hand-knit garments—reinforcing seams, washing and carefully storing winter clothes; protecting shawls and coverlets from moths; unravelling, re-knitting and recycling an old sweater—are also thrifty acts. Such "plain work" creates clothes with identities and memories that are, in the end, much more meaningful than those of any designer item. Perhaps rather than being merely economical, then, thrifty knitting now involves creating value of a different kind.

**With thanks to Noreen and Mandy
Powers, Celia Pym, and Eleanor Farrell
at the Imperial War Museum.**

homespun

Inspired by a remote and rustic
Mallorcan finca, HOMESPUN is a
collection of easy, unstructured and
loosely fitted garments, worked in
natural textures with a handcrafted
feel – just perfect for relaxed,
warm summer days.

WHOLESOME
Denim & Pima Cotton DK
Jennie Atkinson
🧶 152

HOME
Denim
Martin Storey
🧶121

ALLAY
Pima Cotton DK
Lisa Richardson
🧶 136

SOOTHE
Lenpur™ Linen
Marie Wallin
137

COMFORT
Pima Cotton DK
Erika Knight
110

POISE
Pima Cotton DK
Sarah Hatton
⟿ 128

RUSTIC
Summer Tweed
Marie Wallin
🧶141

EARTHY
Purelife Revive
Erika Knight
🧶130

UNWIND WRAP
Summer Tweed & Kidsilk Haze
Kaffe Fassett
🧶 151

Photographer: Sheila Rock.
Styling: Marie Wallin.
Hair & Make Up: Carol Morley (One Photographic).
Art Direction: Marie Wallin.
Models: Sara Karen (Profile Model Management),
Tomas (Kitchentable Model Agency, Palma de Mallorca).
Location: Finca Son Burguet, Puigpunyent, Mallorca.
Many thanks to Cem and Olaf at Watson Production, Palma de Mallorca.

travel journal

words by Marie Wallin

MALLORCA
SON BURGUET, PUIGPUNYENT
Homespun location

This beautiful, charming and rustic finca situated just north of Palma was a perfect location for our *Homespun* story. This stately manor house dates back to the 13th century and is situated in the Tramuntana Mountains surrounded by ancient olive, carob, fig and oak trees. The working estate farms over 300 hectares of land, centred mainly on the rearing of sheep and the production of almonds, olives and carobs. Agroturismo Son Burguet would make an idyllic and relaxing base for exploring the rest of Mallorca.

Agroturismo Son Burguet, Ctra. Palma-Puigpunyent, Km 10,800, PUIGPUNYENT, Mallorca.
Tel: 971 61 42 41 or 971 46 60 62
www.sonburguet.com

The Rowan crew stayed at the Hotel Zhero, Palma de Mallorca.

MALLORCA
DEIA & SINEU
Illusion locations

Deia lies on the North West coast of Mallorca and is built on a hill in the middle of a valley in the 'Serra de Tramuntana' mountain range. This beautiful village is renown not only for its incredible surroundings but also for the American painter Norman Yanikun who spent many long summers at the Pension Sa Fonda in Deia during the 1950's.

The area has always been a favourite of artists, writers, musicians and celebrities; Andrew Lloyd Webber, Pierce Brosnan, Bob Geldolf and the late Princess of Wales to name a few.

The exceptional beauty of the winding cobbled streets, the many flowers and the crumbling walls of the ancient church made Deia a very special location for our ethereal *Illusion* story.

Sineu was the second location we used for the *Illusion* story. This interesting and ancient agricultural hill top town boasts over 1000 years of history and once was the capital of Mallorca. Situated in the centre of rural Mallorca, the wide streets of Sineu with its elegant sandstone buildings evoke an atmosphere of an ancient French rural town. Today Sineu is renown for its weekly market. Started in 1306 by King Jaume II, the Sineu market is celebrated in the main square each Wednesday and is one of the oldest and most interesting markets of Mallorca.

what's new

Rowan Savannah Collection

The *Savannah Collection* is a brochure which epitomises the key trend for relaxed, easy to wear knits that drape and also fit the body. This fabulous collection of 12 designs by Marie Wallin showcases one of the new yarns for the summer season. Savannah is a lovely matt cotton and silk blended yarn which has a summery dry handle. Available in 8 lovely desert shades, this collection features easy to knit textures, open work stitches and simple crochet in little summer tops, beach cover ups and draping cardigans.

Rowan Savannah Collection is available from Rowan stockists from 1st February 2011.

Order code: ZB102

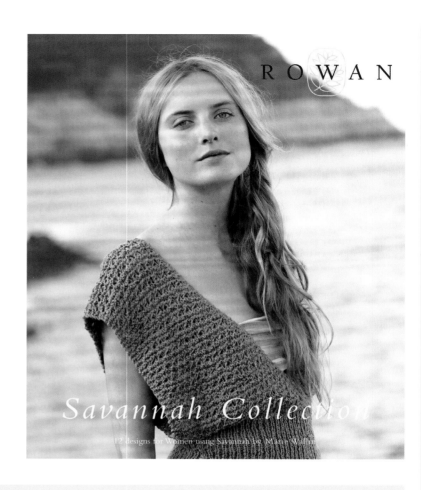

Rowan Panama Collection

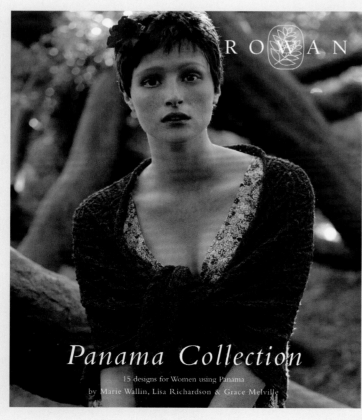

The *Panama Collection* introduces the second new addition to the Rowan yarn range for the summer season. Available in 12 jewel colours, this beautiful fine cotton, linen and viscose blended yarn has a lovely, soft draping nature with a subtle sheen. The collection of 15 exquisite designs by the Rowan design team features the key trends for open work stitches, fine crochet and stripes. This is a brochure full of easy to wear, contemporary styles and is a 'must have' for the essential summer wardrobe.

Rowan Panama Collection is available from Rowan stockists from 1st February 2011.

Order code: ZB101

A whole season's worth of knitting books, magazines and exhibitions covering all aspects of knitting and textile design.

Rowan Summer Baby

Summer Baby is a beautiful brochure full of fun and colourful knits for little girls and boys aged 0-3 months to 4 years. Designed by the Rowan design team using Rowan's favourite cotton yarns, this lovely brochure is sure to be a hit with mums and grannies alike. The collection includes pretty floral dresses, party dress cardigans and crochet tees for the girls and animal, stripes and star patterns for the boys.

Rowan Summer Baby is available from Rowan stockists from 1st February 2011.

Order code: ZB100

Rowan Purelife Classics

Purelife Classics is a beautiful collection of 12 designs for women by Martin Storey. Using the Purelife Organic Cotton DK, 4 ply and Revive, this brochure is a response to the increasing demand for organic and sustainable clothing. The collection features stunning textured and plain knits perfect for balmy summer days and evenings.

Rowan Purelife Classics is available from Rowan stockists from 1st February 2011.

Order code: ZCB42

featuring Handknit Cotton and All Seasons Cotton

Rowan Cotton Classics

Following the strong and aspirational trend for coastal living, *Cotton Classics* is a brochure full of beautifully crafted, nautical cabled sweaters, perfect for a relaxed and casual look. Using Rowan Handknit Cotton and All Seasons Cotton, *Cotton Classics* is a fabulous collection of 16 'coastal-chic' designs for both women and men by Martin Storey.

Rowan Cotton Classics is available from Rowan stockists from 1st February 2011.

Order code: ZCB41

Rowan by Amy Butler River Camp Knits

River Camp Knits is a brochure of 15 garment, accessory and homeware designs using Belle Organic Aran and DK. Designed exclusively by renowned textile designer Amy Butler, this inspirational brochure is full of ideas for relaxed summer knitting.

River Camp Knits is available from Rowan stockists from 1st February 2011.

Order code: ZK36

Lacy Knits

Alison Crowther-Smith
21 stylish accessories in Rowan's Kidsilk yarns

Lacy Knits is the sequel to Alison's popular *Little Luxury Knits*. In her workshops, she is often asked for lacy design, and she has now created an exquisite collection of special lacy knits for you and your home. Ideal for knitting whilst travelling each project takes no more than a few balls of yarn.

Lacy Knits is available from Rowan stockists from spring 2011.

Order code: 978-1-907544-04-0
£14.99

Savile Row

James Sherwood
Forward by Tom Ford

The Master Tailors of British Bespoke

This superbly produced volume tells the rich history of the tailors, the personalities, the clothes and the street synonymous with elegance, sophistication and timeless attitudes. Including rare and archival material and previously unpublished images alongside specially commissioned photography and fashion shoots, it brings together Savile Row's highlights and low-lifes, the dramas and private tales, the suits and their accoutrements, the fabric and the cuts, the history and the future, as never before.

Published by Thames & Hudson

ISBN: 978-0-500-515242
£45.00

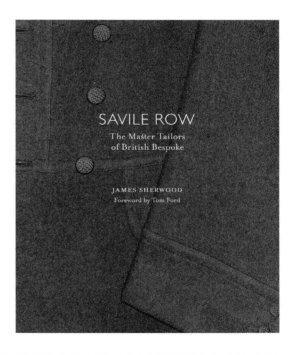

Empress' festive robe, Guangxu reign period (1875-1908). © The Palace Museum, Beijing.

Imperial Chinese Robes from the Forbidden City

This exhibition will show the sumptuous robes and accessories worn by the emperors and empresses of the Qing Dynasty, the last ruling dynasty of China (1644-1911). These costumes are on display for the first time in Europe. Official, festive, and travelling dress for rituals, celebrations, weddings and royal visits will be on show as well as beautifully patterned fabrics crafted for the fashion-conscious court ladies.

The Victoria and Albert Museum, London

www.vam.ac.uk

7th December 2010 – 27th February 2011

Admission charge will apply

ROWAN SIZING GUIDE

When you knit and wear a Rowan design we want you to look and feel fabulous. This all starts with the size and fit of the design you choose. To help you to achieve a great knitting experience we have looked at the sizing of our womens and menswear patterns. This has resulted in the introduction of our new sizing guide which includes the following exciting features:

Our sizing now conforms to standard clothing sizes. Therefore if you buy a standard size 12 in clothing, then our size 12 or Medium patterns will fit you perfectly.

We have extended the size range of our womenswear patterns, with over half of the designs shown being available to knit from size 8 to 26, or Small through to XXLarge, with XXLarge being equivalent to sizes 24/26.

The menswear designs are now available to knit in menswear sizes XSmall through to 2XL ie. 38" to 50" chest.

Dimensions in the charts below are body measurements, not garment dimensions, therefore please refer to the measuring guide to help you to determine which is the best size for you to knit.

STANDARD SIZING GUIDE FOR WOMEN

UK SIZE	8	10	12	14	16	18	20	22	24	26	
USA Size	6	8	10	12	14	16	18	20	22	24	
EUR Size	34	36	38	40	42	44	46	48	50	52	
To fit bust	32	34	36	38	40	42	44	46	48	50	inches
	81	86	91	97	102	107	112	117	122	127	cm
To fit waist	24	26	28	30	32	34	36	38	40	42	inches
	61	66	71	76	81	86	91	97	101	106	cm
To fit hips	34	36	38	40	42	44	46	48	50	52	inches
	86	91	97	102	107	112	117	122	127	132	cm

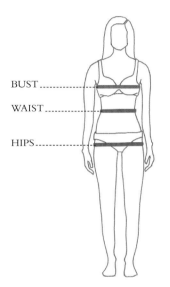

CASUAL SIZING GUIDE FOR WOMEN

As there are some designs that are intended to fit more generously, we have introduced our casual sizing guide. The designs that fall into this group can be recognised by the size range: Small, Medium, Large, Xlarge & XXlarge. Each of these sizes cover two sizes from the standard sizing guide, ie. Size S will fit sizes 8/10, size M will fit sizes 12/14 and so on.

The sizing within this chart is also based on the larger size within the range, ie. M will be based on size 14.

UK SIZE	S	M	L	XL	XXL	
DUAL SIZE	8/10	12/14	16/18	20/22	24/26	
To fit bust	32 – 34	36 – 38	40 – 42	44 – 46	48 – 50	inches
	81 – 86	91 - 97	102 – 107	112 – 117	122 – 127	cm
To fit waist	24 – 26	28 – 30	32 – 34	36 – 38	40 – 42	inches
	61 – 66	71 – 76	81 – 86	91 – 97	102 – 107	cm
To fit hips	34 – 36	38 – 40	42 – 44	46 – 48	50 – 52	inches
	86 – 91	97 – 102	107 – 112	117 – 122	127 – 132	cm

STANDARD SIZING GUIDE FOR MEN

UK SIZE	XS	S	M	L	XL	XXL	2XL	
EUR Size	48	50	52	54	56	58	60	
To fit chest	38	40	42	44	46	48	50	inches
	97	102	107	112	117	122	127	cm
To fit waist	30	32	34	36	38	40	42	inches
	76	81	86	91	97	102	107	cm

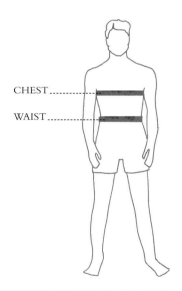

MEASURING GUIDE

For maximum comfort and to ensure the correct fit when choosing a size to knit, please follow the tips below when checking your size.

Measure yourself close to your body, over your underwear and don't pull the tape measure too tight!

Bust/chest – measure around the fullest part of the bust/chest and across the shoulder blades.

Waist – measure around the natural waistline, just above the hip bone.

Hips – measure around the fullest part of the bottom.

If you don't wish to measure yourself, note the size of a favourite jumper that you like the fit of. Our sizes are now comparable to the clothing sizes from the major high street retailers, so if your favourite jumper is a size Medium or size 12, then our casual size Medium and standard size 12 should be approximately the same fit.

To be extra sure, measure your favourite jumper and then compare these measurements with the Rowan size diagram given at the end of the individual instructions.

Finally, once you have decided which size is best for

you, please ensure that you achieve the tension required for the design you wish to knit.

Remember if your tension is too loose, your garment will be bigger than the pattern size and you may use more yarn. If your tension is too tight, your garment could be smaller than the pattern size and you will have yarn left over.

Furthermore if your tension is incorrect, the handle of your fabric will be too stiff or floppy and will not fit properly. It really does make sense to check your tension before starting every project.

FANCY

ERIKA KNIGHT

Main image page 12

YARN

S	M	L	XL	XXL

To fit bust
81–86 91–97 102–107 112–117 122–127 cm
32–34 36–38 40–42 44–46 48–50 in

Rowan Kidsilk Haze
4   4   5   5   5   x 25gm
(photographed in Grace 580)

NEEDLES

1 pair 4½mm (No 7) (US 7) needles

TENSION

22 sts and 22 rows to 10 cm measured over patt
using 4½mm (US 7) needles.

SPECIAL ABBREVIATIONS

Cluster 5 = slip next 5 sts onto right needle
dropping extra loops, slip same 5 sts back onto
left needle. Wrapping yarn twice round needle
for each of next 5 sts and working all 5
elongated sts tog, work (K1 tbl, P1 tbl, K1 tbl,
P1 tbl, K1 tbl) into all 5 sts.

BACK

Using 4½mm (US 7) needles cast on 97 [109:
121: 139: 151] sts **loosely.**
Work in patt as folls:
Row 1 (RS): Knit.
Row 2: P1, ★(P1, wrapping yarn twice round
needle) 5 times, P1, rep from ★ to end.
Row 3: K1, ★cluster 5, K1, rep from ★ to end.
Row 4: P1, ★(K1 dropping extra loop) 5 times,
P1, rep from ★ to end.
Row 5: Knit.
Row 6: P4, ★(P1 wrapping yarn twice around
needle) 5 times, P1, rep from ★ to last 3 sts, P3.
Row 7: K4, ★cluster 5, K1, rep from ★ to last
3 sts, K3.
Row 8: P4, ★(K1 dropping extra loop) 5 times,
P1, rep from ★ to last 3 sts, P3.
These 8 rows form patt.
Cont in patt until back meas 36 [37: 38:
39: 40] cm, ending with RS facing for next row.

Shape armholes

Keeping patt correct, cast off 4 [5: 6: 7: 8] sts at
beg of next 2 rows.
89 [99: 109: 125: 135] sts.★★
Dec 1 st at each end of next 3 [5: 7: 9: 11]
rows, then on foll 4 [5: 5: 7: 6] alt rows, 75 [79:
85: 93: 101] sts.
Cont straight until armhole meas 18 [19: 20: 21:
22] cm, ending with RS facing for next row.

Shape shoulders and back neck

Cast off 5 [6: 7: 9: 10] sts at beg of next 2 rows,
then 5 [6: 7: 9: 11] sts at beg of foll 2 rows.
Cast off rem 55 [55: 57: 57: 59] sts **loosely.**

FRONT

Work as given for back to ★★.
Dec 1 st at each end of next 3 [4: 4: 4: 4] rows.
83 [91: 101: 117: 127] sts.
Work 1 [0: 0: 0: 0] row, ending with RS facing
for next row.

Shape front neck

Next row (RS): Work 2 tog, patt 39 [43: 48:
56: 61] sts and turn, leaving rem sts on a holder.
Work each side of neck separately.
Keeping patt correct, dec 1 st at neck edge of
next 6 [10: 12: 18: 18] rows **and at same time**
dec 1 st at armhole edge on 2nd [2nd: next:
next: next] and foll 0 [0: 1: 3: 5] rows, then on
foll 2 [4: 5: 7: 6] alt rows. 31 [29: 30: 28: 32] sts.
Dec 1 st at neck edge **only** on next 20 [14: 12:
4: 4] rows, then on foll 1 [3: 4: 6: 7] alt rows.
10 [12: 14: 18: 21] sts.
Cont straight until front matches back to beg
of shoulder shaping, ending with RS facing for
next row.

Shape shoulder

Cast off 5 [6: 7: 9: 10] sts at beg of next row.
Work 1 row.
Cast off rem 5 [6: 7: 9: 11] sts.
With RS facing, rejoin yarn to rem sts, work
2 tog, patt to last 2 sts, work 2 tog.
Complete to match first side, reversing
shapings.

SLEEVES

Using 4½mm (US 7) needles cast on 55 [55:
55: 61: 61] sts.
Work in patt as given for back, shaping sides by
inc 1 st at each end of 11th [9th: 7th: 7th: 5th]
and every foll 12th [10th: 8th: 8th: 6th] row
to 59 [69: 71: 67: 65] sts, then on every foll
14th [12th: 10th: 10th: 8th] row until there are
67 [71: 75: 79: 83] sts, taking inc sts into patt.
Cont straight until sleeve meas 41 [42: 43:
43: 43] cm, ending with RS facing for next row.

Shape top

Keeping patt correct, cast off 4 [5: 6: 7: 8] sts at
beg of next 2 rows. 59 [61: 63: 65: 67] sts.
Dec 1 st at each end of next 3 rows, then on
every foll alt row to 39 sts, then on foll 11
rows, ending with RS facing for next row.
Cast off rem 17 sts.

MAKING UP

Press as described on the information page.
Join both shoulder seams using back stitch, or
mattress stitch if preferred.

See information page for finishing instructions,
setting in sleeves using the set-in method.

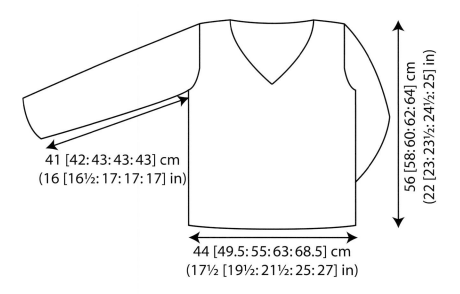

41 [42: 43: 43: 43] cm
(16 [16½: 17: 17: 17] in)

44 [49.5: 55: 63: 68.5] cm
(17½ [19½: 21½: 25: 27] in)

56 [58: 60: 62: 64] cm
(22 [23: 23½: 24½: 25] in)

FOXTAIL
MARTIN STOREY

Main image page 35

●●

YARN

 8 10 12 14 16   18   20   22
To fit bust
 81 86 91 97 102 107 112 117   cm
 32 34 36 38 40   42   44   46   in
Rowan Cotton Glacé
 10 10 11 11 12   13   13   14   x 50gm
(photographed in Bleached 726)

NEEDLES

1 pair 2¾mm (no 12) (US 2) needles
1 pair 3¼mm (no 10) (US 3) needles

TENSION

22 sts and 29 rows to 10 cm measured over patt using 3¼mm (US 3) needles.

BACK

Using 3¼mm (US 3) needles cast on 102 [106: 110: 118: 122: 130: 138: 142] sts.
Row 1 (RS): K2, *P2, K2, rep from * to end.
Row 2: P2, *K2, P2, rep from * to end.
These 2 rows form rib.
Work in rib for a further 30 rows, ending with RS facing for next row.
Now work in patt as folls:
Row 1 (RS): K1, *sl 1, K1, psso, (yfwd) twice, K2tog, rep from * to last st, K1.
Row 2: P2, *(P1, K1) into double yfwd of previous row, P2, rep from * to end.
These 2 rows form patt.
Cont in patt until back meas 23 [23: 22: 25: 24: 26: 25: 27] cm, ending with RS facing for next row.
Keeping patt correct, dec 1 st at each end of next and 2 foll 10th rows, then on 2 foll 8th rows, then on 3 foll 6th rows.
86 [90: 94: 102: 106: 114: 122: 126] sts.
Work 7 rows, ending with RS facing for next row.
Inc 1 st at each end of next and 2 foll 4th rows, then on 5 foll 6th rows, taking inc sts into st st until there are sufficient to work in patt.
102 [106: 110: 118: 122: 130: 138: 142] sts.
Cont straight until back meas 60 [60: 59: 62: 61: 63: 62: 64] cm, ending with RS facing for next row.

Shape armholes

Keeping patt correct, cast off 7 [8: 8: 9: 9: 10: 10: 11] sts at beg of next 2 rows.
88 [90: 94: 100: 104: 110: 118: 120] sts.
Dec 1 st at each end of next 3 [3: 5: 5: 7: 7: 9: 9] rows, then on foll 3 [3: 1: 3: 2: 3: 3: 3] alt rows, then on 2 foll 4th rows.
72 [74: 78: 80: 82: 86: 90: 92] sts.
Cont straight until armhole meas 20 [20: 21: 21: 22: 22: 23: 23] cm, ending with RS facing for next row.

Shape shoulders and back neck

Cast off 3 [3: 4: 4: 4: 5: 6: 6] sts at beg of next 2 rows. 66 [68: 70: 72: 74: 76: 78: 80] sts.
Next row (RS): Cast off 3 [3: 4: 4: 4: 5: 6: 6] sts, patt until there are 7 [8: 8: 9: 9: 9: 9: 10] sts on right needle and turn, leaving rem sts on a holder.
Work each side of neck separately.
Cast off 4 sts at beg of next row.
Cast off rem 3 [4: 4: 5: 5: 5: 5: 6] sts.
With RS facing, rejoin yarn to rem sts, cast off centre 46 [46: 46: 46: 48: 48: 48: 48] sts, patt to end.
Complete to match first side, reversing shapings.

FRONT

Work as given for back until 10 [10: 10: 12: 12: 12: 14: 14] rows less have been worked than on back to beg of shoulder shaping, ending with RS facing for next row.

Shape front neck

Next row (RS): Patt 15 [16: 18: 20: 20: 22: 25: 26] sts and turn, leaving rem sts on a holder.
Work each side of neck separately.
Keeping patt correct, dec 1 st at neck edge of next 4 rows, then on foll 2 [2: 2: 3: 3: 3: 4: 4] alt rows. 9 [10: 12: 13: 13: 15: 17: 18] sts.
Work 1 row, ending with RS facing for next row.

Shape shoulder

Cast off 3 [3: 4: 4: 4: 5: 6: 6] sts at beg of next

rows, then on 2 foll 4th rows.
72 [74: 78: 80: 82: 86: 90: 92] sts.
Cont straight until armhole meas 20 [20: 21: 21: 22: 22: 23: 23] cm, ending with RS facing for next row.

Shape shoulders and back neck

Cast off 3 [3: 4: 4: 4: 5: 6: 6] sts at beg of next 2 rows. 66 [68: 70: 72: 74: 76: 78: 80] sts.
Next row (RS): Cast off 3 [3: 4: 4: 4: 5: 6: 6] sts, patt until there are 7 [8: 8: 9: 9: 9: 9: 10] sts on right needle and turn, leaving rem sts on a holder.
Work each side of neck separately.
Cast off 4 sts at beg of next row.
Cast off rem 3 [4: 4: 5: 5: 5: 5: 6] sts.
With RS facing, rejoin yarn to rem sts, cast off centre 46 [46: 46: 46: 48: 48: 48: 48] sts, patt to end.
Complete to match first side, reversing shapings.

and foll alt row.
Work 1 row.
Cast off rem 3 [4: 4: 5: 5: 5: 5: 6] sts.
With RS facing, rejoin yarn to rem sts, cast off centre 42 [42: 42: 40: 42: 42: 40: 40] sts, patt to end.
Complete to match first side, reversing shapings.

SLEEVES

Using 3¼mm (US 3) needles cast on 76 [78: 80: 82: 84: 86: 88: 90] sts.
Row 1 (RS): P1 [0: 0: 0: 1: 0: 0: 0], K2 [0: 1: 2: 2: 0: 1: 2], *P2, K2, rep from * to last 1 [2: 3: 0: 1: 2: 3: 0] sts, P1 [2: 2: 0: 1: 2: 2: 0], K0 [0: 1: 0: 0: 0: 1: 0].
Row 2: K1 [0: 0: 0: 1: 0: 0: 0], P2 [0: 1: 2: 2: 0: 1: 2], *K2, P2, rep from * to last 1 [2: 3: 0: 1: 2: 3: 0] sts, K1 [2: 2: 0: 1: 2: 2: 0], P0 [0: 1: 0: 0: 0: 1: 0].
These 2 rows form rib.
Work in rib for a further 10 rows, ending with RS facing for next row.
Now work in patt as folls:
Row 1 (RS): K0 [1: 2: 3: 0: 1: 2: 3], *sl 1, K1, psso, (yfwd) twice, K2tog, rep from * to last 0 [1: 2: 3: 0: 1: 2: 3] sts, K0 [1: 2: 3: 0: 1: 2: 3].
Row 2: P0 [1: 2: 3: 0: 1: 2: 3], *P1, (P1, K1) into double yfwd of previous row, P1, rep from * to last 0 [1: 2: 3: 0: 1: 2: 3] sts, P{0 [1: 2: 3: 0: 1: 2: 3].
These 2 rows form patt.
Cont in patt until sleeve meas 15 cm, ending with RS facing for next row.

Shape top

Keeping patt correct, cast off 7 [8: 8: 9: 9: 10: 10: 11] sts at beg of next 2 rows.

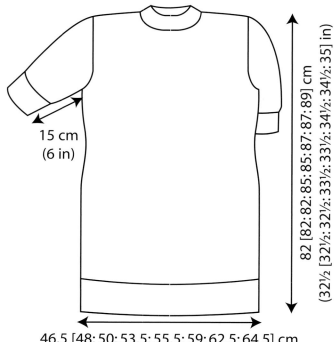

15 cm
(6 in)

82 [82: 82: 85: 85: 87: 87: 89] cm
(32½ [32½: 32½: 33½: 33½: 34½: 34½: 35] in)

46.5 [48: 50: 53.5: 55.5: 59: 62.5: 64.5] cm
(18½ [19: 19½: 21: 22: 23: 24½: 25½] in)

62 [62: 64: 64: 66: 66: 68: 68] sts.
Dec 1 st at each end of next 3 rows, then on foll 3 alt rows, then on 6 foll 4th rows.
38 [38: 40: 40: 42: 42: 44: 44] sts.
Work 1 row.
Dec 1 st at each end of next and every foll alt row until 32 sts rem, then on foll 5 rows, ending with RS facing for next row.
Cast off rem 22 sts.

MAKING UP
Press as described on the information page. Join right shoulder seam using back stitch, or mattress stitch if preferred.
Neckband
With RS facing and using 2¾mm (US 2) needles, pick up and knit 13 [13: 13: 14: 14: 14: 17: 17] sts down left side of neck, 42 [42: 42: 40: 42: 42: 40: 40] sts from front, 13 [13: 13: 14: 14: 14: 17: 17] sts up right side of neck, then 54 [54: 54: 54: 56: 56: 56: 56] sts from back.
122 [122: 122: 122: 126: 126: 130: 130] sts.
Beg with row 2, work in rib as given for back for 11 rows, ending with RS facing for next row.
Cast off **loosely** in rib.
See information page for finishing instructions, setting in sleeves using the set-in method.

DAYDREAM
MARIE WALLIN ● ● ●
Main image page 18 & 19

YARN
| | S | M | L | XL | XXL |
To fit bust
81-86 91-97 102-107 112-117 122-127 cm
32-34 36-38 40-42 44-46 48-50 in
Rowan Purelife Organic Cotton 4 ply
9 9 11 12 13 x 50gm
(photographed in Light Brazilwood 763)

NEEDLES
1 pair 2¾mm (no 12) (US 2) needles

BUTTONS
BUTTONS – 5 x BN1366 (11mm) from Bedecked. Please see information page for contact details.

TENSION
28 sts and 44 rows to 10 cm measured over patt using 2¾mm (US 2) needles.

Pattern note: When working patt from chart, do **NOT** work the inc unless there are sufficient sts to work the corresponding dec. As all increases are next to their corresponding decrease do not work one without the other, so that number of sts remains constant (except where shaping occurs). Where a "sl 1, K2tog, psso" falls at the edge of a row, at beg of rows

replace this with "K2tog" (then work the yfwd), and at end of rows replace this with "sl 1, K1, psso" (after the yfwd).

BACK
Hem border
Using 2¾mm (US 2) needles cast on 18 sts.
Row 1 (RS): K3, yfwd, sl 1, K1, psso, K1, K2tog, (yfwd) twice, sl 1, K1, psso, K2tog, yfwd, K1, K2tog, yfwd, K2tog, K1. 17 sts.
Row 2: K2, yfwd, K1, sl 1 K1, psso, yfwd, K4, P1, sl 1, K1, psso, yfwd, K2, yfwd, K2tog, K1. 18 sts.
Row 3: K3, yfwd, sl 1, K1, psso, K1, yfwd, sl 1, K1, psso, K2tog, (yfwd) twice, (sl 1, K1, psso, K1, yfwd) twice, K2. 19 sts.
Row 4: K2, yfwd, K1, sl 1, K1, psso, yfwd, K4, P1, sl 1, K1, psso, yfwd, K4, yfwd, K2tog, K1. 20 sts.
Row 5: (K3, yfwd, sl 1, K1, psso) twice, K2tog,

(yfwd) twice, (sl 1, K1, psso, K1, yfwd) twice, K2. 21 sts.
Row 6: K2, yfwd, K1, sl 1, K1, psso, yfwd, K4, P1, sl 1, K1, psso, yfwd, K1, yfwd, K2tog, K3, yfwd, K2tog, K1. 22 sts.
Row 7: K3, yfwd, sl 1, K1, psso, K2tog, yfwd, K3, yfwd, sl 1, K1, psso, K2tog, (yfwd) twice, (sl 1, K1, psso, K1, yfwd) twice, K2. 23 sts.
Row 8: K2, yfwd, K1, sl 1, K1, psso, yfwd, K4, P1, sl 1, K1, psso, yfwd, K5, (yfwd, K2tog, K1) twice. 24 sts.
Row 9: K3, yfwd, sl 1, K1, psso, K1, yfwd, sl 1, K1, psso, K1, K2tog, yfwd, K1, yfwd, sl 1, K1, psso, K2tog, (yfwd) twice, (sl 1 K1, psso, K1, yfwd) twice, K2. 25 sts.
Row 10: K2, yfwd, K1, sl 1, K1, psso, yfwd, K4, P1, sl 1, K1, psso, yfwd, K3, yfwd, sl 1, K2tog, psso, yfwd, K4, yfwd, K2tog, K1. 26 sts.
Row 11: K3, yfwd, sl 1, K1, psso, K2, K2tog, yfwd, K5, yfwd, sl 1, K1, psso, K2tog, (yfwd)

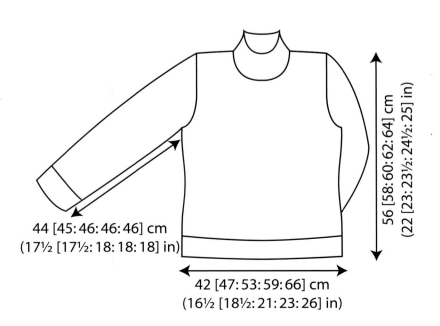

44 [45: 46: 46: 46] cm
(17½ [17½: 18: 18: 18] in)

42 [47: 53: 59: 66] cm
(16½ [18½: 21: 23: 26] in)

56 [58: 60: 62: 64] cm
(22 [23: 23½: 24½: 25] in)

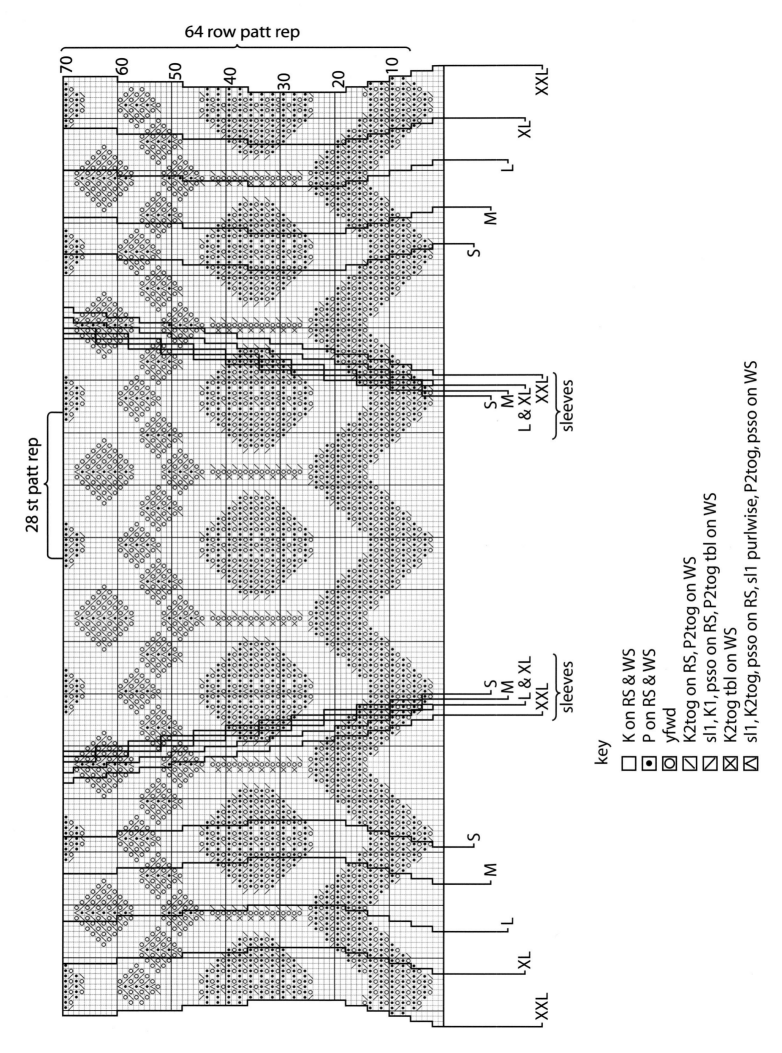

key

☐ K on RS & WS
▣ P on RS & WS
⊙ yfwd
◩ K2tog on RS, P2tog on WS
◪ sl1, K1, psso on RS, P2tog tbl on WS
⊠ K2tog tbl on WS
◩ sl1, K2tog, psso on RS, sl1 purlwise, P2tog, psso on WS

twice, (sl 1, K1, psso, K1, yfwd) twice, K2.
27 sts.
Row 12: K1, K2tog, (yfwd, K2tog, K1) twice,
P1, K3, yfwd, K2tog, K1, sl 1, K1, psso, yfwd,
K1, yfwd, K2tog, K3, yfwd, K2tog, K1. 26 sts.
Row 13: K3, yfwd, sl 1, K1, psso, K2tog, yfwd,
K3, yfwd, sl 1, K2tog, psso, yfwd, K1, K2tog,
(yfwd) twice, sl 1, K1, psso, K2tog, yfwd, K1,
K2tog, yfwd, K2tog, K1. 25 sts.
Row 14: K1, K2tog, (yfwd, K2tog, K1) twice,
P1, K3, yfwd, K2tog, K4, (yfwd, K2tog, K1)
twice. 24 sts.
Row 15: K3, (yfwd, sl 1, K1, psso, K1) twice,
K2tog, yfwd, K1, K2tog, (yfwd) twice, sl 1, K1,
psso, K2tog, yfwd, K1, K2tog, yfwd, K2tog, K1.
23 sts.
Row 16: K1, K2tog, (yfwd, K2tog, K1) twice,
P1, K3, yfwd, sl 1, K2tog, psso, yfwd, K4, yfwd,
K2tog, K1. 22 sts.
Row 17: K3, yfwd, sl 1, K1, psso, K2, K2tog,
yfwd, K1, K2tog, (yfwd) twice, sl 1, K1, psso,
K2tog, yfwd, K1, K2tog, yfwd, K2tog, K1.
21 sts.
Row 18: K1, K2tog, (yfwd, K2tog, K1) twice,
P1, (K3, yfwd, K2tog) twice, K1. 20 sts.
Row 19: K3, yfwd, sl 1, K1, psso, K2tog, yfwd,
K1, K2tog, (yfwd) twice, sl 1, K1, psso, K2tog,
yfwd, K1, K2tog, yfwd, K2tog, K1. 19 sts.
Row 20: K1, K2tog, yfwd, K2tog, K1, yfwd,
K2tog, K1, P1, K3, (yfwd, K2tog, K1) twice.
18 sts.
These 20 rows form patt.
Cont in patt until hem border meas approx
44 [49: 55: 61: 68] cm, ending after patt row 20.
Cast off.

Main section
With RS facing and using 2¾ (US 2) needles,
pick up and knit 115 [129: 147: 163: 183] sts
evenly along straight row-end edge of hem
border.
Next row (WS): Knit.
Beg and ending rows as indicated, working chart
rows 1 to 6 **once only** and then repeating chart
rows 7 to 70 **throughout** (see pattern note),
now work in patt from chart as folls:
Dec 1 st at each end of 3rd and 4 foll 4th rows.
105 [119: 137: 153: 173] sts.
Work 17 rows, ending with RS facing for next
row.
Inc 1 st at each end of next and 5 foll 12th
rows, taking inc sts into patt.
117 [131: 149: 165: 185] sts.
Cont straight until back meas 34 [35: 36:
37: 38] cm from lower edge of hem border,
ending with RS facing for next row.

Shape armholes
Keeping patt correct, cast off 4 [5: 6: 7: 8] sts at
beg of next 2 rows. 109 [121: 137: 151: 169] sts.
Dec 1 st at each end of next 3 [5: 7: 9: 11]
rows, then on foll 4 [5: 7: 8: 10] alt rows.
95 [101: 109: 117: 127] sts.
Cont straight until armhole meas 20 [21: 22:
23: 24] cm, ending with RS facing for next
row.
Shape shoulders and back neck
Next Row (RS): Cast off 6 [7: 8: 9: 9] sts, patt
until there are 28 [30: 32: 35: 38] sts on right
needle and turn, leaving rem sts on a holder.
Work each side of neck separately.
Keeping patt correct, cast off 3 sts at beg of
next row, 6 [7: 8: 9: 9] sts at beg of foll row,
3 sts at beg of next row, 6 [7: 8: 9: 10] sts at beg
of foll row, then 3 sts at beg of next row.
Cast off rem 7 [7: 7: 8: 10] sts.
With RS facing, rejoin yarn to rem sts, cast off
centre 27 [27: 29: 29: 33] sts, patt to end.
Complete to match first side, reversing
shapings.

FRONT
Work as given for back until 28 [28: 32: 32: 36]
rows less have been worked than on back to
beg of shoulder shaping, ending with RS facing
for next row.
Shape neck
Next row (RS): Patt 38 [41: 45: 49: 53] sts
and turn, leaving rem sts on another holder.
Keeping patt correct, dec 1 st at neck edge of
next 6 rows, then on foll 5 alt rows, then on
2 [2: 3: 3: 4] foll 4th rows.
25 [28: 31: 35: 38] sts.
Work 3 rows, ending with RS facing for
next row.
Shape shoulder
Cast off 6 [7: 8: 9: 9] sts at beg of next and
foll alt row, then 6 [7: 8: 9: 10] sts at beg of foll
alt row.
Work 1 row.
Cast off rem 7 [7: 7: 8: 10] sts.
With RS facing, rejoin yarn to rem sts, cast off
centre 19 [19: 19: 19: 21] sts, patt to end.
Complete to match first side, reversing shapings.

SLEEVES
Cuff border
Work as given for hem border, making a strip
approx 21 [21: 22: 22: 23] cm long.
Main section
With RS facing and using 2¾mm (US 2)
needles, pick up and knit 57 [59: 61: 61: 65] sts
evenly along straight row-end edge of cuff
border.
Next row (RS): Knit.
Beg and ending rows as indicated, now work in
patt from chart shaping sides by inc 1 st at each end
of 5th [5th: 5th: 3rd: 3rd] and every foll 6th [6th:
6th: 4th: 4th] row to 95 [101: 105: 69: 73] sts, then
on every foll 8th [8th: 8th: 6th: 6th] row until
there are 101 [105: 109: 113: 117] sts, taking inc
sts into patt.
Cont straight until sleeve meas 44 [45: 46:
46: 46] cm from lower edge of cuff border,
ending with RS facing for next row.
Shape top
Keeping patt correct, cast off 4 [5: 6: 7: 8] sts at
beg of next 2 rows. 93 [95: 87: 99: 101] sts.
Dec 1 st at each end of next 5 rows, then on
foll 4 alt rows, then on 6 foll 4th rows.
63 [65: 67: 69: 71] sts.
Work 1 row.
Dec 1 st at each end of next and every foll alt
row until 51 sts rem, then on foll 8 rows,
ending with RS facing for next row. 33 sts.
Cast off 3 sts at beg of next 2 rows, then 4 sts
at beg of next 2 rows.
Cast off rem 19 sts.

MAKING UP
Press as described on the information page.
Join right shoulder seam using back stitch, or
mattress stitch if preferred.
Neckband
Work as given for hem border, making a strip
that, when slightly stretched, fits neatly around
entire neck edge.
Slip stitch neckband in place.
Back shoulder button border
With RS facing and using 2¾mm (US 2)
needles, pick up and knit 25 sts along back end
of neckband, then 25 [28: 31: 35: 38] sts evenly
along back shoulder edge.
50 [53: 56: 60: 63] sts.
Cast off knitwise (on **WS**).
Front shoulder buttonhole border
With RS facing and using 2¾ (US 2) needles,
pick up and knit 25 [28: 31: 35: 38] sts evenly
along front shoulder edge, then 25 sts along
front end of neckband. 50 [53: 56: 60: 63] sts.
Row 1 (WS): Knit.
Row 2: K6 [9: 8: 8: 7], yfwd, K2tog (to make
first buttonhole), (K8 [8: 9: 10: 11], yfwd, K2tog
- to make a buttonhole) 4 times, K2.
Cast off knitwise (on **WS**).
See information page for finishing instructions,
setting in sleeves using the set-in method.

TEASEL
SARAH HATTON
Main image page 40 & 41

YARN

	S	M	L	XL	XXL
To fit bust					

81-86 91-97 102-107 112-117 122-127 cm
32-34 36-38 40-42 44-46 48-50 in

Rowan Lenpur™ Linen

7 8 8 9 9 x 50gm

(photographed in Blanche 571)

NEEDLES

1 pair 3¼mm (no 10) (US 3) needles
1 pair 4mm (no 8) (US 6) needles

TENSION

22 sts and 30 rows to 10 cm measured over st st using 4mm (US 6) needles.

BACK

Using 3¼mm (US 3) needles cast on 133 [145: 163: 181: 199] sts.
Row 1 (RS): K1, *P2, K1, rep from * to end.
Row 2: P1, *K2, P1, rep from * to end.
These 2 rows form rib.
Work in rib for a further 15 rows, ending with **WS** facing for next row.
Row 18 (WS): P3 [5: 5: 5: 5], (P1, P2tog, P3, P2tog, P1) 14 [15: 17: 19: 21] times, P4 [5: 5: 5: 5]. 105 [115: 129: 143: 157] sts.
Change to 4mm (US 6) needles.
Beg with a K row, work in st st for 2 rows, ending with RS facing for next row.
Next row (RS): K1 [2: 1: 0: 3], K2tog, yfwd, *K2, K2tog, yfwd, rep from * to last 2 [3: 2: 1: 4] sts, K2 [3: 2: 1: 4].
Beg with a P row, work in st st until back meas 35 [36: 37: 38: 39] cm, ending with RS facing for next row.
Place blue markers on needle as folls: place a marker after 18th [20th: 23rd: 26th: 29th] and 25th [27th: 30th: 33rd: 36th] sts in from ends of rows – 4 blue markers in total and 55 [61: 69: 77: 85] sts at centre of row.
Now place vertical lace bands between blue markers as folls:
Row 1 (RS): (K to marker, *slip marker onto right needle, yfwd, K7, yfwd, slip next marker onto right needle) twice, K to end.
Row 2: (P to marker, *slip marker onto right needle, P9, slip next marker onto right needle) twice, P to end.
Row 3: (K to marker, *slip marker onto right needle, yfwd, K9, yfwd, slip marker onto

right needle) twice, K to end.
Row 4: (P to marker, *slip marker onto right needle, P2, K2tog, K3tog, K2tog, P2, slip next marker onto right needle) twice, P to end.
These 4 rows form patt. (**Note:** number of sts between each pair of blue markers varies whilst working patt. All st counts presume there are 7 sts between each pair of markers at all times.)
Cont in patt for a further 2 rows, ending with RS facing for next row.

Shape cap sleeves

Place markers at both ends of last row to denote base of armhole openings.
Work 4 rows, ending with RS facing for next row.
Counting in from both ends of last row, place a red marker 8 sts in from each end of row. (There are now 6 markers within work – 4 blue and 2 red.)
Next row (RS): K to red marker, yfwd (to inc 1 st), slip red marker onto right needle, patt to next red marker, slip marker onto right needle, yfwd (to inc 1 st), K to end.
107 [117: 131: 145: 159] sts.
Working all cap sleeve increases as set by last row, cont as folls:**
Inc 1 st at each end of 8th and 4 foll 8th rows.
117 [127: 141: 155: 169] sts.
Cont straight until armhole meas 23 [24: 25: 26: 27] cm, ending with RS facing for next row.

Shape shoulders and back neck

Cast off 9 [10: 12: 14: 15] sts at beg of next 2 rows. 99 [107: 117: 127: 139] sts.
Next row (RS): Cast off 9 [11: 12: 14: 15] sts, patt until there are 26 [28: 31: 34: 38] sts on right needle and turn, leaving rem sts on a holder.
Work each side of neck separately.
Cast off 3 sts at beg of next row, 10 [11: 12: 14: 16] sts at beg of foll row, then 3 sts at beg of next row.
Cast off rem 10 [11: 13: 14: 16] sts.
With RS facing, rejoin yarn to rem sts, cast off

centre 29 [29: 31: 31: 33] sts, patt to end.
Complete to match first side, reversing shapings.

FRONT

Work as given for back to **.
Work 7 rows, ending with RS facing for next row.
Divide for neck

Next row (RS): K to red marker, yfwd (to inc 1 st), slip red marker onto right needle, patt until there are 50 [55: 62: 69: 76] sts on right needle, K2tog, K2 and turn, leaving rem sts on a holder.
Work each side of neck separately.
Work 1 row.
Next row (RS): Patt to last 4 sts, K2tog, K2. 52 [57: 64: 71: 78] sts.
Working all neck decreases as set by last row, keeping patt between blue markers correct and working armhole increases beyond red markers as set, cont as folls:
Dec 1 st at neck edge of 2nd and foll 12 [11: 11: 10: 10] alt rows, then on 5 [6: 7: 8: 9] foll 4th rows **and at same time** inc 1 st at armhole edge of 6th and 3 foll 8th rows.
38 [43: 49: 56: 62] sts.
Cont straight until front matches back to beg of shoulder shaping, ending with RS facing for next row.
Shape shoulder

Cast off 9 [10: 12: 14: 15] sts at beg of next and foll 1 [0: 2: 2: 1] alt rows, then 10 [11: 0: 0: 16] sts at beg of foll 1 [2: 0: 0: 1] alt rows.
Work 1 row.
Cast off rem 10 [11: 13: 14: 16] sts.
With RS facing, slip centre st onto a holder, rejoin yarn to rem sts, K2, sl 1, K1, psso, patt to next red marker, slip marker onto right needle, yfwd (to inc 1 st), K to end.
Work 1 row.
Next row (RS): K2, sl 1, K1, psso, patt to end.
Working all neck decreases as set by last row, complete to match first side, reversing shapings.

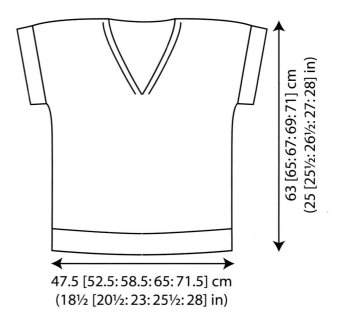

63 [65: 67: 69: 71] cm
(25 [25½: 26½: 27: 28] in)

47.5 [52.5: 58.5: 65: 71.5] cm
(18½ [20½: 23: 25½: 28] in)

MAKING UP

Press as described on the information page. Join right shoulder seam using back stitch, or mattress stitch if preferred.

Neckband

With RS facing and using 3¼mm (US 3) needles, pick up and knit 52 [54: 58: 60: 64] sts down left side of neck, K st on holder at base of V neck, pick up and knit 52 [54: 58: 60: 64] sts up right side of neck, then 41 [41: 43: 43: 45] sts from back. 146 [150: 160: 164: 174] sts.

Row 1 (WS): Knit.

Cast off.

Join left shoulder and neckband seam.

Armhole borders (both alike)

With RS facing and using 3¼mm (US 3) needles, pick up and knit 121 [127: 133: 139: 145] sts evenly along armhole edges between markers.

Beg with row 2, work in rib as given for back for 11 rows, ending with RS facing for next row.

Cast off in rib.

See information page for finishing instructions.

GHOST

AMANDA CRAWFORD

Main image page 52 & 53

YARN

	S	M	L	XL	XXL
To fit bust					
	81-86	91-97	102-107	112-117	122-127 cm
	32-34	36-38	40-42	44-46	48-50 in
Rowan Siena 4 ply					
	14	15	15	16	17 x 50gm

(photographed in Frost 653)

NEEDLES

1 pair 3¾mm (no 9) (US 5) needles
1 pair 3¼mm (no 10) (US 3) needles

TENSION

22 sts and 20 rows to 10 cm measured over lower patt, 24 sts and 23 rows to 10 cm measured over upper patt, both using 3¾mm (US 5) needles.

BACK and FRONT (both alike)
Using 3¾mm (US 5) needles cast on 162 [178: 202: 226: 250] sts.

Row 1 (WS): Knit.

Now work in lower patt as folls:

Row 1 (RS): Knit.

Row 2: K to end, wrapping yarn 3 times round needle for every st.

Row 3: K1 dropping extra loops, *slip next 4 sts onto right needle dropping extra loops, slip same 4 sts back onto left needle, work (K1, P1, K1, P1) into all 4 elongated sts tog, rep from * to last st, K1 dropping extra loops.

Row 4: Knit.

These 4 rows form lower patt.

Cont in lower patt until work meas 37 [38: 39: 40: 41] cm, ending after patt row 2 and with RS facing for next row.

Next row (RS): K1 dropping extra loops, *slip next 4 sts onto right needle dropping extra loops, slip same 4 sts back onto left needle, work (K1, P1, K1) into all 4 elongated sts tog, rep from * to last st, K1 dropping extra loops. 122 [134: 152: 170: 188] sts.

Next row: Knit.

Now work in upper patt as folls:

Row 1 (RS): Knit.

Row 2: K to end, wrapping yarn twice round needle for every st.

Row 3: K1 dropping extra loop, *slip next 3 sts onto right needle dropping extra loops, slip same 3 sts back onto left needle, work (K1, P1, K1) into all 3 elongated sts tog, rep from * to last st, K1 dropping extra loop.

Row 4: Knit.

These 4 rows form upper patt.

Cont in upper patt until work meas 49 [50: 51: 52: 53] cm, ending with RS facing for next row.

Shape armholes

Keeping patt correct, cast off 6 [7: 8: 9: 10] sts at beg of next 2 rows.
110 [120: 136: 152: 168] sts.

Dec 1 st at each end of next 3 [5: 7: 9: 11] rows, then on foll 3 [3: 5: 7: 8] alt rows.
98 [104: 112: 120: 130] sts.

Cont straight until armhole meas 13 [14: 14: 15: 15] cm, ending with RS facing for next row.

Shape neck

Next row (RS): Patt 10 [13: 16: 20: 24] sts and turn, leaving rem sts on a holder.

Work each side of neck separately.

Keeping patt correct, dec 1 st at neck edge of

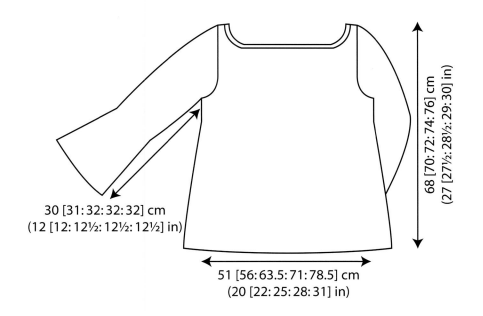

30 [31: 32: 32: 32] cm
(12 [12: 12½: 12½: 12½] in)

51 [56: 63.5: 71: 78.5] cm
(20 [22: 25: 28: 31] in)

68 [70: 72: 74: 76] cm
(27 [27½: 28½: 29: 30] in)

next and foll 2 alt rows.
7 [10: 13: 17: 21] sts.
Cont straight until armhole meas 19 [20: 21: 22: 23] cm, ending with RS facing for next row.

Shape shoulder
Cast off rem 7 [10: 13: 17: 21] sts.
With RS facing, rejoin yarn to rem sts, cast off centre 78 [78: 80: 80: 82] sts, patt to end.
Complete to match first side, reversing shapings.

SLEEVES
Using 3¾mm (US 5) needles cast on 130 [138: 146: 154: 162] sts.
Row 1 (WS): Knit.
Now work in lower patt as given for back and front until sleeve meas 15 cm, ending after patt row 2 and with RS facing for next row.
Next row (RS): K1 dropping extra loops, *slip next 4 sts onto right needle dropping extra loops, slip same 4 sts back onto left needle, work (K1, P1, K1) into all 4 elongated sts tog, rep from * to last st, K1 dropping extra loops. 98 [104: 110: 116: 122] sts.
Next row: Knit.
Now work in upper patt as given for back and front until sleeve meas 30 [31: 32: 32: 32] cm, ending with RS facing for next row.
Shape top
Keeping patt correct, cast off 6 [7: 8: 9: 10] sts at beg of next 2 rows. 86 [90: 94: 98: 102] sts.
Dec 1 st at each end of next 3 rows, then on foll 21 alt rows, then on foll 5 [7: 9: 11: 13] rows, ending with RS facing for next row.
Cast off rem 28 sts.

MAKING UP
Press as described on the information page.
Join right shoulder seam using back stitch, or mattress stitch if preferred.
Neckband
With RS facing and using 3¼mm (US 3) needles, pick up and knit 14 [14: 17: 17: 20] sts down left side of front neck, 78 [78: 80: 80: 82] sts from front, 14 [14: 17: 17: 20] sts up right side of front neck, 14 [14: 17: 17: 20] sts down right side of back neck, 78 [78: 80: 80: 82] sts from back, 14 [14: 17: 17: 20] sts up left side of back neck. 212 [212: 228: 228: 244] sts.
Work in g st for 3 rows, ending with RS facing for next row.
Cast off.
See information page for finishing instructions, setting in sleeves using the set-in method.

ALLURE
LISA RICHARDSON
Main image page 14 & 15

● ● ●

YARN

	S	M	L	XL	XXL
To fit bust					
	81-86	91-97	102-107	112-117	122-127 cm
	32-34	36-38	40-42	44-46	48-50 in

Rowan Purelife Organic Cotton 4 ply

6	7	7	8	8	x 50gm

(photographed in Oak Bark 759)

NEEDLES

2¾mm (no 12) (US 2) circular needle, 40 cm long
3¼mm (no 10) (US 3) circular needle, 80 cm long
1 pair 3¼mm (no 10) (US 3) needles

TENSION

28 sts and 36 rows to 10 cm measured over rev st st using 3¼mm (US 3) needles.

Pattern note: The number of sts varies whilst working patt panels. After cast-on row, all st counts given presume there is just **one** st in patt panels at all times.

PATTERN PANEL (107 sts, decreasing down to 1 st)
Round 1 (RS): *Sl 1, K1, psso, yfwd, (K1, P2) 4 times, K1, yfwd, K2tog**, yfwd, K1, yfwd, rep from * 4 times more, rep from * to ** once more.
Round 2: K3, *(P2, K1) 3 times, P2, K9, rep from * 4 times more, (P2, K1) 3 times, P2, K3.
Round 3: *Sl 1, K1, psso, yfwd, (K1, P2) 4 times, K1, yfwd, K2tog**, yfwd, K3, yfwd, rep from * 4 times more, rep from * to ** once more.
Round 4: K3, *(P2, K1) 3 times, P2, K11, rep from * 4 times more, (P2, K1) 3 times, P2, K3.
Round 5: *Sl 1, K1, psso, yfwd, (K1, P2tog) 4 times, K1, yfwd, K2tog**, yfwd, sl 1, K1, psso, K1, K2tog, yfwd, rep from * 4 times more, rep from * to ** once more.
Round 6: K3,*(P1, K1) 3 times, P1, K11, rep from * 4 times more, (P1, K1) 3 times, P1, K3.
Round 7 : *Sl 1, K1, psso, yfwd, (K1, P1) 4 times, K1, yfwd, K2tog**, yfwd, K1 tbl, yfwd, sl 1, K2tog, psso, yfwd, K1 tbl, yfwd, rep from * 4 times more, rep from * to ** once more.
Round 8: K3, *(P1, K1) 3 times, P1, K13, rep from * 4 times more, (P1, K1) 3 times, P1, K3.
Round 9: *Sl 1, K1, psso, yfwd, (sl 1, K1, psso) twice, K1, (K2tog) twice, yfwd, K2tog**, yfwd, K3, yfwd, K1, yfwd, K3, yfwd, rep from * 4 times more, rep from * to ** once more.
Round 10: Knit.
Round 11: *Sl 1, K1, psso, yfwd, sl 1, K1, psso, K1, K2tog, yfwd, K2tog**, yfwd, sl 1, K1, psso, K1, K2tog, yfwd, K1, yfwd, sl 1, K1, psso, K1, K2tog, yfwd, rep from * 4 times more, rep from * to ** once more.
Round 12: Knit.
Round 13: *Sl 1, K1, psso, yfwd, sl 1, K2tog, psso, yfwd, K2tog**, yfwd, K1 tbl, yfwd, sl 1, K2tog, psso, yfwd, K3, yfwd, sl 1, K2tog, psso, yfwd, K1 tbl, yfwd, rep from * 4 times more, rep from * to ** once more.
Round 14: Knit.
Round 15: Sl 1, K2tog, psso, yfwd, sl 1, K2tog, psso, *(P2, K1) 4 times, yfwd, K2tog, yfwd, K1, yfwd, sl 1, K1, psso, yfwd, K1, rep from * 3 times more, (P2, K1) 3 times, P2, K3tog, yfwd, K3tog. 97 sts.
Rounds 16 to 28: as round 2 to 14 but repeating rep 3 times more, instead of 4 times.
Round 29: Sl 1, K2tog, psso, yfwd, sl 1, K2tog, psso, *(P2, K1) 4 times, yfwd, K2tog, yfwd, K1, yfwd, sl 1, K1, psso, yfwd, K1, rep from * twice

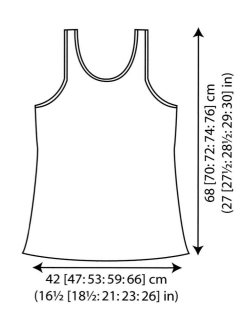

42 [47: 53: 59: 66] cm
(16½ [18½: 21: 23: 26] in)

68 [70: 72: 74: 76] cm
(27 [27½: 28½: 29: 30] in)

more, (P2, K1) 3 times, P2, K3tog, yfwd, K3tog. 77 sts.

Rounds 30 to 42: As rounds 2 to 14 but repeating rep twice more, instead of 4 times.

Round 43: Sl 1, K2tog, psso, yfwd, sl 1, K2tog, psso, ★(P2, K1) 4 times, yfwd, K2tog, yfwd, K1, yfwd, sl 1, K1, psso, yfwd, K1, rep from ★ once more, (P2, K1) 3 times, P2, K3tog, yfwd, K3tog. 57 sts.

Rounds 44 to 56: As rounds 2 to 14 but repeating rep once more, instead of 4 times.

Round 57: Sl 1, K2tog, psso, yfwd, sl 1, K2tog, psso, (P2, K1) 4 times, yfwd, K2tog, yfwd, K1, yfwd, sl 1, K1, psso, yfwd, K1, (P2, K1) 3 times, P2, K3tog, yfwd, K3tog. 37 sts.

Round 58: K3, (P2, K1) 3 times, P2, K9, (P2, K1) 3 times, P2, K3.

Round 59: ★Sl 1, K1, psso, yfwd, (K1, P2) 4 times, K1, yfwd, K2tog★★, yfwd, K3, yfwd, rep from ★ to ★★ once more.

Round 60: K3, (P2, K1) 3 times, P2, K11, (P2, K1) 3 times, P2, K3.

Round 61: ★Sl 1, K1, psso, yfwd, (K1, P2tog) 4 times, K1, yfwd, K2tog★★, yfwd, sl 1, K1, psso, K1, K2tog, yfwd, rep from ★ to ★★ once more.

Round 62: K3, (P1, K1) 3 times, P1, K11, (P1, K1) 3 times, P1, K3.

Round 63: ★Sl 1, K1, psso, yfwd, (K1, P1) 4 times, K1, yfwd, K2tog★★, yfwd, K1 tbl, yfwd, sl 1, K2tog, psso, yfwd, K1 tbl, yfwd, rep from ★ to ★★ once more.

Round 64: K3, (P1, K1) 3 times, P1, K13, (P1, K1) 3 times, P1, K3.

Round 65: ★Sl 1, K1, psso, yfwd, (sl 1, K1, psso) twice, K1, (K2tog) twice, yfwd, K2tog★★, yfwd, K3, yfwd, K1, yfwd, K3, yfwd, rep from ★ to ★★ once more.

Round 66: Knit.

Round 67: ★Sl 1, K1, psso, yfwd, sl 1, K1, psso, K1, K2tog, yfwd, K2tog★★, yfwd, sl 1, K1, psso, K1, K2tog, yfwd, K1, yfwd, sl 1, K1, psso, K1, K2tog, yfwd, rep from ★ to ★★ once more.

Round 68: Knit.

Round 69: ★Sl 1, K1, psso, yfwd, sl 1, K2tog, psso, yfwd, K2tog★★, yfwd, K1 tbl, yfwd, sl 1, K2tog, psso, yfwd, K3, yfwd, sl 1, K2tog, psso, yfwd, K1 tbl, yfwd, rep from ★ to ★★ once more.

Round 70: Knit.

Round 71: Sl 1, K2tog, psso, yfwd, sl 1, K2tog, psso, (Ps, K1) 3 times, P2, K3tog, yfwd, K3tog. 17 sts.

Round 72: K3, (P2, K1) 3 times, P2 K3.

Round 73: Sl 1, K1, psso, yfwd, (K1, P2) 4 times, K1, yfwd, K2tog.

Round 74: K3, (P2, K1) 3 times, P2, K3.

Round 75: Sl 1, K1, psso, yfwd, (K1, P2tog) 4 times, K1, yfwd, K2tog.

Round 76: K3, (P1, K1) 3 times, P2, K3.

Round 77: Sl 1, K1, psso, yfwd, (K1, P1) 4 times, K1, yfwd, K2tog.

Round 78: K3, (P1, K1) 3 times, P1, K3.

Round 79: Sl 1, K1, psso, yfwd, (sl 1, K1, psso) twice, K1, (K2tog) twice, yfwd, K2tog.

Round 80: Knit.

Round 81: Sl 1, K1, psso, yfwd, sl 1, K1, psso, K1, K2tog, yfwd, K2tog.

Round 82: Knit.

Round 83: Sl 1, K1, psso, yfwd, sl 1, K2tog, psso, yfwd, K2tog.

Round 84: Knit.

Round 85: Sl 1, K1, psso, K1, K2tog

Round 86: K3.

Round 87: Sl 1, K2tog, psso, 1 st.

Round 88: K1.

Round 89 onwards: P1.

BODY (worked in one piece to armholes)
Using 3¼mm (US 3) circular needle cast on 552 [580: 616: 648: 688] sts.
Taking care not to twist cast-on edge, now work in rounds as folls:

Round 1 (RS): P19 [21: 24: 27: 30], work next 107 sts as round 1 of patt panel, P77 [87: 99: 109: 123], work next 107 sts as round 1 of patt panel, P19 [21: 24: 27: 30], place marker on needle (to denote base of right side seam), P58 [65: 74: 82: 92], work next 107 sts as round 1 of patt panel, P58 [65: 74: 82: 92].
This round sets position of sts – 3 patt panels with all other sts in rev st st (P every round).
Keeping sts correct as now set and working appropriate rounds of patt panels, cont as folls:
Work 15 rounds.

Round 17 (RS): P2, P2tog, patt to within 4 sts of marker, P2tog tbl, P4 (marker is at centre of these 4 sts), P2tog, patt to last 4 sts, P2tog tbl, P2. 230 [258: 294: 326: 366] sts (see pattern note).
Work 9 rounds.
Rep last 10 rounds 4 times more, then round 17 (the dec round) again.
210 [238: 274: 306: 346] sts.
Work 11 rounds.

Round 79 (RS): P2, M1, patt to within 2 sts of marker, M1, P4 (marker is at centre of these 4 sts), M1, patt to last 2 sts, M1, P2.
214 [242: 278: 310: 350] sts.
Work 7 rounds.
Rep last 8 rounds 4 times more, then first of these rounds (the inc round) again.
234 [262: 298: 330: 370] sts. (All sts are now in rev st st.)
Con straight until work meas 44 [45: 46: 47: 48] cm.

Divide for back and front
Next round(RS): Cast off 8 [10: 11: 13: 14] sts, P until there are 101 [111: 127: 139: 157] sts on right needle and slip these sts onto a holder for front, cast off next 16 [20: 22: 26: 28] sts, P until there are 101 [111: 127: 139: 157] sts on right needle and slip these sts onto a holder for back, cast off rem 8 [10: 11: 13: 14] sts.
Break yarn.

Shape front
Slip 101 [111: 127: 139: 157] sts left on front holder onto 3¼mm (US 3) needles, rejoin yarn with **WS** facing and K to end.
Beg with a P row, now work in rows in rev st st as folls:
Dec 1 st at each end of next 9 [9: 11: 13: 15] rows, then foll 8 [10: 9: 10: 9] alt rows.
67 [73: 87: 93: 109] sts.
Work 1 row, ending with RS facing for next row.

Shape neck
Next Row (RS): (P2tog) 0 [0: 1: 1: 1] times, P22 [25: 30: 33: 41] and turn, leaving rem sts on a holder.
Work each side of neck separately.
Dec 1 st at neck edge of next 8 rows, then on foll 2 alt rows, then 2 [2: 3: 3: 4] foll 4th rows, then on 2 foll 6th rows **and at same time** dec 0 [0: 1: 1: 1] st at armhole edge of 0 [0: 2nd: 2nd: 2nd] and foll 0 [0: 1: 0: 3] alt rows.
8 [11: 14: 18: 22] sts.
Cont straight until armhole meas 23 [24: 25: 26: 27] cm, ending with RS facing for next row.

Shape shoulder
Cast off 4 [6: 7: 9: 11] sts at beg of next row.
Work 1 row.
Cast off rem 4 [6: 7: 9: 11] sts.
With RS facing, rejoin yarn to rem sts of front, cast off centre 23 sts, P to last 0 [0: 2: 2: 2] sts, (P2tog) 0 [0: 1: 1: 1] times.
Complete to match first side, reversing shapings.

Shape back
Slip 101 [111: 127: 139: 157] sts left on back holder onto 3¼mm (US 3) needles, rejoin yarn with **WS** facing and K to end.
Complete to match front.

MAKING UP
Press as described on the information page.
Join both shoulder seams using back stitch, or mattress stitch if preferred.

Neckband
With RS facing and using ¾mm (US 2) circular needle, pick up and knit 56 [56: 60: 60: 64] sts down left side of front neck, 23 sts from front, 56 [56: 60: 60: 64] sts up right side of front neck, 56 [56: 60: 60: 64] sts down right side of back neck, 23 sts from back, then 56 [56: 60: 60: 64] sts up left side of back neck.
270 [270: 286: 286: 302] sts.
Round 1 (RS): Purl.
Round 2: Knit.
Cast off purlwise (on RS).

Armhole borders (both alike)
With RS facing and using 2¾mm (US 2) circular needle, beg and ending at underarm point, pick up and knit 144 [154: 162: 172: 180] sts evenly all round armhole edge.
Round 1 (RS): Purl.
Round 2: Knit.
Cast off purlwise (on RS).
See information page for finishing instructions.

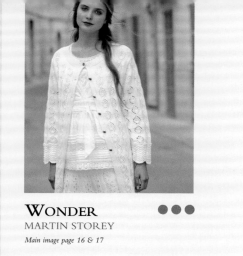

WONDER

MARTIN STOREY

Main image page 16 & 17

YARN

S	M	L	XL	XXL

To fit bust
81-86 91-97 102-107 112-117 122-127 cm
32-34 36-38 40-42 44-46 48-50 in
Rowan Fine Milk Cotton

14	16	18	19	21	x 50gm

(photographed in Snow 493)

NEEDLES

1 pair 2mm (no 14) (US 0) needles
1 pair 2¾mm (no 12) (US 2) needles

BUTTONS - 6 x RW5021 from Bedecked.
Please see information page for contact details.

TENSION

30 sts and 38 rows to 10 cm measured over st st
using 2¾mm (US 2) needles.

SPECIAL ABBREVIATIONS

inc 2 = (K1 tbl, K1) into next st, insert left
needle point behind vertical strand that runs
downwards from between the 2 sts just made
and K1 tbl into this strand - 3 sts made from 1
st; **dec 4** = K2tog tbl, K3tog, lift 2nd st on
right needle (the K2tog tbl) over first st (the
K3tog) and off right needle - 4 sts decreased.

MOTIF PANEL (13 sts)
Row 1 (RS): K13.
Row 2 and every foll alt row: P13.
Row 3: K5, keeping yarn at back (WS) of
work, slip next 3 sts onto right needle, bring
yarn to front (RS) of work then slip same 3 sts
back onto left needle, take yarn back to back
(WS) of work and K the 3 wrapped sts, K5.
Row 5: K3, K3tog, yfwd, inc 2, yfwd, K3tog
tbl, K3.
Row 7: K1, K3tog, yfwd, K2tog, yfwd, inc 2,
yfwd, sl 1, K1, psso, yfwd, K3tog tbl, K1.
Row 9: (K2tog, yfwd) 3 times, K1 tbl, (yfwd,
sl 1, K1, psso) 3 times.
Row 11: K1, (yfwd, K2tog) twice, yfwd, sl 1,
K2tog, psso, yfwd, (sl 1, K1, psso, yfwd) twice,
K1.
Row 13: (sl 1, K1, psso, yfwd) 3 times, K1 tbl,
(yfwd, K2tog) 3 times.
Row 15: K1, inc in next st, yfwd, sl 1, K1, psso,
yfwd, dec 4, yfwd, K2tog, yfwd, inc in next st,
K1.
Row 17: K3, inc in next st, yfwd, dec 4, yfwd,
inc in next st, K3.

Row 18: P13.
These 18 rows form motif panel and are
repeated.

BACK
Using 2¾mm (US 2) needles cast on 154 [170:
190: 210: 232] sts.
Row 1 (RS): Knit.
Row 2: Purl.
Row 3: K5 [13: 5: 15: 8], *(K2tog) 3 times,
(yfwd, K1) 6 times, (K2tog) 3 times, rep from
* to last 5 [13: 5: 15: 8] sts, K5 [13: 5: 15: 8].
Row 4: Knit.
Rep these 4 rows 8 times more, then rows 1 to
3 again, ending with **WS** facing for next row.
Row 40 (WS): K6 [4: 4: 6: 3], K2tog,
(K12 [14: 13: 12: 12], K2tog) 10 [10: 12: 14: 16]
times, K6 [4: 4: 6: 3].
143 [159: 177: 195: 215] sts.
Now work in patt, placing motif panels as folls:
Row 1 (RS): K9 [1: 10: 3: 13], *work next
13 sts as row 1 of motif panel, K3, rep from
* to last 22 [14: 23: 16: 26] sts, work next 13 sts
as row 1 of motif panel, K9 [1: 10: 3: 13].
Row 2: P9 [1: 10: 3: 13], *work next 13 sts as
row 2 of motif panel, P3, rep from * to last
22 [14: 23: 16: 26] sts, work next 13 sts as row
2 of motif panel, P9 [1: 10: 3: 13].
These 2 rows set the sts - 8 [10: 10: 12: 12]
motif panels on a background of st st.
Working appropriate rows of motif panels, cont
as folls:
Cont in patt until back meas 23 [24: 25: 26: 27] cm,
ending with RS facing for next row.
Keeping patt correct, dec 1 st at each end of
next and 2 foll 14th rows, then on 5 foll 12th
rows. 127 [143: 161: 179: 199] sts.
Work 11 rows, ending with RS facing for

next row.
Inc 1 st at each end of next and 4 foll 12th
rows. 137 [153: 171: 189: 209] sts.
Cont straight until back meas 66 [67: 68:
69: 70] cm, ending with RS facing for next
row.
Shape armholes
Keeping patt correct, cast off 5 sts at beg of
next 2 rows. 127 [143: 161: 179: 199] sts.
Dec 1 st at each end of next and foll 6 alt rows.
113 [129: 147: 165: 185] sts.
Cont straight until armhole meas 20 [21: 22:
23: 24] cm, ending with RS facing for next
row.
Shape shoulders and back neck
Cast off 7 [10: 13: 16: 19] sts at beg of next
2 rows. 99 [109: 121: 133: 147] sts.
Next row (RS): Cast off 7 [10: 13: 16: 19] sts,
patt until there are 12 [14: 16: 19: 22] sts on
right needle and turn, leaving rem sts on a
holder.
Work each side of neck separately.
Cast off 4 sts at beg of next row.
Cast off rem 8 [10: 12: 15: 18] sts.
With RS facing, rejoin yarn to rem sts, cast off
centre 61 [61: 63: 63: 65] sts, patt to end.
Complete to match first side, reversing
shapings.

LEFT FRONT
Using 2¾mm (US 2) needles cast on 77 [85:
95: 105: 116] sts.
Row 1 (RS): Knit.
Row 2: Purl.
Row 3: K5 [13: 5: 15: 8], *(K2tog) 3 times,
(yfwd, K1) 6 times, (K2tog) 3 times, rep from
* to end.
Row 4: Knit.

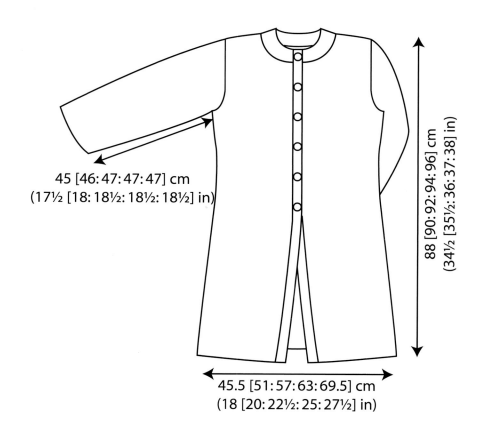

45 [46: 47: 47: 47] cm
(17½ [18: 18½: 18½: 18½] in)

88 [90: 92: 94: 96] cm
(34½ [35½: 36: 37: 38] in)

45.5 [51: 57: 63: 69.5] cm
(18 [20: 22½: 25: 27½] in)

Rep these 4 rows 8 times more, then rows 1 to 3 again, ending with **WS** facing for next row.

Row 40 (WS): K7 [7: 6: 6: 4], K2tog, (K13 [15: 14: 13: 13], K2tog) 4 [4: 5: 6: 7] times, K8 [8: 7: 7: 5]. 72 [80: 89: 98: 108] sts.

Now work in patt, placing motif panels as folls:

Row 1 (RS): K9 [1: 10: 3: 13], *work next 13 sts as row 1 of motif panel, K3, rep from * to last 15 sts, work next 13 sts as row 1 of motif panel, K2.

Row 2: P2, *work next 13 sts as row 2 of motif panel, P3, rep from * to last 22 [14: 23: 16: 26] sts, work next 13 sts as row 2 of motif panel, P9 [1: 10: 3: 13].

These 2 rows set the sts – 4 [5: 5: 6: 6] motif panels on a background of st st.

Working appropriate rows of motif panels, cont as folls:

Cont in patt until left front meas 23 [24: 25: 26: 27] cm, ending with RS facing for next row.

Keeping patt correct, dec 1 st at beg of next and 2 foll 14th rows, then on 5 foll 12th rows. 64 [72: 81: 90: 100] sts.

Work 11 rows, ending with RS facing for next row.

Inc 1 st at beg of next and 4 foll 12th rows. 69 [77: 86: 95: 105] sts.

Cont straight until left front matches back to beg of armhole shaping, ending with RS facing for next row.

Shape armhole

Keeping patt correct, cast off 5 sts at beg of next row. 64 [72: 81: 90: 100] sts.

Work 1 row.

Dec 1 st at armhole edge of next and foll 6 alt rows. 57 [65: 74: 83: 93] sts.

Cont straight until 25 [25: 29: 29: 33] rows less have been worked than on back to beg of shoulder shaping, ending with **WS** facing for next row.

Shape front neck

Keeping patt correct, cast off 15 sts at beg of next row, then 5 sts at beg of foll alt row. 37 [45: 54: 63: 73] sts.

Dec 1 st at neck edge of next 9 rows, then on foll 6 alt rows, then on 0 [0: 1: 1: 2] foll 4th rows. 22 [30: 38: 47: 56] sts.

Work 1 row, ending with RS facing for next row.

Shape shoulder

Cast off 7 [10: 13: 16: 19] sts at beg of next and foll alt row.

Work 1 row.

Cast off rem 8 [10: 12: 15: 18] sts.

RIGHT FRONT

Using 2¾mm (US 2) needles cast on 77 [85: 95: 105: 116] sts.

Row 1 (RS): Knit.

Row 2: Purl.

Row 3: *(K2tog) 3 times, (yfwd, K1) 6 times, (K2tog) 3 times, rep from * to last 5 [13: 5: 15: 8] sts, K5 [13: 5: 15: 8].

Row 4: Knit.

Rep these 4 rows 8 times more, then rows 1 to 3 again, ending with **WS** facing for next row.

Row 40 (WS): K7 [7: 6: 6: 4], K2tog, (K13 [15: 14: 13: 13], K2tog) 4 [4: 5: 6: 7] times, K8 [8: 7: 7: 5]. 72 [80: 89: 98: 108] sts.

Now work in patt, placing motif panels as folls:

Row 1 (RS): K2, *work next 13 sts as row 1 of motif panel, K3, rep from * to last 22 [14: 23: 16: 26] sts, work next 13 sts as row 1 of motif panel, K9 [1: 10: 3: 13].

Row 2: P9 [1: 10: 3: 13], *work next 13 sts as row 2 of motif panel, P3, rep from * to last 15 sts, work next 13 sts as row 2 of motif panel, P2.

These 2 rows set the sts – 4 [5: 5: 6: 6] motif panels on a background of st st.

Working appropriate rows of motif panels, cont as folls:

Cont in patt until right front meas 23 [24: 25: 26: 27] cm, ending with RS facing for next row.

Keeping patt correct, dec 1 st at end of next and 2 foll 14th rows, then on 5 foll 12th rows. 64 [72: 81: 90: 100] sts.

Complete to match left front, reversing shapings.

SLEEVES

Using 2¾mm (US 2) needles cast on 100 [104: 106: 106: 110] sts.

Row 1 (RS): Knit.

Row 2: Purl.

Row 3: K5 [7: 8: 8: 10], *(K2tog) 3 times, (yfwd, K1) 6 times, (K2tog) 3 times, rep from * to last 5 [7: 8: 8: 10] sts, K5 [7: 8: 8: 10].

Row 4: Knit.

Rep these 4 rows 8 times more, then rows 1 to 3 again, ending with **WS** facing for next row.

Row 40 (WS): K9 [9: 10: 10: 10], K2tog, (K18 [19: 19: 19: 20], K2tog) 4 times, K9 [9: 10: 10: 10]. 95 [99: 101: 101: 105] sts.

Now work in patt, placing motif panels as folls:

Row 1 (RS): K1 [3: 4: 4: 6], *work next 13 sts as row 1 of motif panel, K3, rep from * to last 14 [16: 17: 17: 19] sts, work next 13 sts as row 1 of motif panel, K1 [3: 4: 4: 6].

Row 2: P1 [3: 4: 4: 6], *work next 13 sts as row 2 of motif panel, P3, rep from * to last 14 [16: 17: 17: 19] sts, work next 13 sts as row 2 of motif panel, P1 [3: 4: 4: 6].

These 2 rows set the sts – 6 motif panels on a background of st st.

Working appropriate rows of motif panels, cont as set, shaping sides by inc 1 st at each end of 5th [5th: 3rd: 3rd: next] and every foll 8th [8th: 6th: 6th: 6th] row to 115 [125: 111: 135: 145] sts, then on every foll 10th [10th: 8th: 8th: –] row until there are 121 [127: 133: 139: –] sts, taking inc sts into st st.

Cont straight until sleeve meas 45 [46: 47: 47: 47] cm, ending with RS facing for next row.

Shape top

Keeping patt correct, cast off 5 sts at beg of next 2 rows. 111 [117: 123: 129: 135] sts.

Dec 1 st at each end of next and foll 7 alt rows, then on foll row, ending with RS facing for next row.

Cast off rem 93 [99: 105: 111: 117] sts.

MAKING UP

Press as described on the information page. Join both shoulder seams using back stitch, or mattress stitch if preferred.

Neckband

With RS facing and using 2mm (US 0) needles, beg and ending at front opening edges, pick up and knit 42 [42: 46: 46: 50] sts up right side of neck, 69 [69: 71: 71: 73] sts from back, then 42 [42: 46: 46: 50] sts down left side of neck. 153 [153: 163: 163: 173] sts.

Row 1 (WS): K1, *P1, K1, rep from * to end.

Row 2: K2, *P1, K1, rep from * to last st, K1.

These 2 rows form rib.

Cont in rib for a further 13 rows, ending with RS facing for next row.

Cast off in rib.

Button band

Using 2mm (US 0) needles cast on 11 sts.

Beg with row 2, work in rib as given for neckband until band, when slightly stretched, fits up entire left front opening edge, from cast-on edge to top of neckband, ending with RS facing for next row.

Cast off in rib.

Slip stitch band in place.

Mark positions for 6 buttons on this band – first to come 42 cm up from cast-on edge, last to come 2 cm below top of neckband, and rem 4 buttons evenly spaced between.

Buttonhole band

Work to match button band, with the addition of 6 buttonholes worked to correspond with positions marked for buttons as folls:

Buttonhole row (RS): Rib 5, cast off 2 sts (to make a buttonhole – cast on 2 sts over these cast-off sts on next row), rib to end.

See information page for finishing instructions, setting in sleeves using the shallow set-in method.

COMFORT
ERIKA KNIGHT
Main image page 76

YARN

XS S M L XL XXL 2XL

To fit chest

97 102 107 112 117 122 127 cm
38 40 42 44 46 48 50 in

Rowan Pima Cotton DK

11 12 13 14 14 15 16 x 50gm
(photographed in Bark 073)

NEEDLES

1 pair 3¾mm (no 9) (US 5) needles
1 pair 4mm (no 8) (US 6) needles

BUTTONS - 4 x BN1124 from Bedecked.
Please see information page for contact details.

TENSION

23 sts and 30 rows to 10 cm measured over patt
using 4mm (US 6) needles.

BACK

Using 3¾mm (US 5) needles cast on 117 [125:
131: 139: 145: 151: 159] sts.
Row 1 (RS): K0 [0: 0: 0: 0: 1: 1] sts, P2 [2: 1: 1:
0: 2: 2], *K2, P2, rep from * to last 3 [3: 2: 2: 1:
0: 0] sts, K2 [2: 2: 2: 1: 0: 0], P1 [1: 0: 0: 0: 0: 0].
Row 2: K0 [0: 1: 1: 0: 0: 0], P0 [0: 2: 2: 2: 1: 1],
*K2, P2, rep from * to last 1 [1: 0: 0: 3: 2: 2] sts,
K1 [1: 0: 0: 2: 2: 2], P0 [0: 0: 0: 1: 0: 0].
These 2 rows form patt.
Work in patt for a further 2 rows, ending with
RS facing for next row.
Change to 4mm (US 6) needles.
Cont in patt until back meas 47 [48: 49: 48: 49:
48: 49] cm, ending with RS facing for next
row.
Shape armholes
Keeping patt correct, cast off 5 sts at beg of
next 2 rows.
107 [115: 121: 129: 135: 141: 149] sts.
Next row (RS): P1, K2, K2tog, patt to last
5 sts, sl 1, K1, psso, K2, P1.
Next row: K2, P1, P2tog tbl, patt to last 5 sts,
P2tog, P1, K2.
Rep last 2 rows 0 [1: 1: 2: 2: 3: 3] times more.
103 [107: 113: 117: 123: 125: 133] sts.
Next row (RS): P1, K2, K2tog, patt to last
5 sts, sl 1, K1, psso, K2, P1.
Next row: K2, P1, patt to last 3 sts, P1, K2.
Rep last 2 rows 4 [4: 6: 6: 8: 7: 9] times more.
93 [97: 99: 103: 105: 109: 113] sts.
Next row (RS): P1, K2, patt to last 3 sts,
K2, P1.

Next row: K2, P1, patt to last 3 sts, P1, K2.
Last 2 rows set the sts for rest of back.
Cont straight until armhole meas 23 [24: 25:
26: 27: 28: 29] cm, ending with RS facing for
next row.
Shape shoulders and back neck
Cast off 9 [10: 10: 10: 11: 11: 12] sts at beg of
next 2 rows. 75 [77: 79: 83: 83: 87: 89] sts.
Next row (RS): Cast off 9 [10: 10: 10: 11:
11: 12] sts, patt until there are 13 [12: 13: 14:
13: 14: 14] sts on right needle and turn, leaving
rem sts on a holder.
Work each side of neck separately.
Cast off 3 sts at beg of next row.
Cast off rem 10 [9: 10: 11: 10: 11: 11] sts.
With RS facing, rejoin yarn to rem sts, cast off
centre 31 [33: 33: 35: 35: 37: 37] sts, patt to
end.
Complete to match first side, reversing
shapings.

POCKET LININGS (make 2)
Using 4mm (US 6) needles cast on 29 [33: 33:
33: 37: 37: 37] sts.
Row 1 (RS): *P2, K2, rep from * to last st, P1.
Row 2: *K2, P2, rep from * to last st, K1.
These 2 rows form patt.
Cont in patt for a further 33 rows, ending with
WS facing for next row.
Break yarn and leave sts on a holder.

LEFT FRONT
Using 3¾mm (US 5) needles cast on 68 [72:
75: 79: 82: 85: 89] sts.
Row 1 (RS): K0 [0: 0: 0: 0: 1: 1], P2 [2: 1: 1: 0:
2: 2], *K2, P2, rep from * to last 6 sts, (K1, P1)
3 times.
Row 2: (K1, P1) twice, K1, P2, *K2, P2, rep
from * to last 1 [1: 0: 0: 3: 2: 2] sts, K1 [1: 0: 0:
2: 2: 2], P0 [0: 0: 0: 1: 0: 0].
These 2 rows form patt.
Work in patt for a further 2 rows, ending with
RS facing for next row.
Change to 4mm (US 6) needles.

Cont in patt until left front meas 3 [4: 5: 4: 5:
4: 5] cm, ending with RS facing for next row.
Next row (buttonhole row) (RS): Patt to
last 11 sts, cast off 3 sts (to make a buttonhole -
cast on 3 sts over these cast-off sts on next
row), patt to end.
Making a further 3 buttonholes in this way
12 cm after each previous buttonhole and
noting that no further reference will be made
to buttonholes, cont as folls:
Cont straight until left front meas 18 cm,
ending with RS facing for next row.
Place pocket
Next row (RS): Patt 12 [12: 15: 15: 18:
17: 21] sts, cast off next 29 [33: 33: 33: 37:
37: 37] sts in patt, patt to end.
Next row: Patt 27 [27: 27: 31: 27: 31: 31] sts,
with **WS** facing patt across 29 [33: 33: 33: 37:
37: 37] sts of first pocket lining, patt to end.
Cont straight until 18 rows less have been
worked than on back to beg of armhole
shaping, ending with RS facing for next row.
(All 4 buttonholes should now have been
worked.)
Shape front slope
Next row (RS): Patt to last 8 sts, P2tog,
patt 6 sts.
Next row: Patt 6 sts, K1, patt to end.
Keeping sts correct as now set and working all
decreases as set by first of last 2 rows, cont as
folls:
Dec 1 st at front slope edge of next [next: 3rd:
next: 3rd: 3rd: 3rd] and foll 0 [1: 0: 0: 0: 0: 0] alt
row, then on 3 foll 4th rows.
63 [66: 70: 74: 77: 80: 84] sts.
Work 3 [1: 1: 3: 1: 1: 1] rows, ending with RS
facing for next row.
Shape armhole
Keeping patt correct, cast off 5 sts at beg and
dec 1 [0: 0: 1: 0: 0: 0] st at end of next row.
57 [61: 65: 68: 72: 75: 79] sts.
Work 1 row.
Working all armhole decrease (and armhole
edge) as set by back, cont as folls:

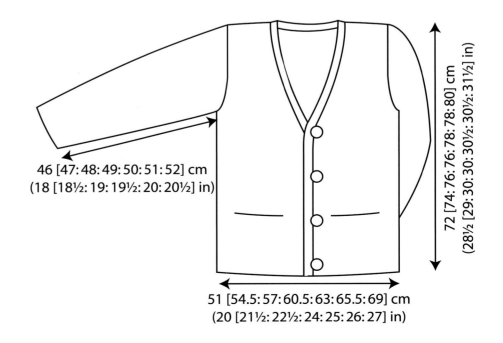

46 [47: 48: 49: 50: 51: 52] cm
(18 [18½: 19: 19½: 20: 20½] in)

51 [54.5: 57: 60.5: 63: 65.5: 69] cm
(20 [21½: 22½: 24: 25: 26: 27] in)

72 [74: 76: 76: 78: 78: 80] cm
(28½ [29: 30: 30: 30½: 30½: 31½] in)

Dec 1 st at armhole edge of next 3 [5: 5: 7: 7: 9: 9] rows, then on foll 4 [4: 6: 6: 8: 7: 9] alt rows **and at same time** dec 1 st at front slope edge of 3rd [next: next: 3rd: next: next: next] and 2 [3: 4: 4: 5: 5: 6] foll 4th rows.
47 [48: 49: 50: 51: 53: 54] sts.
Dec 1 st at front slope edge **only** on 4th [4th: 4th: 4th: 2nd: 2nd: 2nd] and 11 [11: 11: 11: 10: 12: 9] foll 4th rows, then on 0 [0: 0: 0: 1: 0: 2] foll 6th rows. 35 [36: 37: 38: 39: 40: 42] sts.
Cont straight until left front matches back to beg of shoulder shaping, ending with RS facing for next row.

Shape shoulders and back neck
Cast off 9 [10: 10: 10: 11: 11: 12] sts at beg of next and foll alt row, then 10 [9: 10: 11: 10: 11: 11] sts at beg of foll alt row.
Cont as set on rem 7 sts only (for back neck border extension) for a further 7.5 [8: 8: 8.5: 8.5: 9: 9] cm, ending with RS facing for next row.
Cast off.

RIGHT FRONT
Using 3¾mm (US 5) needles cast on 68 [72: 75: 79: 82: 85: 89] sts.
Row 1 (RS): (P1, K1) twice, P1, ★K2, P2, rep from ★ to last 3 [3: 2: 2: 1: 0: 0] sts, K2 [2: 2: 2: 1: 0: 0], P1 [1: 0: 0: 0: 0: 0].
Row 2: K0 [0: 1: 1: 0: 0: 0], P0 [0: 2: 2: 2: 1: 1], ★K2, P2, rep from ★ to last 8 sts, K2, (P1, K1) 3 times.
These 2 rows form patt.

Work in patt for a further 2 rows, ending with RS facing for next row.
Change to 4mm (US 6) needles.
Cont in patt until right front meas 18 cm, ending with RS facing for next row.

Place pocket
Next row (RS): Patt 27 [27: 27: 31: 27: 31: 31] sts, cast off next 29 [33: 33: 33: 37: 37: 37] sts in patt, patt to end.
Next row: Patt 12 [12: 15: 15: 18: 17: 21] sts, with **WS** facing patt across 29 [33: 33: 33: 37: 37: 37] sts of second pocket lining, patt to end.
Cont straight until 18 rows less have been worked than on back to beg of armhole shaping, ending with RS facing for next row.

Shape front slope
Next row (RS): Patt 6 sts, P2tog tbl, patt to end.
Next row: Patt to last 7 sts, K1, patt 6 sts.
Keeping sts correct as now set and working all decreases as set by first of last 2 rows, complete to match left front, reversing shapings.

SLEEVES
Using 3¾mm (US 5) needles cast on 55 [55: 59: 59: 63: 63: 67] sts.
Row 1 (RS): P1, K2, ★P2, K2, rep from ★ to end.
Row 2: K1, P2, ★K2, P2, rep from ★ to end.
These 2 rows form patt.
Work in patt for a further 2 rows, ending with RS facing for next row.

Change to 4mm (US 6) needles.
Cont in patt, shaping sides by inc 1 st at each end of 3rd [next: 3rd: 3rd: 3rd: 3rd: 3rd] and every foll 8th row to 81 [87: 79: 87: 77: 85: 75] sts, then on every foll 10th [–: 10th: 10th: 10th: 10th: 10th] row until there are 85 [–: 89: 91: 93: 95: 97] sts, taking inc sts into patt.
Cont straight until sleeve meas 46 [47: 48: 49: 50: 51: 52] cm, ending with RS facing for next row.

Shape top
Keeping patt correct, cast off 5 sts at beg of next 2 rows. 75 [77: 79: 81: 83: 85: 87] sts.
Working all shaping (and edge sts) in same way as armhole shaping, dec 1 st at each end of next 3 rows, then on foll 3 alt rows, then on 3 foll 4th rows. 57 [59: 61: 63: 65: 67: 69] sts.
Work 1 row.
Dec 1 st at each end of next and every foll alt row to 47 sts, then on foll 9 rows, ending with RS facing for next row. 29 sts.
Cast off 5 sts at beg of next 2 rows.
Cast off rem 19 sts.

MAKING UP
Press as described on the information page.
Join both shoulder seams using back stitch, or mattress stitch if preferred. Join cast-off ends of back neck border extensions, then sew in place to back neck.
See information page for finishing instructions, setting in sleeves using the set-in method.

BEWITCH
GRACE MELVILLE
Main image page 22 & 23

●●

YARN

S	M	L	XL	XXL

To fit bust
81-86 91-97 102-107 112-117 122-127 cm
32-34 36-38 40-42 44-46 48-50 in
Rowan Fine Milk Cotton

9	10	10	11	12	x 50gm

(photographed in Pastille 494)

NEEDLES
1 pair 2¼mm (no 13) (US 1) needles
1 pair 2¾mm (no 12) (US 2) needles
2¼mm (no 13) (US 1) circular needle, 80 cm long
2¾mm (no 12) (US 2) circular needle, 80 cm long

TENSION
26 sts and 42 rows to 10 cm measured over patt, 30 sts and 38 rows to 10 cm measured over st st, both using 2¾mm (US 2) needles.

SPECIAL ABBREVIATIONS
sL2togK = slip next 2 sts as though to K2tog;

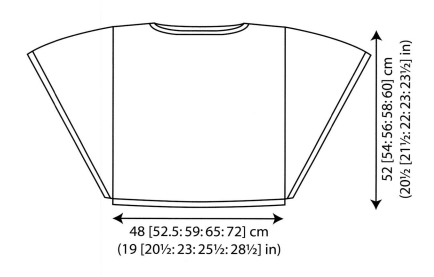

52 [54: 56: 58: 60] cm
(20½ [21½: 22: 23: 23½] in)

48 [52.5: 59: 65: 72] cm
(19 [20½: 23: 25½: 28½] in)

p2sso = pass 2 slipped sts over; **MK** = (K1, P1, K1, P1, K1) all into next st, lift 2nd, 3rd, 4th and 5th sts on right needle over first st and off right needle.

BACK

Using 2¼mm (US 1) needles cast on 125 [137: 153: 169: 187] sts.
Work in g st for 8 rows, ending with RS facing for next row.
Place markers at both ends of last row.
Change to 2¾mm (US 2) needles.
Following appropriate chart for size being knitted, working first 8 [5: 4: 3: 3] sts and last 9 [6: 5: 4: 4] sts as shown on chart, repeating the 18 st patt rep 6 [: 7: 8: 9: 10] times across each row and repeating the 24 row patt rep throughout, now work in patt from chart as folls:
Cont straight until back meas 50 [52: 54: 56: 58] cm, ending with RS facing for next row.
Shape shoulders and back neck
Cast off 8 [10: 11: 13: 15] sts at beg of next 2 rows. 109 [117: 131: 143: 157] sts.
Next row (RS): Cast off 8 [10: 12: 14: 16] sts, patt until there are 24 [26: 30: 34: 38] sts on right needle and turn, leaving rem sts on a holder.
Work each side of neck separately.
Cast off 3 sts at beg of next row, 9 [10: 12: 14: 16] sts at beg of foll row, then 3 sts at beg of next row.
Cast off rem 9 [10: 12: 14: 16] sts.

With RS facing, rejoin yarn to rem sts, cast off centre 45 [45: 47: 47: 49] sts, patt to end.
Complete to match first side, reversing shapings.

FRONT

Work as given for back until 6 [6: 10: 10: 14] rows less have been worked than on back to beg of shoulder shaping, ending with RS facing for next row.
Shape front neck
Next row (RS): Patt 40 [46: 54: 62: 71] sts and turn, leaving rem sts on a holder.
Work each side of neck separately.
Keeping patt correct, dec 1 st at neck edge of next 4 rows, then on foll 0 [0: 2: 2: 2] alt rows, then on 0 [0: 0: 0: 1] foll 4th row.
36 [42: 48: 56: 64] sts.
Work 1 row, ending with RS facing for next row.
Shape shoulder
Cast off 8 [10: 11: 13: 15] sts at beg of next row, 8 [10: 12: 14: 16] sts at beg of foll alt row, then 9 [10: 12: 14: 16] sts at beg of foll alt row **and at same time** dec 1 st at neck edge of next [next: 3rd: 3rd: 3rd] and foll 1 [1: 0: 0: 0] alt row.
Work 1 row.
Cast off rem 9 [10: 12: 14: 16] sts.
With RS facing, rejoin yarn to rem sts, cast off centre 45 sts, patt to end.
Complete to match first side, reversing shapings.

SLEEVE SECTIONS

Using 2¼mm (US 1) circular needle cast on 279 [291: 303: 315: 327] sts.
Work in g st for 8 rows, inc 1 st at each end of 3rd and foll 5 rows and ending with RS facing for next row. 291 [303: 315: 327: 339] sts.
Place markers at both ends of last row.
Change to 2¾mm (US 2) circular needle.
Beg with a K row, now work in st st as folls:
Cast off 3 sts at beg of next 52 [40: 28: 16: 4] rows, then 4 sts at beg of foll 26 [38: 50: 62: 74] rows.
Cast off rem 31 sts.

MAKING UP

Press as described on the information page.
Join right shoulder seam using the back stitch, or mattress stitch if preferred.
Neckband
With RS facing and using 2¼mm (US 1) needles, pick up and knit 6 [6: 10: 10: 14] sts down left side of neck, 45 sts from front, 6 [6: 10: 10: 14] sts up right side of neck, then 57 [57: 59: 59: 61] sts from back.
114 [114: 124: 124: 134] sts.
Work in g st for 6 rows, ending with **WS** facing for next row.
Cast off knitwise (on **WS**).
Join left shoulder and neckband seam.
Matching markers, sew sleeve sections to back and front. Join row-end edges of sleeve g st sections. Join side seams below markers.
See information page for finishing instructions.

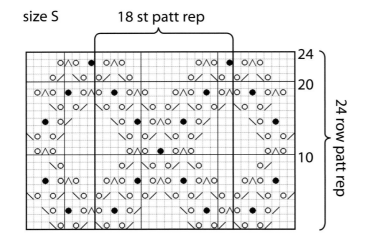

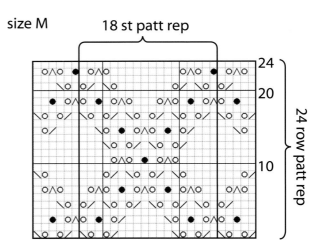

key

☐ K on RS, P on WS
☑ K2tog
◺ sl1, K1, psso
◢ sl2togK, K1, p2sso
⊙ yfwd
● MK

size L | 18 st patt rep

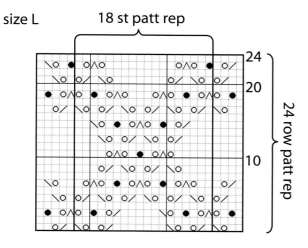

24 row patt rep

size XL & XXL | 18 st patt rep

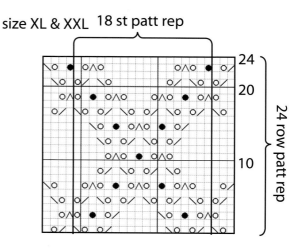

24 row patt rep

HELLEBORE
MARTIN STOREY

Main image page 44 & 45

YARN

S	M	L	XL	XXL

To fit bust
81-86 91-97 102-107 112-117 122-127 cm
32-34 36-38 40-42 44-46 48-50 in

Rowan Cotton Glacé

11	11	12	12	13	x 50gm

(photographed in Oyster 730)

NEEDLES

1 pair 2³⁄4mm (no 12) (US 2) needles
1 pair 3¹⁄4mm (no 10) (US 3) needles
2³⁄4mm (no 12) (US 2) circular needle,
100 cm long

TENSION

28 sts and 35 rows to 10 cm measured over patt
using 3¹⁄4mm (US 3) needles.

BODY

Using 3¹⁄4mm (US 3) needles cast on 135 [149:
163: 177: 205] sts.
Work in patt as folls:
Row 1 (RS): K8, ★(P1, K1) 3 times, P1, K7,
rep from ★ to last st, K1.

Row 2: P1, ★P7, (K1, P1) 3 times, K1, rep
from ★ to last 8 sts, P8.
Row 3: P8, ★(P1, K1) 3 times, P8, rep from ★
to last st, P1.
Row 4: As row 2.
Row 5: As row 1.
Row 6: K1, ★K8, (P1, K1) 3 times, rep from ★
to last 8 sts, K8.
Rows 7 to 9: As rows 1 to 3.
Row 10: As row 2.
Row 11: As row 1.
Row 12: P1, ★(K1, P1) 3 times, K1, P7, rep
from ★ to last 8 sts, (K1, P1) 4 times.
Row 13: (K1, P1) 4 times, ★K7, (P1, K1) 3
times, P1, rep from ★ to last st, K1.
Row 14: P1, ★(K1, P1) 3 times, K8, rep from ★
to last 8 sts, (K1, P1) 4 times.
Row 15: As row 13.
Row 16: As row 12.
Row 17: (K1, P1) 4 times, ★P8, (K1, P1) 3
times, rep from ★ to last st, K1.
Rows 18 to 20: As rows 12 to 14.
Row 21: As row 13.

Row 22: As row 12.
These 22 rows form patt.
Cont in patt until body meas 46 [51: 56: 61:
66] cm, ending with RS facing for next row.
Cast off.

SLEEVES
Using 2³⁄4mm (US 2) needles cast on 128 [142:
156: 170: 184] sts.
Work in g st for 4 rows, ending with RS facing
for next row.
Change to 3¹⁄4mm (US 3) needles.
Work in patt as folls:
Row 1 (RS): K1, ★(P1, K1) 3 times, P1, K7,
rep from ★ to last st, K1.
Row 2: P1, ★P7, (K1, P1) 3 times, K1, rep
from ★ to last st, P1.
Row 3: P1, ★(P1, K1) 3 times, P8, rep from ★
to last st, P1.
Row 4: As row 2.
Row 5: As row 1.
Row 6: K1, ★K8, (P1, K1) 3 times, rep from ★
to last st, K1.

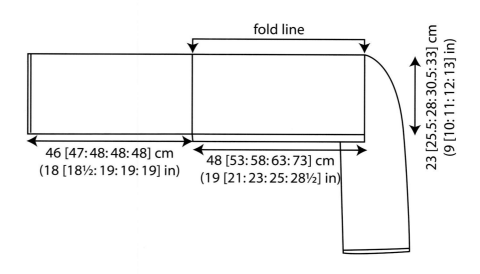

fold line

23 [25.5: 28: 30.5: 33] cm
(9 [10: 11: 12: 13] in)

46 [47: 48: 48: 48] cm
(18 [18½: 19: 19: 19] in)

48 [53: 58: 63: 73] cm
(19 [21: 23: 25: 28½] in)

Rows 7 to 9: As rows 1 to 3.
Row 10: As row 2.
Row 11: As row 1.
Row 12: P1, ★(K1, P1) 3 times, K1, P7, rep from ★ to last st, K1.
Row 13: P1, ★K7, (P1, K1) 3 times, P1, rep from ★ to last st, K1.
Row 14: P1, ★(K1, P1) 3 times, K8, rep from ★ to last st, K1.
Row 15: As row 13.
Row 16: As row 12.
Row 17: P1, ★P8, (K1, P1) 3 times, rep from ★ to last st, K1.
Rows 18 to 20: As rows 12 to 14.
Row 21: As row 13.
Row 22: As row 12.
These 22 rows form patt.
Cont in patt until sleeve meas 46 [47: 48: 48: 48] cm, ending with RS facing for next row.
Cast off.

MAKING UP
Press as described on the information page.
Sew cast-off edges of sleeves to row-end edges of body using back stitch, or mattress stitch if preferred. Join sleeve seams.
Body edging
With RS facing and using 2¾mm (US 2) circular needle, pick up and knit 136 [150: 164: 178: 206] sts from cast-on edge of body, then 136 [150: 164: 178: 206] sts from cast-off edge of body. 272 [300: 328: 356: 412] sts.
Round 1 (RS): ★K2, P2, rep from ★ to end.
Rep this round 5 times more.
Cast off in rib.
See information page for finishing instructions.

EASE
BRANDON MABLY
Main image page 84

YARN

	XS	S	M	L	XL	XXL	2XL	
To fit chest								
	97	102	107	112	117	122	127	cm
	38	40	42	44	46	48	50	in

Rowan Purelife Revive

A Pumice 461								
	4	4	5	5	5	5	6	x 50gm
B Basalt 462								
	2	3	3	3	3	3	3	x 50gm
C Rock 465								
	2	2	2	2	3	3	3	x 50gm
D Marble 466								
	1	2	2	2	2	2	2	x 50gm
E Flint 469								
	2	2	2	2	2	2	2	x 50gm
F Pink Granite 463								
	2	2	2	2	2	2	2	x 50gm
G Granite 464								
	2	2	2	2	3	3	3	x 50gm

NEEDLES
1 pair 3¼mm (no 10) (US 3) needles
1 pair 4mm (no 8) (US 6) needles

TENSION
22 sts and 30 rows to 10 cm measured over st st using 4mm (US 6) needles.

Pattern note: Stripe sequences are an **ODD** number of rows. On first and every foll alt rep of stripe sequence, odd numbered rows are K rows and even numbered rows are P rows. On 2nd and every foll alt rep of stripe sequence, odd numbered rows are **P** rows and even numbered rows are **K** rows.

STRIPE SEQUENCE A
Rows 1 to 3: Using yarn A.
Rows 4 to 6: Using yarn G.
Rows 7 to 18: As rows 1 to 6, twice.
Rows 19 to 21: Using yarn A.
Rows 22 to 24: Using yarn B.
Rows 25 to 30: As rows 19 to 24.
Rows 31 to 33: Using yarn C.
Rows 34 to 36: Using yarn G.
Rows 37 to 39: Using yarn A.
Rows 40 to 43: Using yarn G.
Rows 44 to 47: Using yarn D.
Rows 48 to 51: Using yarn G.
Rows 52 to 55: Using yarn A.
Rows 56 to 59: Using yarn B.
These 59 rows form stripe sequence A and are repeated.

STRIPE SEQUENCE B
Rows 1 to 3: Using yarn B.
Rows 4 to 6: Using yarn C.
Rows 7 to 12: As rows 1 to 6.
Rows 13 to 15: Using yarn E.
Rows 16 to 18: Using yarn C.
Rows 19 to 21: Using yarn B.
Rows 22 to 24: Using yarn A.
Rows 25 to 30: As rows 19 to 24.
Rows 31 to 33: Using yarn B.
Rows 34 to 36: Using yarn D.
Rows 37 to 39: Using yarn F.
Rows 40 to 43: Using yarn D.
Rows 44 to 47: Using yarn B.
Rows 48 to 51: Using yarn C.
Rows 52 to 55: Using yarn E.
Rows 56 to 59: Using yarn A.
These 59 rows form stripe sequence B and are repeated.

STRIPE SEQUENCE C
Rows 1 to 3: Using yarn F.
Rows 4 to 6: Using yarn D.
Rows 7 to 18: As rows 1 to 6, twice.

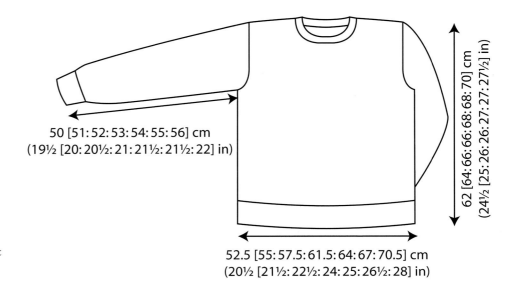

50 [51: 52: 53: 54: 55: 56] cm
(19½ [20: 20½: 21: 21½: 21½: 22] in)

62 [64: 66: 66: 68: 68: 70] cm
(24½ [25: 26: 26: 27: 27: 27½] in)

52.5 [55: 57.5: 61.5: 64: 67: 70.5] cm
(20½ [21½: 22½: 24: 25: 26½: 28] in)

Rows 19 to 21: Using yarn E.
Rows 22 to 24: Using yarn C.
Rows 25 to 27: Using yarn F.
Rows 28 to 30: Using yarn C.
Rows 31 to 33: Using yarn E.
Rows 34 to 36: Using yarn C.
Rows 37 to 39: Using yarn E.
Rows 40 to 43: Using yarn A.
Rows 44 to 47: Using yarn F.
Rows 48 to 51: Using yarn C.
Rows 52 to 55: Using yarn E.
Rows 56 to 59: Using yarn C.
These 59 rows form stripe sequence C and are repeated.

BACK

Using 3¼mm (US 3) needles and yarn A, cast on 114 [122: 126: 134: 142: 146: 154] sts.
Row 1 (RS): K2, *P2, K2, rep from * to end.
Row 2: P2, *K2, P2, rep from * to end.
These 2 rows form rib.
Work in rib for a further 22 rows, inc [dec: inc: inc: dec: inc: inc] 1 st at end of last row and ending with RS facing for next row. 115 [121: 127: 135: 141: 147: 155] sts.
Change to 4mm (US 6) needles.**
Beg with a K row, now work in st st in patt, placing stripe sequences as folls:
Row 1 (RS): Work first 23 [23: 23: 27: 27: 30: 31] sts as row 1 of stripe sequence A, work next 23 [25: 27: 27: 29: 29: 31] sts as row 1 of stripe sequence B, work next 23 [25: 27: 27: 29: 29: 31] sts as row 1 of stripe sequence A, work next 23 [25: 27: 27: 29: 29: 31] sts as row 1 of stripe sequence C, work last 23 [23: 23: 27: 27: 30: 31] sts as row 1 of stripe sequence A.
Row 2: Work first 23 [23: 23: 27: 27: 30: 31] sts as row 2 of stripe sequence A, work next 23 [25: 27: 27: 29: 29: 31] sts as row 2 of stripe sequence C, work next 23 [25: 27: 27: 29: 29: 31] sts as row 2 of stripe sequence A, work next 23 [25: 27: 27: 29: 29: 31] sts as row 2 of stripe sequence B, work last 23 [23: 23: 27: 27: 30: 31] sts as row 2 of stripe sequence A.
These 2 rows set the sts – 5 vertical bands of stripe sequences.
Working appropriate rows of stripe sequences, cont as now set until back meas 37 [38: 39: 38: 39: 38: 39] cm, ending with RS facing for next row.

Shape armholes
Keeping patt correct, cast off 4 sts at beg of next 2 rows.
107 [113: 119: 127: 133: 139: 147] sts.
Dec 1 st at each end of next and foll 4 alt rows. 97 [103: 109: 117: 123: 129: 137] sts.
Cont straight until armhole meas 23 [24: 25: 26: 27: 28: 29] cm, ending with RS facing for next row.

Shape shoulders and back neck
Next row (RS): Cast off 10 [11: 12: 13: 14: 14: 16] sts, patt until there are 26 [27: 29: 31: 33: 35: 37] sts on right needle and turn, leaving rem sts on a holder.
Work each side of neck separately.
Cast off 3 sts at beg of next row, 10 [11: 12: 13: 14: 14: 16] sts at beg of foll row, then 3 sts at

beg of next row.
Cast off rem 10 [10: 11: 12: 13: 15: 15] sts.
With RS facing, rejoin appropriate yarns to rem sts, cast off centre 25 [27: 27: 29: 29: 31: 31] sts, patt to end.
Complete to match first side, reversing shapings.

FRONT
Work as given for back to **.
Beg with a K row, now work in st st in patt, placing stripe sequences as folls:
Row 1 (RS): Work first 23 [23: 23: 27: 27: 30: 31] sts as row 1 of stripe sequence A, work next 23 [25: 27: 27: 29: 29: 31] sts as row 1 of stripe sequence C, work next 23 [25: 27: 27: 29: 29: 31] sts as row 1 of stripe sequence A, work next 23 [25: 27: 27: 29: 29: 31] sts as row 1 of stripe sequence B, work last 23 [23: 23: 27: 27: 30: 31] sts as row 1 of stripe sequence A.
Row 2: Work first 23 [23: 23: 27: 27: 30: 31] sts as row 2 of stripe sequence A, work next 23 [25: 27: 27: 29: 29: 31] sts as row 2 of stripe sequence B, work next 23 [25: 27: 27: 29: 29: 31] sts as row 2 of stripe sequence A, work next 23 [25: 27: 27: 29: 29: 31] sts as row 2 of stripe sequence C, work last 23 [23: 23: 27: 27: 30: 31] sts as row 2 of stripe sequence A.
These 2 rows set the sts – 5 vertical bands of stripe sequences.
Working appropriate rows of stripe sequences, cont as now set until front matches back to beg of armhole shaping, ending with RS facing for next row.

Shape armholes
Keeping patt correct, cast off 4 sts at beg of next 2 rows.
107 [113: 119: 127: 133: 139: 147] sts.
Dec 1 st at each end of next and foll 4 alt rows. 97 [103: 109: 117: 123: 129: 137] sts.
Work as given for back until 18 [18: 18: 20: 20: 22: 22] rows less have been worked than on back to beg of shoulder shaping, ending with RS facing for next row.

Shape neck
Next row (RS): Patt 40 [42: 45: 49: 52: 55: 59] sts and turn, leaving rem sts on a holder.
Work each side of neck separately.
Keeping patt correct, dec 1 st at neck edge of next 6 rows, then on foll 4 [4: 4: 5: 5: 6: 6] alt rows. 30 [32: 35: 38: 41: 43: 47] sts.
Work 3 rows, ending with RS facing for next row.

Shape shoulder
Cast off 10 [11: 12: 13: 14: 14: 16] sts at beg of next and foll alt row.
Work 1 row.
Cast off rem 10 [10: 11: 12: 13: 15: 15] sts.
With RS facing, rejoin appropriate yarns to rem sts, cast off centre 17 [19: 19: 19: 19: 19: 19] sts, patt to end.
Complete to match first side, reversing shapings.

SLEEVES
Using 3¼mm (US 3) needles and yarn A, cast on 46 [46: 50: 50: 54: 54: 58] sts.
Work in rib as given for back for 24 rows, dec [inc: dec: inc: dec: inc: dec] 1 st at end of last

row and ending with RS facing for next row. 45 [47: 49: 51: 53: 55: 57] sts.
Change to 4mm (US 6) needles.
Beg with a K row, now work in st st in patt, placing stripe sequences as folls:
Left sleeve only
Row 1 (RS): Work first 11 [11: 11: 12: 12: 13: 13] sts as row 1 of stripe sequence C, work next 23 [25: 27: 27: 29: 29: 31] sts as row 1 of stripe sequence A, work last 11 [11: 11: 12: 12: 13: 13] sts as row 1 of stripe sequence B.
Row 2: Work first 11 [11: 11: 12: 12: 13: 13] sts as row 2 of stripe sequence B, work next 23 [25: 27: 27: 29: 29: 31] sts as row 2 of stripe sequence A, work last 11 [11: 11: 12: 12: 13: 13] sts as row 2 of stripe sequence C.
Right sleeve only
Row 1 (RS): Work first 11 [11: 11: 12: 12: 13: 13] sts as row 1 of stripe sequence B, work next 23 [25: 27: 27: 29: 29: 31] sts as row 1 of stripe sequence A, work last 11 [11: 11: 12: 12: 13: 13] sts as row 1 of stripe sequence C.
Row 2: Work first 11 [11: 11: 12: 12: 13: 13] sts as row 2 of stripe sequence C, work next 23 [25: 27: 27: 29: 29: 31] sts as row 2 of stripe sequence A, work last 11 [11: 11: 12: 12: 13: 13] sts as row 2 of stripe sequence B.
Both sleeves
These 2 rows set the sts – 3 vertical bands of stripe sequences.
Working appropriate rows of stripe sequences, cont in patt, shaping sides by inc 1 st at each end of 3rd [next: next: next: next: next: next] and foll 0 [0: 0: 1: 3: 4: 4] alt rows, then on every foll 4th row until there are 101 [105: 109: 113: 119: 123: 127] sts, taking inc sts into stripe sequences as set by edge sts.
Cont straight until sleeve meas 50 [51: 52: 53: 54: 55: 56] cm, ending with RS facing for next row.

Shape top
Keeping patt correct, cast off 4 sts at beg of next 2 rows.
93 [97: 101: 105: 111: 115: 119] sts.
Dec 1 st at each end of next and foll 3 alt rows, then on foll row, ending with RS facing for next row.
Cast off rem 83 [87: 91: 95: 101: 105: 109] sts.

MAKING UP
Press as described on the information page.
Join right shoulder seam using back stitch, or mattress stitch if preferred.
Neckband
With RS facing, using 3¼mm (US 3) needles and yarn A, pick up and knit 18 [18: 18: 19: 21: 22: 22] sts down left side of neck, 17 [19: 19: 19: 19: 19: 19] sts from front, 18 [18: 18: 19: 21: 22: 22] sts up right side of neck, then 37 [39: 39: 41: 41: 43: 43] sts from back. 90 [94: 94: 98: 102: 106: 106] sts.
Beg with row 2, work in rib as given for back for 7 rows, ending with RS facing for next row.
Cast off in rib.
See information page for finishing instructions, setting in sleeves using the shallow set-in method.

MIRAGE
MARIE WALLIN
Main image page 10 & 11

●●

YARN

	S–M	L–XL	XXL	
To fit bust				
	81–97	102–117	122–127	cm
	32–38	40–46	48–50	in

Rowan Kidsilk Haze

3	3	4	x 25gm

(photographed in Ghost 642)

NEEDLES

1 pair 3¾mm (no 9) (US 5) needles
1 pair 4½mm (no 7) (US 7) needles

TENSION

18½ sts and 28 rows to 10 cm measured over patt using 4½mm (US 7) needles.

BACK

Using 3¾mm (US 5) needles cast on 81 [105: 117] sts.
Work in g st for 5 rows, ending with **WS** facing for next row.
Change to 4½mm (US 7) needles.
Now work in patt as folls:
Row 1 (WS): Purl.
Row 2: K2, *K2tog, yfwd, K1, rep from * to last st, K1.
Row 3: Purl.
Row 4: K2, *yfwd, K1, K2tog, rep from * to last st, K1.
These 4 rows form patt.
Cont in patt, shaping side seams by inc 1 st at each end of 2nd and 6 [3: 2] foll 4th rows, then on 3 [6: 7] foll 6th rows, then on foll 4th row, then on foll 2 alt rows, then on foll 5 rows, ending with RS facing for next row and taking

inc sts into st st until there are sufficient to work in patt. 117 [141: 153] sts. (Back should meas 23 [25: 26] cm.)
Cast on 6 sts at beg of next 2 rows.
129 [153: 165] sts.
Place markers at both ends of last row to denote base of armhole openings.★★
Cont straight until work meas 23 [25: 26] cm from markers, ending with RS facing for next row.

Shape shoulders and back neck

Next row (RS): Cast off 16 [19: 21] sts, patt until there are 37 [45: 48] sts on right needle and turn, leaving rem sts on a holder.
Work each side of neck separately.
Keeping patt correct, cast off 3 sts at beg of next row, 16 [19: 21] sts at beg of foll row, then 3 sts at beg of next row.
Cast off rem 15 [20: 21] sts.
With RS facing, rejoin yarn to rem sts, cast off centre 23 [25: 27] sts, patt to end.
Complete to match first side, reversing shapings.

FRONT

Work as given for back to ★★.
Inc 1 st at each end of 5th and 8 foll 6th rows, taking inc sts into st st until there are sufficient to work in patt. 147 [171: 183] sts.
Cont straight until front matches back to beg of shoulder shaping, ending with RS facing for next row.

Shape shoulders and front neck

Next row (RS): Cast off 16 [19: 21] sts, patt

until there are 39 [47: 50] sts on right needle and turn, leaving rem sts on a holder.
Work each side of neck separately.
Keeping patt correct, cast off 4 sts at beg of next row, 16 [19: 21] sts at beg of foll row, then 4 sts at beg of next row.
Cast off rem 15 [20: 21] sts.
With RS facing, rejoin yarn to rem sts, cast off centre 37 [39: 41] sts, patt to end.
Complete to match first side, reversing shapings.

MAKING UP

Press as described on the information page.
Join right shoulder seam using back stitch, or mattress stitch if preferred.

Neckband

With RS facing and using 3¾mm (US 5) needles, pick up and knit 78 [81: 84] sts from front, then 54 [57: 60] sts from back.
132 [138: 144] sts.
Work in g st for 2 rows, ending with **WS** facing for next row.
Cast off knitwise (on **WS**).
Join left shoulder and neckband seam.

Armhole borders (both alike)

With RS facing and using 3¾mm (US 5) needles, pick up and knit 101 [110: 114] sts evenly along armhole row-end edge between markers.
Work in g st for 2 rows, ending with **WS** facing for next row.
Cast off knitwise (on **WS**).
See information page for finishing instructions.

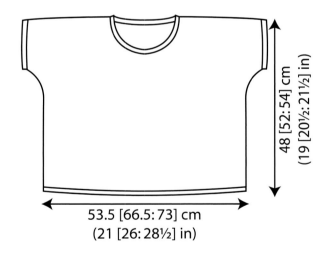

48 [52: 54] cm
(19 [20½: 21½] in)

53.5 [66.5: 73] cm
(21 [26: 28½] in)

PIMPERNEL
MARTIN STOREY

Main image page 50 & 51

●●

YARN

S	M	L	XL	XXL

To fit bust
81-86 91-97 102-107 112-117 122-127 cm
32-34 36-38 40-42 44-46   48-50 in

Rowan Kidsilk Haze

7	7	8	8	8	x 25gm

(photographed in Cream 634)

NEEDLES

1 pair 2¾mm (no 12) (US 2) needles
1 pair 3¼mm (no 10) (US 3) needles
2¾mm (no 12) (US 2) circular needles, one 40
cm long and one 100 cm long

TENSION

26 sts and 36 rows to 10 cm measured over patt
using 3¼mm (US 3) needles.

BACK and FRONT (both alike - knitted sideways)

Using 3¼mm (US 3) needles cast on 105 [111:

117: 123: 129] sts.
Work in patt as folls:
Row 1 (RS): K2, *yfwd, sl 1, K2, lift the
slipped st over the 2 K sts and off right needle,
rep from * to last st, K1.
Row 2: Purl.
Row 3: K1, *sl 1, K2, lift the slipped st over
the 2 K sts and off right needle, yfwd, rep from
* to last 2 sts, K2.
Row 4: Purl.
These 4 rows form patt.
Cont in patt until work meas 50 [53: 56:
59: 62] cm, ending with RS facing for next
row.

Shape neck

Keeping patt correct, dec 1 st at beg of next
row then at same edge on foll 8 rows.
96 [102: 108: 114: 120] sts.
Cont straight until work meas 23 [23: 24:
24: 25] cm **from last dec**, ending with RS
facing for next row.
Inc 1 st at neck edge of next 9 rows, taking inc
sts into patt and ending with **WS** facing for
next row.
105 [111: 117: 123: 129] sts.
(Neck shaping now complete.)
Cont straight until work meas 50 [53: 56:
59: 62] cm **from last inc**, ending with RS
facing for next row.
Cast off.

MAKING UP

Press as described on the information page.
Join both shoulder/overarm seams using back
stitch, or mattress stitch if preferred.

Neckband

With RS facing and using shorter 2¾mm (US
2) circular needle, pick up and knit 80 [80: 83:
83: 86] sts along front neck edge, then 80 [80:

83: 83: 86] sts along back neck edge.
160 [160: 166: 166: 172] sts.
Round 1 (RS): Knit.
Rep this round 5 times more.
Cast off.

Cuffs (both alike)

Mark points along side seam edges 10 [10.5:
11: 11: 11.5] cm either side of
shoulder/overarm seams.
With RS facing and using 2¾mm (US 2)
needles, pick up and knit 66 [70: 74: 74: 78] sts
along edge between markers.
Row 1 (WS): P2, *K2, P2, rep from * to end.
Row 2: K2, *P2, K2, rep from * to end.
These 2 rows form rib.
Cont in rib until cuff meas 24 cm from pick-
up row, ending with RS facing for next row.
Cast off in rib.

Side borders (both alike)

Using 2¾mm (US 2) needles cast on 9 sts.
Work in g st until border, when slightly
stretched, fits along entire side seam and
armhole edge of back and front, between lower
row-end edges and ending with RS facing for
next row.
Cast off.
Slip stitch borders in place, attaching them over
pick-up rows along top of cuffs, then join row-
end edges of cuffs.

Hem borders (both alike)

With RS facing and using longer 2¾mm
(US 2) circular needle, beg and ending at outer
edge of side borders, pick up and knit
350 [366: 384: 400: 418] sts evenly along entire
lower edge of back (or front).
Work in g st for 8 rows, ending with **WS**
facing for next row.
Cast off knitwise (on **WS**).
See information page for finishing instructions.

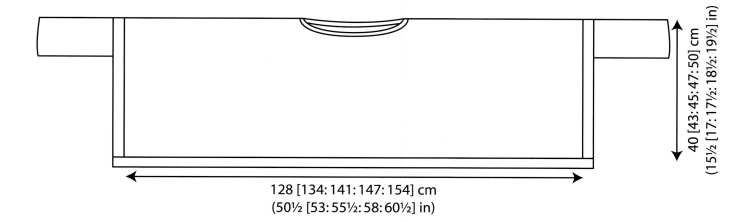

128 [134: 141: 147: 154] cm
(50½ [53: 55½: 58: 60½] in)

40 [43: 45: 47: 50] cm
(15½ [17: 17½: 18½: 19½] in)

VISION
MARIE WALLIN

Main image page 20 & 21

●●

YARN

	S–M	L–XL	
To fit bust			
	81-97	102-117	cm
	32-38	40-46	in

Rowan Kidsilk Haze

| | 3 | 3 | x 25gm |

(photographed in Majestic 589)

NEEDLES

1 pair 3¼mm (no 10) (US 3) needles

TENSION

25 sts and 34 rows to 10 cm measured over st st using 3¼mm (US 3) needles.

MAIN SECTION

Using 3¼mm (US 3) needles cast on 52 [60] sts.
Row 1 (RS): Knit.
Row 2: K1, P to last st, K1.
Rows 3 to 10: As rows 1 and 2, 4 times.
Row 11: K13 [15], wrap next st (by slipping next st on left needle onto right needle, taking yarn to opposite side of work between needles and then slipping same st back onto left needle – when working back across wrapped sts, work the wrapped st and the wrapping loop tog as one st) and turn.
Row 12: P to last st, K1.
Row 13: K26 [30], wrap next st and turn.
Row 14: P to last st, K1.
Row 15: K39 [45], wrap next st and turn.
Row 16: P to last st, K1.
Rows 17 to 26: As rows 1 and 2, 5 times.
Rep last 26 rows 20 [22] times more, ending with RS facing for next row.
Cast off.

BACK SECTIONS (make 2)

Using 3¼mm (US 3) needles cast on 36 sts.

Row 1 (WS): K1, P to last st, K1.
Row 2: K2, ★yfwd, K2tog, yfwd, (K2tog) 3 times, K2, yfwd, K3, yfwd, sl 1, K1, psso, yfwd, K2, rep from ★ once more.
Row 3: As row 1.
Row 4: K2, ★yfwd, K2tog, (K3tog) twice, yfwd, K1, yfwd, K2. (sl 1, K1, psso, yfwd) twice, K2, rep from ★ once more. 32 sts.
Row 5: K1, P10, P2tog, P13, P2tog, P3, K1. 30 sts.
Row 6: K2, ★yfwd, K3tog, yfwd, K3, yfwd, K2, (sl 1, K1, psso, yfwd) twice, K2, rep from ★ once more. 32 sts.
Row 7: As row 1.
Row 8: K2, ★yfwd, K2tog, yfwd, K1, (yfwd, K2, sl 1, K1, psso) twice, yfwd, sl 1, K1, psso, yfwd, K2, rep from ★ once more. 36 sts.
Row 9: As row 1.
Row 10: K2, ★yfwd, K2tog, yfwd, K3, yfwd, K2, (sl 1, K1, psso) 3 times, yfwd, sl 1, K1, psso, yfwd, K2, rep from ★ once more.
Row 11: As row 1.
Row 12: K2, ★(yfwd, K2tog) twice, K2, yfwd, K1, yfwd, (sl 1, K2tog, psso) twice, sl 1, K1, psso, yfwd, K2, rep from ★ once more. 32 sts.
Row 13: K1, P3, P2tog tbl, P13, P2tog tbl, P10, K1. 30 sts.
Row 14: K2, ★(yfwd, K2tog) twice, K2, yfwd, K3, yfwd, sl 1, K2tog, psso, yfwd, K2, rep from ★ once more. 32 sts.
Row 15: As row 1.
Row 16: K2, ★yfwd, K2tog, yfwd, (K2tog, K2, yfwd) twice, K1, yfwd, sl 1, K1, psso, yfwd, K2, rep from ★ once more. 36 sts.
These 16 rows form patt.
Cont in patt until work meas 22 cm, ending

with RS facing for next row.
Next row (RS): Knit.
Next row: K1, P to last st, K1.
Rep last 2 rows until strip meas 44 cm, ending with RS facing for next row.
Cast off.

MAKING UP

Press as described on the information page. Join cast-on and cast-off edges of main section using back stitch, or mattress stitch if preferred – this seam forms lower centre back seam. Mark point midway along shorter row-end edge of resulting loop – this point is centre back neck point. Longer row-end edge of loop forms lower back hem edge and front opening edge. Using diagram as a guide, now form back mock cable section as folls: Form one back section into an upside-down "U" shape so that cast-on and cast-off edges meet but keeping RS uppermost at both ends of strip. Now make same shape with second back section, threading through loop formed by first section. (On this section, overlap lace section over st st section for approx 3 cm where cast-on and cast-off edges meet.) There are now 2 interlocking loops – lace sections should be at bottom right and top left. Place marker at centre of each joined cast-on/cast-off edge – points A and B on diagram. Matching point A to top of lower centre back seam, sew this joined cast-on/cast-off edge to inner (shorter) row-end edge of main section. Matching point B to marked centre back neck point, sew other joined cast-on/cast-off edge to inner (shorter) row-end edge of main section at back neck edge.

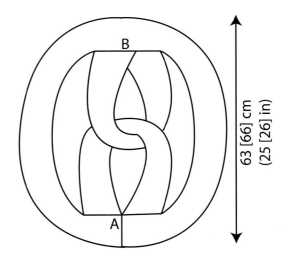

63 [66] cm
(25 [26] in)

CAMPION
MARIE WALLIN

Main image page 46

YARN

S	M	L	XL	XXL

To fit bust
81–86 91–97 102–107 112–117 122–127 cm
32–34 36–38 40–42 44–46 48–50 in

Rowan Siena 4 ply

11 12 14 16 17 x 50gm

(photographed in Cream 652)

NEEDLES

1 pair 2¼mm (no 13) (US 1) needles
1 pair 7mm (no 2) (US 10½) needles

TENSION

14½ sts and 17 rows to 10 cm measured over st
st using 7mm (US 10½) needles and yarn
DOUBLE.

BACK

Using 2¼mm (US 1) needles and yarn
SINGLE cast on 114 [122: 138: 150: 166] sts.
Row 1 (RS): K2, *P2, K2, rep from * to end.
Row 2: P2, *K2, P2, rep from * to end.
These 2 rows form rib.
Work in rib for a further 38 rows, – [inc: –:
–: dec] – [1: –: –: 1] st at end of last row and
ending with RS facing for next row.
114 [123: 138: 150: 165] sts.
Change to 7mm (US 10½) needles.
Join in 2nd strand of yarn.
Now using yarn DOUBLE throughout, cont as
folls:
Next row (RS): *K1, K2tog, rep from * to
end. 76 [82: 92: 100: 110] sts.
Beg with a P row, now work in st st, shaping
side seams by dec 1 st at each end of 20th and
2 foll 16th rows. 70 [76: 86: 94: 104] sts.
Cont straight until back meas 56 [57: 58:
59: 60] cm, ending with RS facing for
next row.
Shape for cap sleeves
Inc 1 st at each end of next and foll 4th row,
then on foll 2 alt rows, then on foll row, ending
with RS facing for next row.
80 [86: 96: 104: 114] sts.
Cast on 2 sts at beg of next 2 rows.
84 [90: 100: 108: 118] sts.
Place markers at both ends of last row to
denote base of armholes.

Cont straight until armhole meas 22 [23: 24:
25: 26] cm, ending with RS facing for next
row.
Shape shoulders and back neck
Next row (RS): Cast off 13 [14: 16: 18: 21]
sts, K until there are 16 [18: 20: 22: 24] sts on
right needle and turn, leaving rem sts on a
holder.
Work each side of neck separately.
Cast off 3 sts at beg of next row.
Cast off rem 13 [15: 17: 19: 21] sts.
With RS facing, rejoin yarn DOUBLE to rem
sts, cast off centre 26 [26: 28: 28: 28] sts,
K to end.
Complete to match first side, reversing
shapings.

FRONT
Work as given for back until 20 [20: 22:
22: 24] rows less have been worked than on
back to beg of shoulder shaping, ending with
RS facing for next row.
Shape front neck
Next row (RS): K34 [37: 42: 46: 52] and
turn, leaving rem sts on a holder.
Work each side of neck separately.
Dec 1 st at neck edge of next 4 rows, then on
foll 2 [2: 3: 3: 4] alt rows, then on 2 foll 4th
rows. 26 [29: 33: 37: 42] sts.
Work 3 rows, ending with RS facing for
next row.
Shape shoulder
Cast off 13 [14: 16: 18: 21] sts at beg of
next row.

Work 1 row.
Cast off rem 13 [15: 17: 19: 21] sts.
With RS facing, rejoin yarn DOUBLE to
rem sts, cast off centre 16 [16: 16: 16: 14] sts,
K to end.
Complete to match first side, reversing
shapings.

MAKING UP
Press as described on the information page.
Join right shoulder seam using back stitch, or
mattress stitch if preferred.
Neckband
With RS facing, using 2¼mm (US 1) needles
and yarn SINGLE, pick up and knit 45 [45: 49:
49: 53] sts down left side of neck, 30 sts from
front, 45 [45: 49: 49: 53] sts up right side of
neck, then 62 [62: 66: 66: 66] sts from back.
182 [182: 194: 194: 202] sts.
Beg with row 2, work in rib as given for
back for 15 rows, ending with RS facing for
next row.
Cast off in rib.
Join left shoulder and neckband seam.
Armhole borders (both alike)
With RS facing, using 2¼mm (US 1) needles
and yarn SINGLE, pick up and knit 122 [130:
134: 142: 146] sts evenly along armhole row-
end edges between markers.
Beg with row 2, work in rib as given for
back for 11 rows, ending with RS facing for
next row.
Cast off in rib.
See information page for finishing instructions.

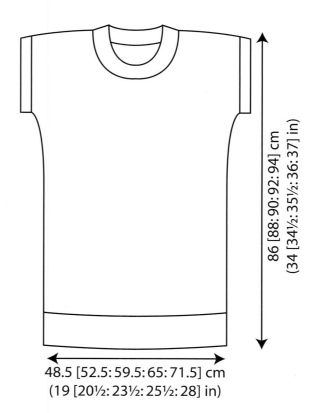

86 [88: 90: 92: 94] cm
(34 [34½: 35½: 36: 37] in)

48.5 [52.5: 59.5: 65: 71.5] cm
(19 [20½: 23½: 25½: 28] in)

BALSAM
LISA RICHARDSON

●●

Main image page 48 & 49

YARN

S	M	L	XL	XXL

To fit bust
81-86 91-97 102-107 112-117 122-127 cm
32-34 36-38 40-42 44-46 48-50 in

Rowan Lenpur™ Linen

7 7 8 9 10 x 50gm

(photographed in Blanche 571)

NEEDLES

1 pair 3¼mm (no 10) (US 3) needles
1 pair 7mm (no 2) (US 10½) needles

BUTTONS – 1 x RW5019 from Bedecked.
Please see information page for contact details.

TENSION

14 sts and 14 rows to 10 cm measured over st st
using 7mm (US 10½) needles.

Tension note: As garment is knitted loosely,
fabric will drop when worn and tension will
change. Pattern is calculated to tension in wear
of 16 sts and 12 rows to 10 cm. All
measurements given relate to length of knitting
when hanging from needles, **NOT** when
laid flat.

BACK

Using 3¼mm (US 3) needles cast on 99 [111:
123: 135: 153] sts.
Row 1 (RS): K3, ★P3, K3, rep from ★ to end.
Row 2: P3, ★K3, P3, rep from ★ to end.
These 2 rows form rib.
Work in rib for a further 24 [24: 26: 26: 24]
rows, ending with RS facing for next row.
Change to 7mm (US 10½) needles.
Next row (RS): K3 [2: 4: 7: 2], K2tog,
(K2, K2tog, K1, K2tog) 13 [15: 16: 17: 21]
times, K3 [2: 5: 7: 2]. 72 [80: 90: 100: 110] sts.
Beg with a P row, now work in st st as folls:
Dec 1 st at each end of 4th and foll 4th row.
68 [76: 86: 96: 106] sts.★★
Work 7 rows, ending with RS facing for
next row.
Inc 1 st at each end of next and foll 8th row.
72 [80: 90: 100: 110] sts.
Work 7 [9: 9: 11: 13] rows, ending with RS
facing for next row. (Back should meas approx
35 [36: 37: 38: 39] cm - see tension note.)
Shape armholes
Cast off 3 sts at beg of next 2 rows.
66 [74: 84: 94: 104] sts.
Dec 1 st at each end of next and foll 3 alt rows.

58 [66: 76: 86: 96] sts.
Cont straight until armhole meas 21 [22: 23:
24: 25] cm, ending with RS facing for next
row. (See tension note.)
Shape back neck and shoulders
Next row (RS): Cast off 7 [9: 11: 14: 16] sts,
K until there are 11 [13: 15: 17: 19] sts on right
needle and turn, leaving rem sts on a holder.
Work each side of neck separately.
Cast off 3 sts at beg of next row.
Cast off rem 8 [10: 12: 14: 16] sts.
With RS facing, rejoin yarn to rem sts, cast off
centre 22 [22: 24: 24: 26] sts, K to end.
Complete to match first side, reversing
shapings.

FRONT
Work as given for back to ★★.
Work 5 rows, ending with RS facing for next
row.
Divide for neck
Next row (RS): K30 [34: 39: 44: 49] and
turn, leaving rem sts on a holder.
Work each side of neck separately.
Dec 1 st at neck edge of next 4 rows, then on
foll 2 [2: 3: 3: 4] alt rows, then on 2 [2: 1: 1: 1]
foll 4th rows **and at same time** inc 1 st at
side seam edge of 2nd and foll 8th row.
24 [28: 33: 38: 42] sts.
Work 1 [3: 5: 7: 7] rows, dec 1 st at neck edge
on 0 [0: 4th: 4th: 4th] row and ending with RS
facing for next row. 24 [28: 32: 37: 41] sts.
Shape armhole
Cast off 3 sts at beg of next row.
21 [25: 29: 34: 38] sts.
Work 1 row.
Dec 1 st at neck edge of next and foll 6th row
and at same time dec 1 st at armhole edge of
next and foll 3 alt rows. 15 [19: 23: 28: 32] sts.
Cont straight until front matches back to beg
of shoulder shaping, ending with RS facing for
next row.
Shape shoulder
Cast off 7 [9: 11: 14: 16] sts at beg of next row.
Work 1 row.
Cast off rem 8 [10: 12: 14: 16] sts.

With RS facing, rejoin yarn to rem sts, cast off
centre 8 sts, K to end.
Complete to match first side, reversing
shapings.

SLEEVES
Using 3¼mm (US 3) needles, cast on 39 [41:
43: 45: 47] sts.
Row 1 (RS): P0 [1: 2: 0: 1], K3, ★P3, K3, rep
from ★ to last 0 [1: 2: 0: 1] sts, P0 [1: 2: 0: 1].
Row 2: K0 [1: 2: 0: 1], P3, ★K3, P3, rep from
★ to last 0 [1: 2: 0: 1] sts, K0 [1: 2: 0: 1].
These 2 rows form rib.
Cont in rib for a further 24 rows, ending with
RS facing for next row.
Change to 7mm (US 10½) needles.
Row 27 (RS): K1 [2: 3: 1: 2], K2tog, (K2,
K2tog, K1 [1: 1: 2: 2], K2tog) 5 times, K1 [2: 3:
2: 3]. 28 [30: 32: 34: 36] sts.
Beg with a P row, now work in st st, shaping
sides by inc 1 st at each end of next 2 [2: 2:
2: 4] rows, then on every foll alt row until there
are 68 [70: 74: 76: 80] sts.
Cont straight until sleeve meas 44 [45: 46:
46: 46] cm, ending with RS facing for next
row.
Shape top
Cast off 3 sts at beg of next 2 rows.
62 [64: 68: 70: 74] sts.
Dec 1 st at each end of next and foll 2 alt rows,
then on foll row, ending with RS facing for
next row.
Cast off rem 54 [56: 60: 62: 66] sts.

MAKING UP
Press as described on the information page.
Join right shoulder seam using back stitch, or
mattress stitch if preferred.
Neckband
With RS facing and using 3¼mm (US 3)
needles, pick up and knit 93 [93: 95: 98: 100] sts
down left side of neck, 11 sts from front,
93 [93: 95: 98: 100] sts up right side of neck,
then 40 [40: 42: 42: 44] sts from back.
237 [237: 243: 249: 255] sts.
Beg with row 2, work in rib as given for

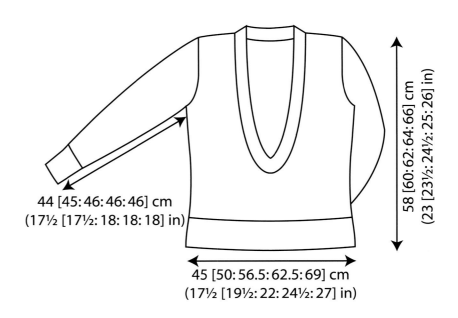

44 [45: 46: 46: 46] cm
(17½ [17½: 18: 18: 18] in)

58 [60: 62: 64: 66] cm
(23 [23½: 24½: 25: 26] in)

45 [50: 56.5: 62.5: 69] cm
(17½ [19½: 22: 24½: 27] in)

back for 15 rows, ending with RS facing for next row.
Cast off in rib.

See information page for finishing instructions, setting in sleeves using the shallow set-in method. Make button loop and attach button

to inside on pick-up row, level with beg of armhole shaping, to fasten fronts as in photograph.

HOME
MARTIN STOREY
Main image page 70 & 71

YARN

8	10	12	14	16	18	

To fit bust

81	86	91	97	102	107	cm
32	34	36	38	40	42	in

Rowan Denim

A Memphis 229

10	11	11	11	12	12	x 50gm

B Ecru 324

1	1	1	1	2	2	x 50gm

C Nashville 225

1	1	1	1	2	2	x 50gm

NEEDLES
1 pair 3¼mm (no 10) (US 3) needles
1 pair 4mm (no 8) (US 6) needles
4mm (no 8) (US 6) circular needle, 80 cm long

BUTTONS – 6 x RW5030 (18mm) from Bedecked. Please see information page for contact details.

TENSION
Before washing: 20 sts and 28 rows to 10 cm measured over st st, 22 sts and 27 rows to 10 cm measured over patt, both using 4mm (US 6) needles.

Tension note: Denim will shrink in length when washed for the first time. Allowances have been made in the pattern for shrinkage (see size diagram for after washing measurements).

Pattern note: When working patt, slip all sts with yarn held at WS of work - this is back on RS rows, and front on WS rows.

BACK
Frills (make 4)
Using 4mm (US 6) circular needle and yarn A cast on 344 [360: 376: 400: 432: 448] sts.
Row 1 (RS): *K2, lift first of these sts on right needle over 2nd st and off right needle, rep from * to end.
172 [180: 188: 200: 216: 224] sts.
Row 2: *P2tog, rep from * to end.
86 [90: 94: 100: 108: 112] sts.
Break yarn and leave sts on a holder.
Main section
Using 3¼mm (US 3) needles and yarn A cast on 85 [89: 93: 99: 107: 111] sts.
Row 1 (RS): K1, *P1, K1, rep from * to end.
Row 2: As row 1.
These 2 rows form moss st.
Work in moss st for a further 8 rows, inc 1 st at end of last row and ending with RS facing for next row. 86 [90: 94: 100: 108: 112] sts.
Change to 4mm (US 6) needles.
Beg with a K row, work in st st for 4 rows, ending with RS facing for next row.
Row 5 (RS): Holding WS of one frill against

RS of main section, K tog first st of frill with first st of main section, *K tog next st of frill with next st of main section, rep from * to end.
86 [90: 94: 100: 108: 112] sts.
Beg with a P row, work in st st for 7 rows, ending with RS facing for next row.
Rep last 8 rows twice more, then row 5 again – all 4 frills now attached.
Next row (WS): P4 [1: 3: 4: 2: 4], M1P, (P7 [8: 8: 7: 8: 8], M1P) 11 [11: 11: 13: 13: 13] times, P5 [1: 3: 5: 2: 4].
98 [102: 106: 114: 122: 126] sts.
Now work in patt as folls:
Row 1 (RS): Using yarn B, K1, sl 1, *K2, sl 2, rep from * to last 4 sts, K2, sl 1, K1.
Row 2: Using yarn B, P1, sl 1, *P2, sl 2, rep from * to last 4 sts, P2, sl 1, P1.
Row 3: Using yarn A, knit.
Row 4: Using yarn C, P2, *sl 2, P2, rep from * to end.
Row 5: Using yarn C, K2, *sl 2, K2, rep from * to end.
Row 6: Using yarn A, purl.
These 6 rows form patt.
Work in patt for a further 24 [24: 22: 30: 28: 34] rows, ending with RS facing for next row.
Shape armholes
Keeping patt correct, cast off 6 [7: 7: 8: 8: 9] sts

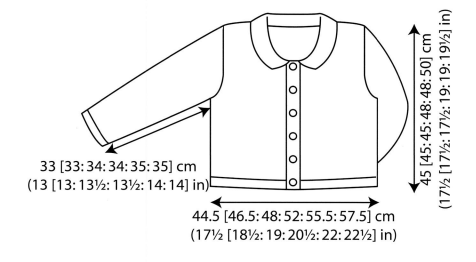

33 [33: 34: 34: 35: 35] cm
(13 [13: 13½: 13½: 14: 14] in)

44.5 [46.5: 48: 52: 55.5: 57.5] cm
(17½ [18½: 19: 20½: 22: 22½] in)

45 [45: 45: 48: 48: 50] cm
(17½ [17½: 17½: 19: 19: 19½] in)

at beg of next 2 rows.
86 [88: 92: 98: 106: 108] sts.
Dec 1 st at each end of next 3 [3: 5: 5: 7: 7] rows, then on foll 3 [3: 2: 3: 4: 3] alt rows, then on 2 foll 4th rows. 70 [72: 74: 78: 80: 84] sts.
Cont straight until armhole meas 23.5 [23.5: 24.5: 24.5: 25.5: 25.5] cm, ending with RS facing for next row.

Shape shoulders and back neck
Cast off 6 [6: 7: 7: 7: 8] sts at beg of next 2 rows. 58 [60: 60: 64: 66: 68] sts.
Next row (RS): Cast off 6 [6: 7: 7: 7: 8] sts, patt until there are 10 [11: 10: 12: 12: 12] sts on right needle and turn, leaving rem sts on a holder.
Work each side of neck separately.
Cast off 4 sts at beg of next row.
Cast off rem 6 [7: 6: 8: 8: 8] sts.
With RS facing, rejoin appropriate yarn to rem sts, cast off centre 26 [26: 26: 26: 28: 28] sts, patt to end.
Complete to match first side, reversing shapings.

LEFT FRONT
Frills (make 4)
Using 4mm (US 6) needles and yarn A cast on 172 [180: 188: 200: 216: 224] sts.
Row 1 (RS): *K2, lift first of these sts on right needle over 2nd st and off right needle, rep from * to end.
86 [90: 94: 100: 108: 112] sts.
Row 2: *P2tog, rep from * to end.
43 [45: 47: 50: 54: 56] sts.
Break yarn and leave sts on a holder.
Main section
Using 3¼mm (US 3) needles and yarn A cast on 43 [45: 47: 49: 53: 55] sts.
Work in moss st as given for back for 10 rows, inc 0 [0: 0: 1: 1: 1] st at end of last row and ending with RS facing for next row.
43 [45: 47: 50: 54: 56] sts.
Change to 4mm (US 6) needles.
Beg with a K row, work in st st for 4 rows, ending with RS facing for next row.
Row 5 (RS): Holding WS of one frill against RS of main section, K tog first st of frill with first st of main section, *K tog next st of frill with next st of main section, rep from * to end. 43 [45: 47: 50: 54: 56] sts.
Beg with a P row, work in st st for 7 rows, ending with RS facing for next row.
Rep last 8 rows twice more, then row 5 again – all 4 frills now attached.
Next row (WS): P4 [2: 3: 4: 3: 4], M1P, (P7 [8: 8: 7: 8: 8], M1P) 5 [5: 5: 6: 6: 6] times, P4 [3: 4: 4: 3: 4]. 49 [51: 53: 57: 61: 63] sts.★★
Now work in patt as folls:
Row 1 (RS): Using yarn B, K1, sl 1, *K2, sl 2, rep from * to last 3 [1: 3: 3: 3: 1] sts, K3 [1: 3: 3: 3: 1].
Row 2: Using yarn B, P3 [1: 3: 3: 3: 1], *sl 2, P2, rep from * to last 2 sts, sl 1, P1.

Row 3: Using yarn A, knit.
Row 4: Using yarn C, P1 [3: 1: 1: 1: 3], *sl 2, P2, rep from * to end.
Row 5: Using yarn C, *K2, sl 2, rep from * to last 1 [3: 1: 1: 1: 3] sts, K1 [3: 1: 1: 1: 3].
Row 6: Using yarn A, purl.
These 6 rows form patt.
Work in patt for a further 24 [24: 22: 30: 28: 34] rows, ending with RS facing for next row.
Shape armhole
Keeping patt correct, cast off 6 [7: 7: 8: 8: 9] sts at beg of next row. 43 [44: 46: 49: 53: 54] sts.
Work 1 row.
Dec 1 st at armhole edge of next 3 [3: 5: 5: 7: 7] rows, then on foll 3 [3: 2: 3: 4: 3] alt rows, then on 2 foll 4th rows.
35 [36: 37: 39: 40: 42] sts.
Cont straight until 21 [21: 21: 23: 23: 23] rows less have been worked than on back to beg of shoulder shaping, ending with **WS** facing for next row.
Shape front neck
Keeping patt correct, cast off 9 [9: 9: 8: 9: 9] sts at beg of next row. 26 [27: 28: 31: 31: 33] sts.
Dec 1 st at neck edge of next 3 rows, then on foll 2 [2: 2: 3: 3: 3] alt rows, then on 3 foll 4th rows. 18 [19: 20: 22: 22: 24] sts.
Work 1 row, ending with RS facing for next row.
Shape shoulder
Cast off 6 [6: 7: 7: 7: 8] sts at beg of next and foll alt row.
Work 1 row.
Cast off rem 6 [7: 6: 8: 8: 8] sts.

RIGHT FRONT
Work as given for left front to ★★.
Now work in patt as folls:
Row 1 (RS): Using yarn B, K3 [1: 3: 3: 3: 1], *sl 2, K2, rep from * to last 2 sts, sl 1, K1.
Row 2: Using yarn B, P1, sl 1, *P2, sl 2, rep from * to last 3 [1: 3: 3: 3: 1] sts, P3 [1: 3: 3: 3: 1].
Row 3: Using yarn A, knit.
Row 4: Using yarn C, *P2, sl 2, rep from * to last 1 [3: 1: 1: 1: 3] sts, P1 [3: 1: 1: 1: 3].
Row 5: Using yarn C, K1 [3: 1: 1: 1: 3], *sl 2, K2, rep from * to end.
Row 6: Using yarn A, purl.
These 6 rows form patt.
Complete to match left front, reversing shapings.

SLEEVES
Using 3¼mm (US 3) needles and yarn A cast on 55 [55: 57: 57: 59: 59] sts.
Work in moss st as given for back for 10 rows, inc 1 st at end of last row and ending with RS facing for next row. 56 [56: 58: 58: 60: 60] sts.
Change to 4mm (US 6) needles.
Beg with a K row, work in st st, shaping sides by inc 1 st at each end of 19th [15th: 15th:

13th: 13th: 11th] and every foll 20th [16th: 16th: 14th: 14th: 12th] row to 62 [62: 62: 68: 68: 70] sts, then on every foll 22nd [18th: 18th: 16th: 16th: 14th] row until there are 64 [66: 68: 70: 72: 74] sts.
Cont straight until sleeve meas 37.5 [37.5: 39: 39: 40: 40] cm, ending with RS facing for next row.
Shape top
Cast off 6 [7: 7: 8: 8: 9] sts at beg of next 2 rows. 52 [52: 54: 54: 56: 56] sts.
Dec 1 st at each end of next 3 rows, then on every foll alt row until 40 sts rem.
Work 3 rows, ending with RS facing for next row.
Dec 1 st at each end of next and 3 foll 4th rows, then 3 foll 6th rows, then foll 3 rows, ending with RS facing for next row.
Cast off rem 20 sts.

MAKING UP
Press as described on the information page.
Join both shoulder seams using back stitch, or mattress stitch if preferred.
Button band
Using 3¼mm (US 3) needles and yarn A cast on 9 sts.
Work in moss st as given for back until button band, when slightly stretched, fits up entire left front opening edge, from cast-on edge to neck shaping, ending with RS facing for next row.
Cast off in moss st.
Slip st band in place. Mark positions for 6 buttons on this band - first to come 1.5 cm up from cast-on edge, last to come 1.5 cm below neck shaping, and rem 4 buttons evenly spaced between.
Buttonhole band
Work to match button band, with the addition of 6 buttonholes worked to correspond with positions marked for buttons on button band as folls:
Buttonhole row (RS): Moss st 4 sts, cast off 2 sts (to make a buttonhole - cast on 2 sts over these cast-off sts on next row), moss st to end.
When band is complete, slip st in place.
Collar
Using 3¼mm (US 3) needles and yarn A cast on 101 [101: 101: 103: 107: 107] sts.
Work in moss st as given for back until collar meas 10 cm, ending with RS facing for next row.
Cast off 11 sts at beg of next 6 rows.
Cast off rem 35 [35: 35: 37: 41: 41] sts in moss st.
Machine wash all pieces before completing sewing together.
See information page for finishing instructions, setting in sleeves using the set-in method and attaching shaped cast-off edge of collar to neck edge, placing ends of collar half way across top of bands.

GENTIAN
GRACE MELVILLE

Main image page 32 & 34

●●

YARN

8	10	12	14	16	18	20	22

To fit bust

81	86	91	97	102	107	112	117	cm
32	34	36	38	40	42	44	46	in

Rowan Siena 4 ply

5	6	6	7	7	7	8	8	x 50gm

(photographed in Cream 652)

NEEDLES

1 pair 2³/4mm (no 12) (US 2) needles
1 pair 3¹/4mm (no 10) (US 3) needles

TENSION

32 sts and 24 rows to 10 cm measured over patt using 3¹/4mm (US 3) needles.

BACK and FRONT (both alike)
Using 2³/4mm (US 2) needles, cast on
122 [130: 134: 146: 150: 162: 170: 178] sts.
Row 1 (RS): K2, *P2, K2, rep from * to end.
Row 2: P2, *K2, P2, rep from * to end.
These 2 rows form rib.
Work in rib for a further 4 rows, ending with RS facing for next row.
Change to 3¹/4mm (US 3) needles.
Row 7 (RS): K1 [5: 7: 5: 8: 5: 4: 5], M1,
*K7 [8: 7: 8: 7: 8: 7: 8], M1, rep from * to last
2 [5: 8: 5: 9: 5: 5: 5] sts, K to end.
140 [146: 152: 164: 170: 182: 194: 200] sts.
Now work in patt, shaping side seams as folls:
Row 1 (WS): K2tog, P5, *P5tog, (K1, P1, K1,
P1, K1) all into next st, rep from * to last 7 sts,
P5, K2tog.
138 [144: 150: 162: 168: 180: 192: 198] sts.
Row 2: Purl.
Row 3: K2tog, P4, *(K1, P1, K1, P1, K1) all
into next st, P5tog, rep from * to last 6 sts, P4,
K2tog.
136 [142: 148: 160: 166: 178: 190: 196] sts.
Row 4: Purl.
Row 5: Wrapping yarn round needle 3 times
for every st: K2tog, K to last 2 sts, K2tog.
Row 6: K to end, dropping extra loops.
134 [140: 146: 158: 164: 176: 188: 194] sts.
Row 7: K2tog, P2, *P5tog, (K1, P1, K1, P1,
K1) all into next st, rep from * to last 4 sts, P2,
K2tog.

132 [138: 144: 156: 162: 174: 186: 192] sts.
Row 8: Purl.
Row 9: K2tog, P1, *(K1, P1, K1, P1, K1) all
into next st, P5tog, rep from * to last 3 sts, P1,
K2tog.
130 [136: 142: 154: 160: 172: 184: 190] sts.
Row 10 to 12: As rows 4 to 6.
128 [134: 140: 152: 158: 170: 182: 188] sts.
Row 13: K3tog, P4, *P5tog, (K1, P1, K1, P1,
K1) all into next st, rep from * to last 7 sts, P4,
K3tog.
124 [130: 136: 148: 154: 166: 178: 184] sts.
Row 14: Purl.
Row 15: K3tog, P2, *(K1, P1, K1, P1, K1) all
into next st, P5tog, rep from * to last 5 sts, P2,
K3tog.
120 [126: 132: 144: 150: 162: 174: 180] sts.
Row 16: Purl.
Row 17: Wrapping yarn round needle 3 times
for every st: K to end.
Row 18: K to end, dropping extra loops.
Row 19: K1, P2, *P5tog, (K1, P1, K1, P1, K1)
all into next st, rep from * to last 3 sts, P2, K1.
Row 20: Purl.
Row 21: K1, P2, *(K1, P1, K1, P1, K1) all into
next st, P5tog, rep from * to last 3 sts, P2, K1.
Last 6 rows form patt.
Cont in patt, inc 1 st at each end of 6th and
3 foll 8th rows, taking inc sts into patt when
there are sufficient sts.
128 [134: 140: 152: 158: 170: 182: 188] sts.
Cont straight until back meas 28 [28: 27: 30:
29: 31: 30: 32] cm, ending with RS facing for
next row.

Shape armholes

Keeping patt correct, cast off 4 [4: 5: 6: 6: 7: 8:
9] sts at beg of next 2 rows.
120 [126: 130: 140: 146: 156: 166: 170] sts.
Dec 1 st at each end of next 5 [5: 5: 7: 7: 7:
9: 9] rows, then on foll 2 [4: 4: 5: 5: 8: 8: 8] alt
rows.

106 [108: 112: 116: 122: 126: 132: 136] sts.
Cont straight until armhole meas 20 [20: 21:
21: 22: 22: 23: 23] cm, ending with RS facing
for next row.

Shape back neck and shoulders

Next row (RS): Cast off 5 [6: 7: 8: 9: 10:
11: 12] sts, patt until there are 9 [9: 10: 11: 12:
13: 15: 16] sts on right needle and turn, leaving
rem sts on a holder.
Work each side of neck separately.
Cast off 3 sts at beg of next row.
Cast off rem 6 [6: 7: 8: 9: 10: 12: 13] sts.
With RS facing, rejoin yarn to rem sts, cast
off centre 78 [78: 78: 78: 80: 80: 80: 80] sts,
patt to end.
Complete to match first side, reversing
shapings.

MAKING UP

Press as described on the information page.
Join right shoulder seam using back stitch, or
mattress stitch if preferred.

Neckband
With RS facing and using 2³/4mm (US 2)
needles, pick up and knit 75 [75: 75: 75: 77: 77:
77: 77] sts from front, then 75 [75: 75: 75: 77:
77: 77: 77] sts from back.
150 [150: 150: 150: 154: 154: 154: 154] sts.
Beg with row 2, work in rib as given for back
for 5 rows, ending with RS facing for next row.
Cast off in rib.
Join left shoulder and neckband seam.

Armhole borders (both alike)
With RS facing and using 2³/4mm (US 2)
needles, pick up and knit 118 [118: 126: 130:
134: 138: 142: 146] sts evenly all round
armhole edge.
Beg with row 2, work in rib as given for back
for 5 rows, ending with RS facing for next row.
Cast off in rib.
See information page for finishing instructions.

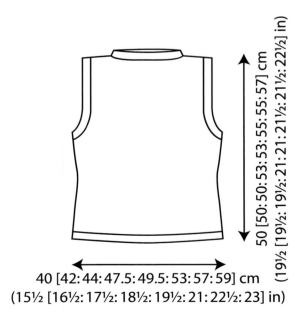

50 [50: 50: 53: 53: 55: 55: 57] cm
(19½ [19½: 19½: 21: 21: 21½: 21½: 22½] in)

40 [42: 44: 47.5: 49.5: 53: 57: 59] cm
(15½ [16½: 17½: 18½: 19½: 21: 22½: 23] in)

CLEAVERS
ERIKA KNIGHT
Main image page 36 & 37

YARN

S	M	L	XL	XXL

To fit bust
81-86 91-97 102-107 112-117 122-127 cm
32-34 36-38 40-42 44-46 48-50 in

Rowan Lenpur™ Linen

11	12	13	15	16	x 50gm

(photographed in Blanche 571)

NEEDLES

1 pair 3¾mm (no 9) (US 5) needles
1 pair 4mm (no 8) (US 6) needles

EXTRAS - Piece of silk fabric approx 15 cm wide and 150 cm long

TENSION

22 sts and 30 rows to 10 cm measured over st st using 4mm (US 6) needles.

BACK and SIDE FRONTS

Using 3¾mm (US 5) needles cast on 157 [181: 203: 231: 261] sts.
Row 1 (RS): Sl 1, K1, *P1, K1, rep from * to last st, K1.
Row 2: Sl 1, *P1, K1, rep from * to end.
These 2 rows form rib.
Cont in rib for a further 18 rows, ending with RS facing for next row.
Change to 4mm (US 6) needles.
Next row (RS): Sl 1, K to end.
Next row: Sl 1, P to last st, K1.
These 2 rows form patt.
Cont as set until work meas 43 [44: 45: 46: 47] cm, ending with RS facing for next row.
Divide for armholes
Next row (RS): Sl 1, K22 [28: 33: 40: 47] and slip these sts onto a holder for right side front, cast off next 6 sts, K until there are 99 [111: 123: 137: 153] sts on right needle, join in new ball of yarn and cast off next 6 sts, K to end and slip these sts onto another holder for left side front, leaving new ball of yarn with these sts.
Shape back
Cont on centre 99 [111: 123: 137: 153] sts only for back.
Work 1 row, ending with RS facing for next row.
Next row (RS): K2, K2tog, K to last 4 sts, sl 1, K1, psso, K2.
Working all armhole decreases as set by last row, dec 1 st at each end of 2nd and foll 3 alt

rows. 89 [101: 113: 127: 143] sts.
Cont straight until armhole meas 19 [20: 21: 22: 23] cm, ending with RS facing for next row.
Next row (RS): K17 [23: 28: 35: 42], (P1, K1) 27 [27: 28: 28: 29] times, P1, K to end.
Next row: P17 [23: 28: 35: 42], (K1, P1) 27 [27: 28: 28: 29] times, K1, P to end.
These 2 rows set the sts for rest of back - centre sts now in rib with all other sts still in st st.
Shape shoulders
Keeping sts correct as now set, cast off 6 [8: 9: 12: 14] sts at beg of next 4 rows, then 5 [7: 10: 11: 14] sts at beg of foll 2 rows.
Cast off rem 55 [55: 57: 57: 59] sts in rib, placing markers either side of centre 39 [39: 41: 41: 43] sts to denote back neck.
Shape left side front
With **WS** facing and using ball of yarn set aside with left side front, slip left side front 23 [29: 34: 41: 48] sts back onto 4mm (US 6) needles and patt 1 row, ending with RS facing for next row.
Working armhole decreases as set by back, dec 1 st at armhole edge of next and foll 4 alt rows. 18 [24: 29: 36: 43] sts.
Cont straight until left side front matches back to beg of shoulder shaping, ending with RS facing for next row.
Shape shoulder
Cast off 6 [8: 9: 12: 14] sts at beg of next and foll alt row.
Work 1 row.
Cast off rem 6 [8: 11: 12: 15] sts.
Shape right side front
With **WS** facing, slip right side front 23 [29: 34: 41: 48] sts back onto 4mm (US 6) needles, rejoin yarn and patt 1 row, ending with RS facing for next row.
Complete to match left side front, reversing shapings.

CENTRE FRONT

Using 3¾mm (US 5) needles cast on 83 [83:

85: 85: 87] sts.
Work in rib as given for back and side fronts for 20 rows, ending with RS facing for next row.
Change to 4mm (US 6) needles.
Next row (RS): Sl 1, K to end.
Next row: Sl 1, P to last st, K1.
These 2 rows form patt.
Cont as set until centre front meas 62 [64: 66: 68: 70] cm, ending with RS facing for next row.
Change to 3¾mm (US 5) needles.
Beg with row 1, work in rib as given for back and side fronts for 8 rows, ending with RS facing for next row.
Cast off in rib, placing markers 8 sts in from each end of cast-off row.

SLEEVES

Using 3¾mm (US 5) needles cast on 45 [47: 49: 51: 53] sts.
Row 1 (RS): K1, *P1, K1, rep from * to end.
Row 2: P1, *K1, P1, rep from * to end.
These 2 rows form rib.
Cont in rib for a further 18 rows, ending with RS facing for next row.
Change to 4mm (US 6) needles.
Beg with a K row, cont in st st as folls:
Work 2 rows, ending with RS facing for next row.
Next row (RS): K3, M1, K to last 3 sts, M1, K3.
Working all increases as set by last row, inc 1 st at each end of 4th and every foll 4th row to 65 [77: 81: 89: 97] sts, then on every foll 6th row until there are 85 [91: 95: 99: 103] sts.
Cont straight until sleeve meas 44 [45: 46: 46: 46] cm, ending with RS facing for next row.
Shape top
Cast off 3 sts at beg of next 2 rows.
79 [85: 89: 93: 97] sts.
Working all decreases as set by back armhole, dec 1 st at each end of next and foll 3 alt rows, then on foll row, ending with RS facing for next row.
Cast off rem 69 [75: 79: 83: 87] sts.

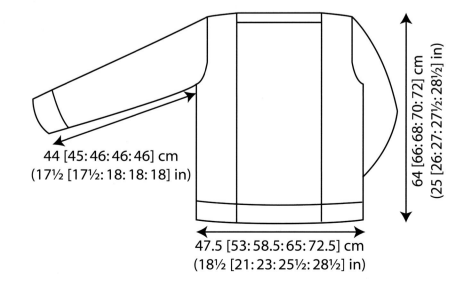

44 [45: 46: 46: 46] cm
(17½ [17½: 18: 18: 18] in)

47.5 [53: 58.5: 65: 72.5] cm
(18½ [21: 23: 25½: 28½] in)

64 [66: 68: 70: 72] cm
(25 [26: 27: 27½: 28½] in)

MAKING UP
Press as described on the information page. Cut silk fabric into 2 equal lengths and gather one end of each piece to approx 12-13 cm.

With **WS** facing (so seam forms ridge on RS of work) and inserting gathered end of fabric into seam at waist level, join side fronts to centre front using back stitch.

Join both shoulder seams beyond markers using back stitch, or mattress stitch if preferred.
See information page for finishing instructions, setting in sleeves using the shallow set-in method.

CHARITY
MARIE WALLIN
Main image page 47

●●

YARN

	S	M	L	XL	XXL	
To fit bust						
	81-86	91-97	102-107	112-117	122-127	cm
	32-34	36-38	40-42	44-46	48-50	in

Rowan Siena 4 ply
A Frost 653

4	4	4	5	5	x 50gm

B White 651

11	11	11	12	12	x 50gm

NEEDLES
1 pair 2¼mm (no 13) (US 1) needles
1 pair 3mm (no 11) (US 2/3) needles
2¼mm (no 13) (US 1) circular needle, 80 cm long
3mm (no 11) (US 2/3) circular needle, 120 cm long

TENSION
28 sts and 38 rows to 10 cm measured over st st using 3mm (US 2/3) needles.

BACK
Using 2¼mm (US 1) needles and yarn A cast on 129 [143: 161: 177: 197] sts.
Row 1 (RS): K1, *P1, K1, rep from * to end.
Row 2: As row 1.
These 2 rows form moss st.
Work in moss st for a further 4 rows, ending with RS facing for next row,
Change to 3mm (US 2/3) needles.
Break off yarn A and join in yarn B.
Beg with a K row, now work in st st, shaping side seams by dec 1 st at each end of 9th [9th: 9th: 9th: 3rd] and 0 [2: 4: 6: 8] foll 6th rows,

then on 10 [8: 6: 4: 2] foll 4th rows.
107 [121: 139: 155: 175] sts.
Work 21 rows, ending with RS facing for next row.
Inc 1 st at each end of next and 4 foll 10th rows. 117 [131: 149: 165: 185] sts.
Work 13 rows, ending with RS facing for next row. (Back should meas 34 [35: 36: 37: 36] cm.)
Shape armholes
Cast off 4 [5: 6: 7: 8] sts at beg of next 2 rows.
109 [121: 137: 151: 169] sts.
Dec 1 st at each end of next 3 [5: 7: 9: 11] rows, then on foll 4 [5: 7: 8: 10] alt rows.
95 [101: 109: 117: 127] sts.
Cont straight until armhole meas 20 [21: 22: 23: 24] cm, ending with RS facing for next row.
Shape shoulders and back neck
Next row (RS): Cast off 6 [7: 8: 10: 11] sts, K until there are 19 [21: 23: 25: 28] sts on right needle and turn, leaving rem sts on a holder.
Work each side of neck separately.
Cast off 3 sts at beg of next row, then 6 [7: 8: 10: 11] sts at beg of foll row, and 3 sts at beg of next row.
Cast off rem 7 [8: 9: 9: 11] sts.
With RS facing, rejoin yarn to rem sts, cast off centre 45 [45: 47: 47: 49] sts, K to end.

Complete to match first side, reversing shapings.

LEFT FRONT
Using 2¼mm (US 1) needles and yarn A cast on 119 [133: 151: 167: 187] sts.
Work in moss st as given for back for 6 rows, dec 1 st at end of last row and ending with RS facing for next row.
118 [132: 150: 166: 186] sts.
Change to 3mm (US 2/3) needles.
Join in yarn B.
Now work in stripe patt as folls:
Row 1 (RS): Using yarn B, K to last 2 sts, moss st 2 sts.
Row 2: Using yarn B, moss st 2 sts, P to end.
These 2 rows set the sts – front opening edge 2 sts still in moss st with all other sts now in st st.
Keeping sts correct as now set, work 4 rows using yarn B, dec 0 [0: 0: 0: 1] st at beg of next row. 118 [132: 150: 166: 185] sts.
Using yarn A, work 6 rows, dec 1 st at beg of 3rd row. 117 [131: 149: 165: 184] sts.
Last 12 rows form stripe patt and beg side seam shaping.
Cont as set, dec 1 st at beg of next [3rd: 3rd: 3rd: 3rd] and 0 [1: 3: 3: 3] foll 6th rows, then on 3 [2: 0: 0: 0] foll 4th rows.

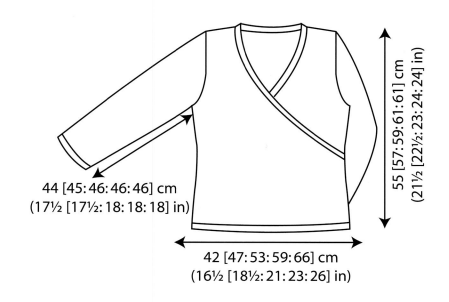

44 [45: 46: 46: 46] cm
(17½ [17½: 18: 18: 18] in)

42 [47: 53: 59: 66] cm
(16½ [18½: 21: 23: 26] in)

55 [57: 59: 61: 61] cm
(21½ [22½: 23: 24: 24] in)

113 [127: 145: 161: 180] sts.

Work 1 [1: 1: 5: 3] rows, ending with RS facing for next row.

Shape tie

Keeping stripes correct, inc 1 st at end of next and foll alt row, then at same edge on foll row, taking inc sts into moss st and ending with RS facing for next row, **and at same time** dec 1 st at beg of 3rd [3rd: 3rd: next: 3rd] row.

115 [129: 147: 163: 182] sts.

Work 1 row, ending with **WS** facing for next row.

Change to 3mm (US 2/3) circular needle.

Next row (WS): Cast on 248 [276: 304: 332: 360] sts, moss st 5 sts, place marker on right needle, P to end.

363 [405: 451: 495: 542] sts.

Next row: (K2tog) 1 [1: 1: 1: 0] times, K to marker, slip marker onto right needle, *K1, P1, rep from * to end. 362 [404: 450: 494: 542] sts.

Next row: *P1, K1, rep from * to marker, slip marker onto right needle, P to end.

Remove marker.

Next row: (K2tog) 0 [0: 0: 0: 1] times, K to last 2 sts, moss st 2 sts. 362 [404: 450: 494: 541] sts.

Next row: Moss st 2 sts, P to end.

Keeping sts correct as set by last 2 rows, dec 1 st at beg of next [next: next: next: 5th] and 3 [3: 3: 3: 2] foll 4th rows.

358 [400: 446: 490: 538] sts.

Work 18 rows, ending with **WS** facing for next row.

Next row (WS): (P1, K1) 127 [141: 155: 169: 183] times, P to end.

Next row: K102 [116: 134: 150: 170], *K1, P1, rep from * to end.

Cast off 255 [283: 311: 339: 367] sts in moss st at beg of next row, placing marker on last cast-off st. 103 [117: 135: 151: 171] sts.

Tie is now completed - change back to straight 3mm (US 2/3) needles.

Shape front slope

Keeping stripes correct, dec 1 st at end of next row and at same edge on foll 44 [53: 53: 53: 53] rows, then on foll 4 [0: 0: 0: 0] alt rows **and at same time** inc 1 st at beg of next and 4 foll 10th rows.

59 [68: 86: 102: 122] sts.

Work 1 [0: 0: 0: 0] row, ending after 4 [2: 6: 4: 2] rows using yarn B [A: A: B: B] and with RS facing for next row.

Shape armhole

Keeping stripes correct, cast off 4 [5: 6: 7: 8] sts at beg and dec 1 st at end of next row.

54 [62: 79: 94: 113] sts.

Work 1 row, dec 0 [0: 1: 1: 1] st at front slope edge. 54 [62: 78: 93: 112] sts.

Dec 1 st at armhole edge of next 3 [5: 7: 9: 11] rows, then on foll 4 [5: 7: 8: 10] alt rows **and at same time** dec 1 st at front slope edge of next 1 [1: 15: 25: 31] rows, then on foll 5 [7: 3: 0: 0] alt rows. 41 [44: 46: 51: 60] sts.

Dec 1 st at front slope edge **only** on 2nd [2nd: 2nd: next: next] and foll 0 [0: 0: 1: 13] rows, then on foll 17 [17: 16: 16: 9] alt rows, then on 3 foll 4th rows, then on foll 6th row.

19 [22: 25: 29: 33] sts.

Cont straight until left front matches back to beg of shoulder shaping, ending with RS facing for next row.

Shape shoulder

Cast off 6 [7: 8: 10: 11] sts at beg of next and foll alt row.

Work 1 row.

Cast off rem 7 [8: 9: 9: 11] sts.

RIGHT FRONT

Using 2¼mm (US 1) needles and yarn A cast on 119 [133: 151: 167: 187] sts.

Work in moss st as given for back for 6 rows, dec 1 st at beg of last row and ending with RS facing for next row.

118 [132: 150: 166: 186] sts.

Change to 3mm (US 2/3) needles.

Break off yarn A and join in yarn B.

Now work in patt as folls:

Row 1 (RS): Moss st 2 sts, K to end.

Row 2: P to last 2 sts, moss st 2 sts.

These 2 rows set the sts - front opening edge 2 sts still in moss st with all other sts now in st st.

Keeping sts correct as now set, dec 1 st at end of 7th [7th: 7th: 7th: next] and 0 [2: 4: 4: 5] foll 6th rows, then on 4 [2: 0: 0: 0] foll 4th rows.

113 [127: 145: 161: 180] sts.

Work 1 [1: 1: 5: 3] rows, ending with RS facing for next row.

Shape tie

Inc 1 st at beg of next and foll alt row, then at same edge on foll row, taking inc sts into moss st and ending with RS facing for next row, **and at same time** dec 1 st at end of 3rd [3rd: 3rd: next: 3rd] row. 115 [129: 147: 163: 182] sts.

Change to 3mm (US 2/3) circular needle.

Next row (RS): Cast on 112 [115: 118: 121: 124] sts, moss st 5 sts, place marker on right needle, K to end.

227 [244: 265: 284: 306] sts.

Next row: P to marker, slip marker onto right needle, moss st to end.

Next row: Moss st to marker, slip marker onto right needle, K to last 2 [2: 2: 2: 0] sts, (K2tog) 1 [1: 1: 1: 0] times. 226 [243: 264: 283: 306] sts.

Remove marker.

Next row: P to last 2 sts, moss st 2 sts.

Next row: Moss st 2 sts, K to last 0 [0: 0: 0: 2] sts, (K2tog) 0 [0: 0: 0: 1] times.

Keeping sts correct as set by last 2 rows, dec 1 st at end of 2nd [2nd: 2nd: 2nd: 6th] and 3 [3: 3: 3: 2] foll 4th rows.

222 [239: 260: 279: 302] sts.

Work 17 rows, ending with RS facing for next row.

Next row (RS): (P1, K1) 60 [61: 63: 64: 66] times, K to end.

Next row: P102 [117: 134: 151: 170], *K1, P1, rep from * to end.

Cast off 119 [122: 125: 128: 131] sts in moss st at beg of next row, placing marker on last cast-off st. 103 [117: 135: 151: 171] sts.

Next row: Purl.

Tie is now completed - change back to straight 3mm (US 2/3) needles.

Complete to match left front from beg of front slope shaping, reversing shapings.

LEFT SLEEVE

Using 2¼mm (US 1) needles and yarn A cast on 51 [53: 57: 57: 59] sts.

Work in moss st as given for back for 6 rows, ending with RS facing for next row.

Change to 3mm (US 2/3) needles.**

Join in yarn B.

Beg with a K row, now work in st st in stripes as folls:

Rows 1 to 6: Using yarn B and inc 1 st at each end of 3rd of these rows.

53 [55: 59: 59: 61] sts.

Rows 7 to 12: Using yarn A and inc 1 st at each end of next and foll 4th row.

57 [59: 63: 63: 65] sts.

These 12 rows form striped st st and beg sleeve shaping.

Cont in striped st st, shaping sides by inc 1 st at each end of 3rd and every foll 4th row to 77 [81: 81: 93: 101] sts, then on every foll 6th row until there are 107 [111: 115: 119: 123] sts.

Cont straight until sleeve meas approx 44 [45: 46: 46: 46] cm, ending after same stripe row as on left front to beg of armhole shaping and with RS facing for next row.

Shape top

Keeping stripes correct, cast off 4 [5: 6: 7: 8] sts at beg of next 2 rows.

99 [101: 103: 105: 107] sts.

Dec 1 st at each end of next 5 rows, then on every foll alt row to 57 sts, then on foll 11 rows, ending with RS facing for next row. 35 sts.

Cast off 4 sts at beg of next 4 rows.

Cast off rem 19 sts.

RIGHT SLEEVE

Work as given for left sleeve to **.

Break off yarn A and join in yarn B.

Using yarn B **throughout**, complete as given for left sleeve.

MAKING UP

Press as described on the information page.

Join both shoulder seams using back stitch, or mattress stitch if preferred.

Front band

With RS facing, using 2¼mm (US 1) circular needle and yarn A, beg and ending at markers, pick up and knit 130 [138: 142: 146: 150] sts up right front slope, 57 [57: 59: 59: 61] sts from back, then 130 [138: 142: 146: 150] sts down left front slope. 317 [333: 343: 351: 361] sts.

Work in moss st as given for back for 5 rows, inc 1 st at each end of every row and ending with RS facing for next row.

327 [343: 353: 361: 371] sts.

Cast off in moss st.

Sew row-end edges of front band to top of tie cast-off edges.

See information page for finishing instructions, setting in sleeves using the set-in method and leaving 10 cm opening in right side seam level with tie.

CICELY

GRACE MELVILLE

Main image page 38

● ● ●

YARN

S	M	L	XL	XXL

To fit bust
81–86 91–97 102–107 112–117 122–127 cm
32–34 36–38 40–42 44–46 48–50 in

Rowan Cotton Glacé

7 8 9 10 12 x 50gm

(photographed in Bleached 726)

NEEDLES

1 pair 2¾mm (no 12) (US 2) needles
1 pair 3¼mm (no 10) (US 3) needles
Cable needle

TENSION

32 sts and 34 rows to 10 cm measured over patt
using 3¼mm (US 3) needles.

SPECIAL ABBREVIATIONS

C6B = slip next 3 sts onto cable needle and
leave at back of work, K3, then K3 from cable
needle.

Pattern note: Lower sections of back and
front are worked in separate panels using
separate balls of yarn. Unlike when working an
intarsia design, where 2 balls of yarn meet the
yarns are **NOT** twisted together – this forms
the holes within each cable.

BACK

Left side panel

Using 3¼mm (US 3) needles cast on 20 [28:
23: 32: 29] sts.

Row 1 (RS): (K3, P3) 3 [4: 3: 5: 4] times,
K2 [3: 3: 2: 3], P0 [1: 2: 0: 2].

Row 2: K0 [1: 2: 0: 2], P2 [3: 3: 2: 3], (K3, P3)
3 [4: 3: 5: 4] times.

These 2 rows form rib.

Work in rib for a further 10 rows, dec 1 st at
end of 3rd and foll 4th row and ending with
RS facing for next row. 18 [26: 21: 30: 27] sts.

Do NOT break yarn but leave these sts and the
attached ball of yarn on left needle.

★★Centre panels

Onto same needle, cast on 15 sts.

Row 1 (RS): (K3, P3) twice, K3.

Row 2: P3, (K3, P3) twice.

These 2 rows form rib.

Work in rib for a further 10 rows, ending with
RS facing for next row.

Do NOT break yarn but leave these sts and the
attached ball of yarn on left needle.

Rep from ★★ 6 [6: 8: 8: 10] times more.

Right side panel

Onto same needle, cast on 20 [28: 23: 32: 29] sts.

Row 1 (RS): P0 [1: 2: 0: 2], K2 [3: 3: 2: 3],
(P3, K3) 3 [4: 3: 5: 4] times.

Row 2: (P3, K3) 3 [4: 3: 5: 4] times, P2 [3: 3:
2: 3], K0 [1: 2: 0: 2].

These 2 rows form rib.

Work in rib for a further 10 rows, dec 1 st at
beg of 3rd and foll 4th row and ending with
RS facing for next row. 18 [26: 21: 30: 27] sts.

There are now 9 [9: 11: 11: 13] separate panels
on left needle. 141 [157: 177: 195: 219] sts in
total.

Now working across each panel on left needle
in turn, using ball of yarn attached to each
panel and remembering **NOT** to twist yarns
together where they meet (so that vertical holes
are formed), cont as folls:

Row 13 (RS): Work 2 tog, rib 13 [21: 16:
25: 22], ★slip next 3 sts onto cable needle and
leave at back of work, using same ball of yarn
as used for previous panel K first 3 sts of next
panel, using ball of yarn with last 3 sts worked
(the first 3 sts of the next panel) K last 3 sts of
previous panel – the 3 sts on cable needle, rib
9, rep from ★ 7 [7: 9: 9: 11] times more, rib
4 [12: 7: 16: 13], work 2 tog.
139 [155: 175: 193: 217] sts.

Using separate balls of yarn for each panel and
making sure holes are formed where panels
meet, work 11 rows, dec 1 st at each end of
4th and foll 4th row.
135 [151: 171: 189: 213] sts.

Last 12 rows form patt and beg side seam
shaping.

Keeping patt correct as now set (linking panels
tog on every cable row **only** and creating
vertical holes between panels on all other
rows), cont as folls:

Dec 1 st at each end of next and 3 foll 4th
rows. 127 [143: 163: 181: 205] sts.

Work 13 rows, ending with RS facing for
next row.

Inc 1 st at each end of next and 2 foll 8th rows,
taking inc sts into rib.
133 [149: 169: 187: 211] sts.

Work 5 rows, ending with RS facing for next
row. (11 rows have now been worked since 5th
cable row.)

Break off all balls of yarn **EXCEPT** ball
attached to first set of sts for next row.

Now using just one ball of yarn (so vertical
holes are **NOT** formed), cont as folls:

Row 73 (RS): Rib 11 [19: 14: 23: 20], (C6B,
rib 9) 7 [7: 9: 9: 11] times, C6B, rib 11 [19: 14:
23: 20].

Keeping sts correct as set, work 11 rows, inc 1
st at each end of 2nd and foll 8th row, taking
inc sts into rib. 137 [153: 173: 191: 215] sts.

Last 12 rows form patt for rest of back.

Cont straight in patt until back meas 29 [30:
31: 32: 33] cm, ending with RS facing for next
row.

Shape armholes

Keeping patt correct, cast off 5 [7: 9: 11: 13] sts
at beg of next 2 rows.
127 [139: 155: 169: 189] sts.★★★

Dec 1 st at each end of next 5 [7: 9: 11: 13]
rows, then on foll 7 [8: 9: 10: 12] alt rows.
103 [109: 119: 127: 139] sts.

Cont straight until armhole meas 22 [23: 24:
25: 26] cm, ending with RS facing for
next row.

Shape shoulders and back neck

Next row (RS): Cast off 7 [8: 9: 10: 11] sts,
patt until there are 19 [21: 23: 26: 29] sts on
right needle and turn, leaving rem sts on a
holder.

Work each side of neck separately.

Cast off 3 sts at beg of next row, 7 [8: 9:
10: 11] sts at beg of foll row, then 3 sts at beg of
next row.

Cast off rem 6 [7: 8: 10: 12] sts.

With RS facing, rejoin yarn to rem sts, cast off
centre 51 [51: 55: 55: 59] sts, patt to end.

Complete to match first side, reversing
shapings.

FRONT

Work as given for back to ★★★.

Dec 1 st at each end of next 5 [6: 6: 6: 6] rows.
117 [127: 143: 157: 177] sts.

Work 1 [0: 0: 0: 0] row, ending with RS facing
for next row.

Divide for front neck

Next row (RS): Work 2 tog, patt 56 [61: 69:

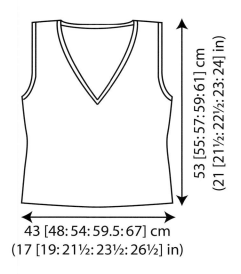

53 [55: 57: 59: 61] cm
(21 [21½: 22½: 23: 24] in)

43 [48: 54: 59.5: 67] cm
(17 [19: 21½: 23½: 26½] in)

76: 86] sts and turn, leaving rem sts on a holder. Work each side of neck separately.

Keeping patt correct, dec 1 st at armhole edge of 2nd [2nd: next: next: next] and foll 0 [0: 1: 3: 5] rows, then on foll 5 [7: 9: 10: 12] alt rows **and at same time** dec 1 st at neck edge of next [next: next: 2nd: 2nd] and foll 5 [1: 1: 0: 0] rows, then on foll 3 [7: 9: 11: 14] alt rows. 42 [45: 48: 51: 54] sts.

Dec 1 st at neck edge **only** on 2nd and foll 21 [21: 21: 19: 19] alt rows, then on 0 [0: 0: 1: 0] foll 4th row. 20 [23: 26: 30: 34] sts.

Cont straight until front matches back to beg of shoulder shaping, ending with RS facing for next row.

Shape shoulder

Cast off 7 [8: 9: 10: 11] sts at beg of next and foll alt row.

Work 1 row.
Cast off rem 6 [7: 8: 10: 12] sts.
With RS facing, slip centre st onto a holder, rejoin yarn to rem sts, patt to last 2 sts, work 2 tog.
Complete to match first side, reversing shapings.

MAKING UP

Press as described on the information page. Join right shoulder seam using back stitch, or mattress stitch if preferred.

Neckband

With RS facing and using 2¾mm (US 2) needles, pick up and knit 66 [70: 74: 78: 80] sts down left side of neck, K st from holder at base of V and mark this st with a coloured thread, pick up and knit 66 [70: 74: 78: 80] sts up right side of neck, then 48 [48: 51: 51: 54] sts from back. 181 [189: 200: 208: 215] sts.

Row 1 (WS): Knit.
Row 2: K to within 2 sts of marked st, K2tog, K marked st, K2tog tbl, K to end.
Rep last 2 rows once more, ending with **WS** facing for next row.
Cast off rem 177 [185: 196: 204: 211] sts knitwise (on **WS**).
Join left shoulder and neckband seam.

Armhole borders (both alike)

With RS facing and using 2¾mm (US 2) needles, pick up and knit 114 [124: 132: 142: 150] sts evenly all round armhole edge.
Work in g st for 4 rows, ending with **WS** facing for next row.
Cast off knitwise (on **WS**).
See information page for finishing instructions.

POISE
SARAH HATTON

Main image page 78 & 79

YARN

8	10	12	14	16	18	20	22	

To fit bust

81	86	91	97	102	107	112	117	cm
32	34	36	38	40	42	44	46	in

Rowan Pima Cotton

8	8	8	9	9	10	10	11	x 50gm

(photographed in Fig 076)

NEEDLES

1 pair 3¼mm (no 10) (US 3) needles
1 pair 3¾mm (no 9) (US 5) needles
3¼mm (no 10) (US 3) circular needle, 100 cm long
3¾mm (no 9) (US 5) circular needle, 100 cm long

TENSION

23 sts and 32 rows to 10 cm measured over st st using 3¾mm (US 5) needles.

BACK

Using 3¾mm (US 5) needles cast on 100 [104: 108: 116: 122: 130: 136: 144] sts.
Beg with a K row, work in st st until back meas 20 [20: 19: 22: 21: 23: 22: 24] cm, ending with RS facing for next row.

Shape armholes

Cast off 5 [6: 6: 7: 7: 8: 8: 9] sts at beg of next 2 rows. 90 [92: 96: 102: 108: 114: 120: 126] sts.
Next row (RS): K1, sl 1, K1, psso, K to last 3 sts, K2tog, K1.
Next row: P1, P2tog, P to last 3 sts, P2tog tbl, P1.
Working all armhole decreases as set by last 2 rows, dec 1 st at each end of next 3 [3: 3: 5: 5: 5: 7: 7] rows, then on foll 1 [1: 2: 2: 2: 4:

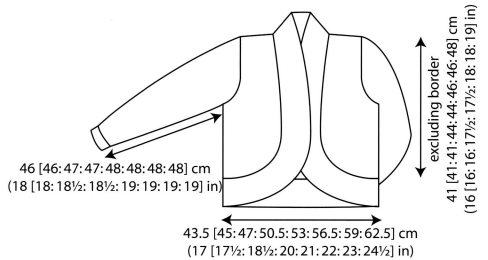

46 [46: 47: 47: 48: 48: 48: 48] cm
(18 [18: 18½: 18½: 19: 19: 19: 19] in)

43.5 [45: 47: 50.5: 53: 56.5: 59: 62.5] cm
(17 [17½: 18½: 20: 21: 22: 23: 24½] in)

41 [41: 41: 44: 44: 46: 46: 48] cm
(16 [16: 16: 17½: 17½: 18: 18: 19] in) excluding border

3: 4] alt rows.
78 [80: 82: 84: 90: 92: 96: 100] sts.
Cont straight until armhole meas 20 [20: 21:
21: 22: 22: 23: 23] cm, ending with RS facing
for next row.

Shape shoulders and back neck
Next row (RS): Cast off 9 [9: 10: 10: 11: 12:
13: 14] sts, K until there are 12 [13: 13: 14: 15:
15: 16: 17] sts on right needle and turn, leaving
rem sts on a holder.
Work each side of neck separately.
Cast off 3 sts at beg of next row.
Cast off rem 9 [10: 10: 11: 12: 12: 13: 14] sts.
With RS facing, rejoin yarn to rem sts, cast
off centre 36 [36: 36: 36: 38: 38: 38: 38] sts,
K to end.
Complete to match first side, reversing
shapings.

LEFT FRONT
Using 3¾mm (US 5) needles cast on 12 [14:
20: 14: 19: 17: 24: 22] sts.
Beg with a K row, work in st st as folls:
Work 1 row, ending with **WS** facing for next
row.
Row 2 (WS): P1, M1P, P to end.
Row 3: K to last st, M1, K1.
Working all increases as set by last 2 rows, inc
1 st at shaped edge of foll 12 [12: 8: 18: 16: 22:
18: 24] rows, then on foll 11 alt rows, then on
3 foll 4th rows.
40 [42: 44: 48: 51: 55: 58: 62] sts.
Cont straight until left front matches back to
beg of armhole shaping, ending with RS facing
for next row.
Shape armhole
Cast off 5 [6: 6: 7: 7: 8: 8: 9] sts at beg of next
row. 35 [36: 38: 41: 44: 47: 50: 53] sts.
Work 1 row.
Shape front slope
Working all armhole and front slope decreases
as set by back armhole decreases, dec 1 st at
armhole edge of next 5 [5: 5: 7: 7: 7: 9: 9] rows,
then on foll 1 [1: 2: 2: 2: 4: 3: 4] alt rows **and
at same time** dec 1 st at front slope edge of
next and 1 [1: 2: 2: 3: 2: 2] foll 4th rows, then
on 0 [0: 0: 0: 0: 0: 1: 1] foll 6th row.
27 [28: 28: 29: 32: 32: 34: 36] sts.
Dec 1 st at front slope edge only on 2nd [2nd:
6th: 4th: 2nd: 2nd: 6th: 4th] and 2 [2: 0: 0: 1: 0:

0: 0] foll 4th rows, then on 6 [6: 7: 7: 7: 7: 7]
foll 6th rows. 18 [19: 20: 21: 23: 24: 26: 28] sts.
Cont straight until left front matches back to
beg of shoulder shaping, ending with RS facing
for next row.

Shape shoulder
Cast off 9 [9: 10: 10: 11: 12: 13: 14] sts at beg of
next row.
Work 1 row.
Cast off rem 9 [10: 10: 11: 12: 12: 13: 14] sts.

RIGHT FRONT
Work as given for left front, reversing shapings.

SLEEVES
Using 3¼mm (US 3) needles cast on 46 [46:
46: 46: 46: 50: 50: 50: 50] sts.
Row 1 (RS): K2, *P2, K2, rep from * to end.
Row 2: P2, *K2, P2, rep from * to end.
Rows 3 to 8: As rows 1 and 2, 3 times.
Rows 9 and 10: Knit.
Row 11: *K2tog, yfwd, rep from * to last
2 sts, K2.
Row 12: K to end, inc 0 [0: 1: 1: 0: 0: 1: 1] st at
each end of row.
46 [46: 48: 48: 50: 50: 52: 52] sts.
Change to 3¾mm (US 5) needles.
Beg with a K row, work in st st, shaping sides
by inc 1 st at each end of 5th and 0 [3: 1: 5:
4: 8: 8: 12] foll 6th rows, then on every foll
8th row until there are 76 [78: 80: 82: 84: 86:
88: 90] sts.
Cont straight until sleeve meas 46 [46: 47: 47:
48: 48: 48: 48] cm, ending with RS facing for
next row.
Shape top
Cast off 5 [6: 6: 7: 7: 8: 8: 9] sts at beg of next
2 rows. 66 [66: 68: 68: 70: 70: 72: 72] sts.
Dec 1 st at each end of next 9 rows, then on
every foll alt row to 28 sts, then on foll 5 rows,
ending with RS facing for next row. 18 sts.
Cast off 4 sts at beg of next 2 rows.
Cast off rem 10 sts.

MAKING UP
Press as described on the information page.
Join both shoulder seams using back stitch, or
mattress stitch if preferred. Join side seams.
Front and hem border
With RS facing and using 3¼mm (US 3)

circular needle, beg and ending at base of right
side seam, pick up and knit 12 [14: 20: 14: 19:
17: 24: 22] sts from right front cast-on edge,
55 [55: 51: 61: 59: 65: 61: 67] sts up shaped
row-end edge to last inc, 13 sts up right front
opening edge to beg of front slope shaping,
57 [57: 61: 61: 63: 63: 67: 67] sts up right front
slope, 42 [42: 42: 42: 44: 44: 44: 44] sts from
back, 57 [57: 61: 61: 63: 63: 67: 67] sts down
left front slope, 13 sts down left front opening
edge to last inc, 55 [55: 51: 61: 59: 65: 61: 67] sts
down shaped row-end edge to cast-on edge,
12 [14: 20: 14: 19: 17: 24: 22] sts from left front
cast-on edge, then 100 [104: 108: 116: 122:
130: 136: 144] sts from back cast-on edge.
416 [424: 440: 456: 474: 490: 510: 526] sts.
Round 1 (RS): Purl.
Round 2: *K2tog, yfwd, rep from * to end.
Round 3: Purl.
Round 4: K12 [14: 20: 14: 19: 17: 24: 22], (inc
in next st, K4) 11 [11: 11: 11: 10: 10: 12: 12]
times, inc in next st, K180 [180: 180: 200: 212:
224: 204: 216], inc in next st, (K4, inc in
next st) 11 [11: 11: 11: 10: 10: 12: 12] times,
K to end.
440 [448: 464: 480: 496: 512: 536: 552] sts.
Round 5: *P2, K2, rep from * to end.
Round 6 and 7: As round 5, twice.
Round 8: Knit.
Rounds 9 to 11: As rounds 1 to 3.
Change to 3¾mm (US 5) circular needle.
Round 12: Knit.
Rounds 13 to 15: *K2, P2, rep from * to end.
Round 16: Knit.
Rounds 17 to 19: As rounds 1 to 3.
Round 20: Knit.
Rounds 21 to 23: As round 5.
Round 24: *P2, K1, M1, K1, P2, K2, rep from
* to end.
495 [504: 522: 540: 558: 576: 603: 621] sts.
Rounds 25 and 26: *P2, K3, P2, K2, rep from
* to end.
Round 27: *P2, K3, P2, K1, M1, K1, rep from
* to end.
550 [560: 580: 600: 620: 640: 670: 690] sts.
Rounds 28 and 29: *P2, K3, rep from
* to end.
Cast off in patt.
See information page for finishing instructions,
setting in sleeves using the set-in method.

EARTHY
ERIKA KNIGHT
Main image page 80 & 81

●●

YARN

	XS	S	M	L	XL	XXL	2XL	
To fit chest								
	97	102	107	112	117	122	127	cm
	38	40	42	44	46	48	50	in

Rowan Purelife Revive

A Basalt 462

4	4	4	4	4	5	5	x 50gm

B Rock 465

4	4	4	5	5	5	5	x 50gm

C Pumice 461

3	4	4	4	4	5	5	x 50gm

NEEDLES

1 pair 3¼mm (no 10) (US 3) needles
1 pair 4mm (no 8) (US 6) needles

TENSION

20 sts and 28 rows to 10 cm measured over patt using 4mm (US 6) needles.

STRIPE SEQUENCE

Rows 1 to 54: Using yarn A.
Row 55: Using yarn B.
Rows 56 to 59: Using yarn A.
Rows 60 and 61: Using yarn B.
Rows 62 to 64: Using yarn A.
Rows 65 to 67: Using yarn B.
Row 68: Using yarn A.
Row 69: Using yarn B.
Cont using yarn B until work meas 43 [44: 45: 44: 45: 44: 45] cm, ending with RS facing for next row. (For sleeves, cont using yarn B until work meas 45 [46: 47: 48: 49: 50: 51] cm.)
Now work rows 55 to 69 once more, **but** using yarn C instead of yarn B, and yarn B instead of yarn A.
Cont using yarn C **only** for rest of knitted section.

BACK

Using 3¼mm (US 3) needles and yarn A, cast on 103 [111: 115: 123: 127: 135: 139] sts.
Work in g st for 2 rows, ending with RS facing for next row.
Change to 4mm (US 6) needles.
Beg with stripe row 1, now work in patt in stripe sequence (see above) as folls:
Row 1 (RS): K2, *yfwd, sl 1, K2tog, psso, yfwd, K1, rep from * to last st, K1.
Row 2: Purl.
Row 3: K1, K2tog, yfwd, K1, *yfwd, sl 1, K2tog, psso, yfwd, K1, rep from * to last 3 sts, yfwd, sl 1, K1, psso, K1.

Row 4: Purl.
These 4 rows form patt.
Working appropriate rows of stripe sequence throughout, cont in patt until back meas 48 [49: 50: 49: 50: 49: 50] cm, ending with RS facing for next row.
Shape armholes
Keeping patt correct, cast off 4 sts at beg of next 2 rows.
95 [103: 107: 115: 119: 127: 131] sts.
Dec 1 st at each end of next 3 [5: 5: 7: 7: 9: 9] rows, then on foll 4 [4: 5: 5: 6: 7: 7] alt rows.
81 [85: 87: 91: 93: 95: 99] sts.
Cont straight until armhole meas 21 [22: 23: 24: 25: 26: 27] cm, ending with RS facing for next row.
Shape shoulders and back neck
Cast off 7 [7: 7: 8: 8: 8: 9] sts at beg of next 2 rows. 67 [71: 73: 75: 77: 79: 81] sts.
Next row (RS): Cast off 7 [7: 7: 8: 8: 8: 9] sts, patt until there are 9 [10: 11: 10: 11: 11: 11] sts on right needle and turn, leaving rem sts on a holder.
Work each side of neck separately.
Cast off 3 sts at beg of next row.
Cast off rem 6 [7: 8: 7: 8: 8: 8] sts.
With RS facing, rejoin yarn to rem sts, cast off centre 35 [37: 37: 39: 39: 41: 41] sts, patt to end.
Complete to match first side, reversing shapings.

FRONT

Work as given for back until 20 [20: 20: 22: 22: 24: 24] rows less have been worked than on back to beg of shoulder shaping, ending with RS facing for next row.
Shape front neck
Next row (RS): Patt 30 [31: 32: 34: 35: 36: 38] sts and turn, leaving rem sts on a holder.
Work each side of neck separately.
Keeping patt correct, dec 1 st at neck edge of next 6 rows, then on foll 3 [3: 3: 4: 4: 5: 5] alt rows, then on foll 4th row.
20 [21: 22: 23: 24: 24: 26] sts.

Work 3 rows, ending with RS facing for next row.
Shape shoulder
Cast off 7 [7: 7: 8: 8: 8: 9] sts at beg of next and foll alt row.
Work 1 row.
Cast off rem 6 [7: 8: 7: 8: 8: 8] sts.
With RS facing, rejoin yarn to rem sts, cast off centre 21 [23: 23: 23: 23: 23: 23] sts, patt to end.
Complete to match first side, reversing shapings.

SLEEVES

Using 3¼mm (US 3) needles and yarn A, cast on 51 [51: 55: 55: 59: 59: 63] sts.
Work in g st for 2 rows, ending with RS facing for next row.
Change to 4mm (US 6) needles.
Working next 2 [6: 6: 12: 12: 16: 16] rows using yarn A and then, beg with stripe row 1, working in stripe sequence (see above) cont as folls:
Work in patt as given for back, shaping sides by inc 1 st at each end of 9th [9th: 11th: 9th: 11th: 9th: 11th] and every foll 10th [10th: 12th: 10th: 12th: 10th: 12th] row to 57 [67: 77: 65: 75: 63: 75] sts, then on every foll 12th [12th: –: 12th: 14th: 12th: 14th] row until there are 73 [75: –: 79: 81: 83: 85] sts, taking inc sts into patt.
Cont straight until sleeve meas 50 [51: 52: 53: 54: 55: 56] cm, ending after same stripe row as on back and front to beg of armhole shaping and with RS facing for next row.
Shape top
Keeping patt correct, cast off 4 sts at beg of next 2 rows. 65 [67: 69: 71: 73: 75: 77] sts.
Dec 1 st at each end of next 3 rows, then on foll 4 alt rows, then on 3 foll 4th rows.
45 [47: 49: 51: 53: 55: 57] sts.
Work 1 row.
Dec 1 st at each end of next and every foll alt row to 37 sts, then on foll 5 rows, ending with RS facing for next row. 27 sts.

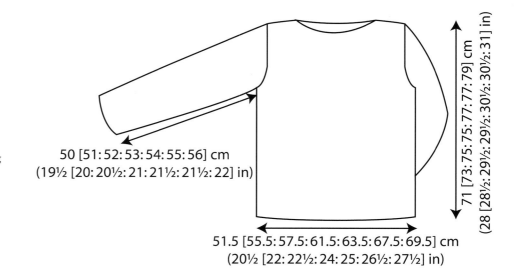

50 [51: 52: 53: 54: 55: 56] cm
(19½ [20: 20½: 21: 21½: 21½: 22] in)

51.5 [55.5: 57.5: 61.5: 63.5: 67.5: 69.5] cm
(20½ [22: 22½: 24: 25: 26½: 27½] in)

71 [73: 75: 75: 77: 77: 79] cm
(28 [28½: 29½: 29½: 30½: 30½: 31] in)

Cast off 4 sts at beg of next 2 rows.
Cast off rem 19 sts.

MAKING UP
Press as described on the information page.
Join right shoulder seam using back stitch, or mattress stitch if preferred.

Neckband
With RS facing, using 3¼mm (US 3) needles and yarn C, pick up and knit 20 [20: 20: 22: 22: 24: 24] sts down left side of neck, 21 [23: 23: 23: 23: 23: 23] sts from front, 20 [20: 20: 22: 22: 24: 24] sts up right side of neck, then 41 [43: 43: 45: 45: 47: 47] sts from back.
102 [106: 106: 112: 112: 118: 118] sts.
Cast off knitwise (on **WS**).

See information page for finishing instructions, setting in sleeves using the set-in method.

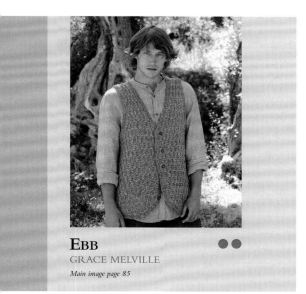

EBB
GRACE MELVILLE
Main image page 85

YARN

	XS	S	M	L	XL	XXL	2XL	
To fit chest								
	97	102	107	112	117	122	127	cm
	38	40	42	44	46	48	50	in

Rowan Purelife Revive

A Basalt 462

5	6	6	6	7	7	7	x 50gm

B Rock 465

5	6	6	6	7	7	7	x 50gm

NEEDLES
1 pair 3¼mm (no 10) (US 3) needles
1 pair 4mm (no 8) (US 6) needles

BUTTONS - 5 x RW5030 (18mm) from Bedecked. Please see information page for contact details.

TENSION
26 sts and 38 rows to 10 cm measured over patt using 4mm (US 6) needles.

Pattern note: When working patt, work all slipped sts purlwise with yarn at **WS** of work - this is back of work on RS rows, and front of work on WS rows.

BACK
Using 4mm (US 6) needles and yarn A, cast on 131 [143: 149: 155: 167: 173: 185] sts.
Now work in patt as folls:
Sizes XS, S, L, XL and 2XL only
Row 1 (RS): Using yarn A, knit.
Row 2: Using yarn A, P4, K3, *P3, K3, rep from * to last 4 sts, P4.
Row 3: Using yarn B, K1, sl 3 (see pattern note), *K3, sl 3, rep from * to last st, K1.
Row 4: Using yarn B, P1, sl 3, *K3, sl 3, rep from * to last st, P1.
Rows 5 to 12: As rows 1 to 4, twice.
Row 13: Using yarn A, knit.
Row 14: Using yarn A, P1, K3, *P3, K3, rep from * to last st, P1.
Row 15: Using yarn B, K4, sl 3, *K3, sl 3, rep from * to last 4 sts, K4.
Row 16: Using yarn B, P1, K3, *sl 3, K3, rep from * to last st, P1.
Rows 17 to 24: As rows 13 to 16, twice.
Sizes M and XXL only
Row 1 (RS): Using yarn A, knit.
Row 2: Using yarn A, P1, K3, *P3, K3, rep from * to last st, P1.
Row 3: Using yarn B, K4, sl 3 (see pattern note), *K3, sl 3, rep from * to last 4 sts, K4.
Row 4: Using yarn B, P1, K3, *sl 3, K3, rep from * to last st, P1.
Rows 5 to 12: As rows 1 to 4, twice.
Row 13: Using yarn A, knit.
Row 14: Using yarn A, P4, K3, *P3, K3, rep from * to last 4 sts, P4.
Row 15: Using yarn B, K1, sl 3, *K3, sl 3, rep from * to last st, K1.
Row 16: Using yarn B, P1, sl 3, *K3, sl 3, rep from * to last st, P1.
Rows 17 to 24: As rows 13 to 16, twice.
All sizes
These 24 rows form patt.
Cont in patt for a further 110 rows, ending after patt row 14 and with RS facing for next row. (Back should meas 35 cm.)
Shape armholes
Keeping patt correct, cast off 8 [9: 10: 10: 11: 12: 13] sts at beg of next 2 rows.

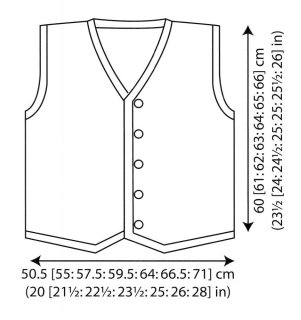

60 [61: 62: 63: 64: 65: 66] cm
(23½ [24: 24½: 25: 25: 25½: 26] in)

50.5 [55: 57.5: 59.5: 64: 66.5: 71] cm
(20 [21½: 22½: 23½: 25: 26: 28] in)

115 [125: 129: 135: 145: 149: 159] sts.
Dec 1 st at each end of next 5 [7: 7: 7: 9: 9: 11] rows, then on foll 7 [8: 8: 8: 10: 11: 11] alt rows, then on 3 foll 4th rows.
85 [89: 93: 99: 101: 103: 109] sts.
Cont straight until armhole meas 23 [24: 25: 26: 27: 28: 29] cm, ending with RS facing for next row.

Shape shoulders and back neck
Cast off 6 [6: 7: 8: 8: 8: 9] sts at beg of next 2 rows. 73 [77: 79: 83: 85: 87: 91] sts.
Next row (RS): Cast off 6 [6: 7: 8: 8: 8: 9] sts, patt until there are 9 [10: 10: 10: 11: 10: 11] sts on right needle and turn, leaving rem sts on a holder.
Work each side of neck separately.
Cast off 3 sts at beg of next row.
Cast off rem 6 [7: 7: 7: 8: 7: 8] sts.
With RS facing, rejoin appropriate yarn to rem sts, cast off centre 43 [45: 45: 47: 47: 51: 51] sts, patt to end.
Complete to match first side, reversing shapings.

LEFT FRONT
Using 4mm (US 6) needles and yarn A cast on 3 sts.
Now work in patt as folls:
Row 1 (RS): Using yarn A, K3.
Row 2: Using yarn A, inc in first st, K1, inc in last st. 5 sts.
Row 3: Using yarn B, inc in first st, K3, inc in last st. 7 sts.
Row 4: Using yarn B, inc in first st, sl 1, K3, sl 1, inc in last st. 9 sts.
Row 5: Using yarn A, inc in first st, K to last st, inc in last st. 11 sts.
Row 6: Using yarn A, inc in first st, P3, K3, P3, inc in last st. 13 sts.
Row 7: Using yarn B, inc in first st, K1, sl 3, K3, sl 3, K1, inc in last st. 15 sts.
Row 8: Using yarn B, inc in first st, K2, sl 3, K3, sl 3, K2, inc in last st. 17 sts.
Row 9: As row 5. 19 sts.
Row 10: Using yarn A, inc in first st, K1, (P3, K3) twice, P3, K1, inc in last st. 21 sts.
Row 11: Using yarn B, inc in first st, K2, (sl 3, K3) twice, sl 3, K2, inc in last st. 23 sts.
Row 12: Using yarn B, inc in first st, (K3, sl 3) 3 times, K3, inc in last st. 25 sts.
This sets position of patt as given for back.
Keeping patt correct, cont as folls:
Sizes XS and S only
Inc 1 st at each end of next 20 rows, ending with RS facing for next row. 65 sts.
Sizes M and L only
Inc 1 st at end (front opening edge) of next row and at same edge of foll 19 rows, ending with RS facing for next row, **and at same time** cast on 3 sts at beg of next and foll 9 alt rows. 75 sts.
Sizes XL, XXL and 2XL only
Inc 1 st at end (front opening edge) of next row and at same edge on foll 19 rows, ending

with RS facing for next row, **and at same time** cast on 3 sts at beg of next row, then 4 sts at beg of foll 9 alt rows. 84 sts.
All sizes
Cast on 6 [12: 5: 8: 5: 8: 14] sts at beg of next row. 71 [77: 80: 83: 89: 92: 98] sts.
Work 3 rows, ending with RS facing for next row.
Next row (buttonhole row) (RS): Patt to last 6 sts, yfwd, K2tog, patt 4 sts.
Work 31 rows.
Rep last 32 rows 3 times more, then first of these rows (the buttonhole row) again - 5 buttonholes made.
Work 1 row, ending with RS facing for next row. (Shorter row-end edge of left front should now match back to beg of armhole shaping.)
Shape armhole
Keeping patt correct, cast off 8 [9: 10: 10: 11: 12: 13] sts at beg of next row.
63 [68: 70: 73: 78: 80: 85] sts.
Work 1 row.
Shape front slope
Dec 1 st at armhole edge of next 5 [7: 7: 7: 9: 9: 11] rows, then on foll 7 [8: 8: 8: 10: 11: 11] alt rows, then on 3 foll 4th rows **and at same time** dec 1 st at front slope edge of next and foll 15 [17: 17: 17: 15: 17: 15] alt rows, then on 0 [0: 0: 0: 2: 2: 3] foll 4th rows.
32 [32: 34: 37: 38: 37: 41] sts.
Dec 1 st at front slope edge **only** on 2nd [2nd: 2nd: 4th: 2nd: 4th: 2nd] and foll 2 [1: 0: 0: 0: 0: 0] alt rows, then on 11 [11: 12: 13: 13: 13: 14] foll 4th rows.
18 [19: 21: 23: 24: 23: 26] sts.
Cont straight until left front matches back to beg of shoulder shaping, ending with RS facing for next row.
Shape shoulder
Cast off 6 [6: 7: 8: 8: 8: 9] sts at beg of next and foll alt row.
Work 1 row.
Cast off rem 6 [7: 7: 7: 8: 7: 8] sts.

RIGHT FRONT
Work to match left front, reversing shapings and omitting buttonholes.

MAKING UP
Press as described on the information page.
Join both shoulder seams using back stitch, or mattress stitch if preferred.
Armhole borders (both alike)
With RS facing, using 3¼mm (US 3) needles and yarn A, pick up and knit 145 [153: 161: 165: 173: 181: 189] sts evenly all round armhole edge.
Row 1 (WS): K1, *P1, K1, rep from * to end.
Row 2: As row 1.
These 2 rows form moss st.
Work in moss st for a further 3 rows, ending with RS facing for next row.
Cast off in moss st.

Join side and armhole border seams.
Front and hem border
Using 3¼mm (US 3) needles and yarn A cast on 5 sts.
Work in moss st as given for armhole borders until strip, when slightly stretched and beg at base of left side seam, fits across cast-on edge of back, then along shaped edge of right front to centre of original set of cast-on sts, ending with RS facing for next row.
***Turn corner**
Row 1 (RS): Moss st 4 sts, wrap next st (by slipping next st on left needle onto right needle, taking yarn to opposite side of work between needles and then slipping same st back onto left needle - when working back across wrapped sts, work the wrapped st and the wrapping loop tog as one st) and turn.
Row 2: Moss st to end.
Row 3: Moss st 3 sts, wrap next st and turn.
Row 4: Moss st to end.
Row 5: Moss st 2 sts, wrap next st and turn.
Row 6: Moss st to end.
Row 7: Moss st 1 st, wrap next st and turn.
Row 8: Moss st to end.
Rows 9 and 10: As rows 5 and 6.
Rows 11 and 12: As rows 3 and 4.
Rows 13 and 14: As rows 1 and 2.
These 14 rows complete corner.***
Cont in moss st until strip, when slightly stretched, fits along shaped edge to base of front opening edge, ending with RS facing for next row.
Turn corner
Row 1 (RS): Moss st 4 sts, wrap next st and turn.
Row 2: Moss st to end.
Row 3: Moss st 3 sts, wrap next st and turn.
Row 4: Moss st to end.
Row 5: Moss st 2 sts, wrap next st and turn.
Row 6: Moss st to end.
Rows 7 and 8: As rows 3 and 4.
Rows 9 and 10: As rows 1 and 2.
These 10 rows complete corner.**
Cont in moss st until strip, when slightly stretched, fits up right front opening edge, up right front slope, across back neck, down left front slope, then down left front opening edge to base of front opening edge, ending with RS facing for next row.
Rep from ** to ** once more.
Cont in moss st until strip, when slightly stretched, fits along shaped edge to centre of original cast-on sts, ending with RS facing for next row.
Rep from *** to *** once more.
Cont in moss st until strip, when slightly stretched, fits along shaped edge to base of left side seam, ending with RS facing for next row.
Cast off.
Slip stitch border in place, joining cast-on and cast-off edges at base of left side seam.
See information page for finishing instructions.

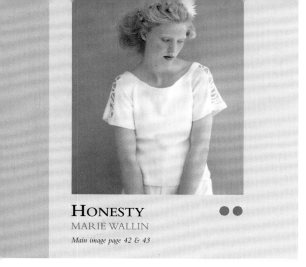

HONESTY
MARIE WALLIN

Main image page 42 & 43

YARN

	S	M	L	XL	XXL
To fit bust					
	81-86	91-97	102-107	112-117	122-127 cm
	32-34	36-38	40-42	44-46	48-50 in

Rowan Siena 4 ply

7	8	9	10	11	x 50gm

(photographed in White 651)

NEEDLES

1 pair 2¼mm (no 13) (US 1) needles
1 pair 3mm (no 11) (US 2/3) needles
2 double-pointed 2¼mm (no 13) (US 1) needles

TENSION

28 sts and 38 rows to 10 cm measured over st st using 3mm (US 2/3) needles.

BACK and FRONT (both alike)
Using 2¼mm (US 1) needles cast on 129 [143: 161: 177: 197] sts.
Row 1 (RS): K1, *P1, K1, rep from * to end.
Row 2: As row 1.
These 2 rows form moss st.
Work in moss st for a further 10 rows, dec 1 st at each end of 7th of these rows and ending with RS facing for next row.
127 [141: 159: 175: 195] sts.
Change to 3mm (US 2/3) needles.
Row 13 (RS): K3, K2tog, K to last 5 sts, sl 1, K1, psso, K3.
Working all side seam decreases as set by last row and beg with a P row, work in st st, dec 1 st at each end of 4th and 8 foll 4th rows.
107 [121: 139: 155: 175] sts.
Work 17 rows, ending with RS facing for next row.
Next row (RS): K3, M1, K to last 3 sts, M1, K3.
Working all side seam increases as set by last row, inc 1 st at each end of 10th and 3 foll 10th rows. 117 [131: 149: 165: 185] sts.
Cont straight until work meas 34 [35: 36: 37: 38] cm, ending with RS facing for next row.
Shape raglan armholes
Cast off 3 sts at beg of next 2 rows.
111 [125: 143: 159: 179] sts.
Sizes S and M only
Next row (RS): K3, K2tog, K to last 5 sts, sl 1, K1, psso, K3.
Work 3 rows.
Rep last 4 rows 5 [0: –: –: –] times more.
99 [123: –: –: –] sts.

Sizes L, XL and XXL only
Next row (RS): K3, K2tog, K to last 5 sts, sl 1, K1, psso, K3.
Next row: P3, P2tog tbl, P to last 5 sts, P2tog, P3.
Rep last 2 rows – [–: 4: 10: 17] times more.
– [–: 123: 115: 107] sts.
All sizes
Next row (RS): K3, K2tog, K to last 5 sts, sl 1, K1, psso, K3.
Next row: Purl.
Rep last 2 rows 9 [21: 20: 16: 11] times more, ending with RS facing for next row.
79 [79: 81: 81: 83] sts.
Cast off.

SLEEVES
Using 2¼mm (US 1) needles, cast on 107 [111: 115: 119: 123] sts.
Work in moss st as given for back and front for 11 rows, ending with **WS** facing for next row.
Left sleeve only
Row 12 (WS): Moss st 45 [47: 49: 51: 53] sts and slip these sts onto a holder, moss st 3 sts and slip these 3 sts onto a 2nd holder, cast off next 14 sts in moss st, moss st to end.
Right sleeve only
Row 12 (WS): Moss 45 [47: 49: 51: 53] sts and slip these sts onto a holder, cast off next 14 sts in moss st, moss st until there are 3 sts on right needle and slip these 3 sts onto a 2nd holder, moss st to end.
Both sleeves
Cont on this last set of 45 [47: 49: 51: 53] sts only for first side of sleeve.
Change to 3mm (US 2/3) needles.
Next row (RS): Knit.
Next row: K1, P to end.
These 2 rows set the sts – sleeve opening edge st worked as a K st on every row with all other sts in st st.
Working all increases as set by back and front, cont as set, inc 1 st at beg of 11th and foll 10th row. 47 [49: 51: 53: 55] sts.
Cont straight until work meas 10 cm from cast-on edge, ending with RS facing for next row.
Shape raglan
Work 1 row.
Cast off 3 sts at beg of next row.
44 [46: 48: 50: 52] sts.
Next row (RS): K to last 5 sts, sl 1, K1, psso, K3.
Next row: P3, P2tog tbl, P to last st, K1.
Rep last 2 rows 5 times more.
32 [34: 36: 38: 40] sts.
Next row (RS): K to last 5 sts, sl 1, K1, psso, K3.
Next row: P to last st, K1.
Rep last 2 rows 15 [17: 19: 21: 23] times more, ending with RS facing for next row.
Cast off rem 16 sts.

Shape raglan
Cast off 3 sts at beg of next row.
44 [46: 48: 50: 52] sts.
Work 1 row.
Next row (RS): K3, K2tog, K to end.
Next row: K1, P to last 5 sts, P2tog, P3.
Rep last 2 rows 5 times more.
32 [34: 36: 38: 40] sts.
Next row (RS): K3, K2tog, K to end.
Next row: K1, P to end.
Rep last 2 rows 15 [17: 19: 21: 23] times more, ending with RS facing for next row.
Cast off rem 16 sts.
Using 3mm (US 2/3) needles and with RS facing, rejoin yarn to 45 [47: 49: 51: 53] sts on holder and work on this set of sts only for second side of sleeve.
Next row (RS): Knit.
Next row: P to last st, K1.
These 2 rows set the sts – sleeve opening edge st worked as a K st on every row with all other sts in st st.
Working all increases as set by back and front, cont as set, inc 1 st at end of 11th and foll 10th row. 47 [49: 51: 53: 55] sts.
Cont straight until work meas 10 cm from cast-on edge, ending with RS facing for next row.

MAKING UP
Press as described on the information page.
Join both front and right back raglan seams

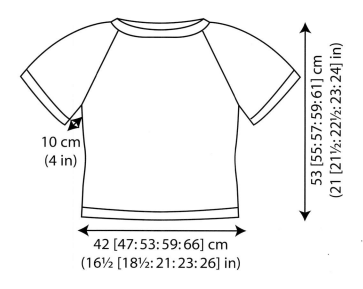

10 cm (4 in)

42 [47: 53: 59: 66] cm (16½ [18½: 21: 23: 26] in)

53 [55: 57: 59: 61] cm (21 [21½: 22½: 23: 24] in)

using back stitch, or mattress stitch if preferred.

Neckband

With RS facing and using 2¼mm (US 1) needles, pick up and knit 16 sts from top of first section of left sleeve, turn and cast on 5 sts, turn and pick up and knit 16 sts from top of second section of left sleeve, 77 [77: 79: 79: 81] sts from front, 16 sts from top of first section of right sleeve, turn and cast on 5 sts, turn and pick up and knit 16 sts from top of second section of right sleeve, then 78 [78: 80: 80: 82] sts from back.

229 [229: 233: 233: 237] sts.

Work in moss st as given for back for 11 rows, ending with RS facing for next row.

Cast off in moss st.

Sleeve trims (both alike)

Slip 3 sts left on holder at base of sleeve opening onto double-pointed 2¼mm (US 1) needles and rejoin yarn with RS facing.

Row 1 (RS): K3, *without turning slip these 3 sts to opposite end of needle and bring yarn to opposite end of work pulling it quite tightly across **WS** of work, K these 3 sts again, rep from * until trim is approx 60 cm long.

Slip these 3 sts back onto a holder but do NOT break off yarn.

Using photograph as a guide, arrange trim into a zigzag shape to fill opening in sleeve and sew in place to edges of sleeve sections. Adjust length of trim (by unravelling a few rows or knitting a few more rows) so it fits neatly to cast-on edge of neckband, then cast off. Sew cast-off edge of trim to cast-on edge of neckband.

See information page for finishing instructions.

LOBELIA
SARAH DALLAS
Main image page 39

YARN

8	10	12	14	16	18	20	22	

To fit bust

81	86	91	97	102	107	112	117	cm
32	34	36	38	40	42	44	46	in

Rowan Cotton Glacé

A Dawn Grey 831

6	6	6	6	7	7	7	8	x 50gm

B Bleached 726

6	6	6	7	7	8	8	8	x 50gm

NEEDLES

1 pair 3mm (no 11) (US 2/3) needles
1 pair 3¾mm (no 9) (US 5) needles

BUTTONS – 7 x RW5022 (15mm) from Bedecked. Please see information page for contact details.

TENSION

23 sts and 32 rows to 10 cm measured over st st using 3¾mm (US 5) needles.

BACK

Using 3mm (US 2/3) needles and yarn A cast on 125 [129: 133: 141: 147: 155: 161: 169] sts.

Break off yarn A and join in yarn B.

Row 1 (RS): K1, *P1, K1, rep from * to end.

Row 2: P1, *K1, P1, rep from * to end.

These 2 rows form rib.

Work in rib for a further 8 rows, ending with RS facing for next row.

Change to 3¾mm (US 5) needles.

Join in yarn A.

Beg with a K row, now work in st st in stripes as folls:

Rows 1 to 10: Using yarn A and dec 1 st at each end of 9th of these rows. 123 [127: 131: 139: 145: 153: 159: 167] sts.

Rows 11 to 20: Using yarn B.

These 20 rows form striped st st and beg side seam shaping.

Cont in striped st st, shaping side seams by dec 1 st at each end of 5th and 4 foll 16th rows. 113 [117: 121: 129: 135: 143: 149: 157] sts.

Cont straight until back meas 35 [35: 34: 37: 36: 38: 37: 39] cm, ending with RS facing for next row.

Shape armholes

Keeping stripes correct, cast off 4 sts at beg of next 2 rows.

105 [109: 113: 121: 127: 135: 141: 149] sts.

Next row (RS): K2, K2tog, K to last 4 sts, sl 1, K1, psso, K2.

Work 1 row.

Rep last 2 rows 4 times more.

95 [99: 103: 111: 117: 125: 131: 139] sts.

Cont straight until armhole meas 20 [20: 21: 21: 22: 22: 23: 23] cm, ending with RS facing for next row.

Shape back neck

Next row (RS): K26 [28: 30: 34: 36: 40: 43: 47] and turn, leaving rem sts on a holder. Work each side of neck separately.

Keeping stripes correct, dec 1 st at neck edge of next row, ending with RS facing for next row. 25 [27: 29: 33: 35: 39: 42: 46] sts.

Shape shoulder

Dec 1 st at neck edge of next 4 rows **and at same time** cast off 7 [8: 8: 10: 10: 12:

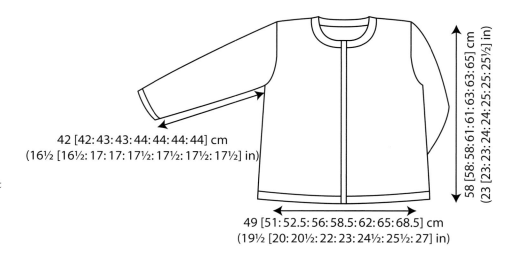

42 [42: 43: 43: 44: 44: 44: 44] cm
(16½ [16½: 17: 17: 17½: 17½: 17½: 17½] in)

58 [58: 58: 61: 61: 63: 63: 65] cm
(23 [23: 23: 24: 24: 25: 25: 25½] in)

49 [51: 52.5: 56: 58.5: 62: 65: 68.5] cm
(19½ [20: 20½: 22: 23: 24½: 25½: 27] in)

13: 14] sts at beg of next and foll alt row.
Cast off rem 7 [7: 9: 9: 11: 11: 12: 14] sts.
With RS facing, rejoin appropriate yarn to rem sts, cast off centre 43 [43: 43: 43: 45: 45: 45: 45] sts, K to end.
Complete to match first side, reversing shapings.

LEFT FRONT
Using 3mm (US 2/3) needles and yarn A cast on 68 [70: 72: 76: 78: 82: 86: 90] sts.
Break off yarn A and join in yarn B.
Row 1 (RS): *K1, P1, rep from * to last 2 sts, K2.
Row 2: *K1, P1, rep from * to end.
These 2 rows form rib.
Work in rib for a further 8 rows, dec 1 [1: 1: 1: 0: 0: 1: 1] st at end of last row and ending with RS facing for next row.
67 [69: 71: 75: 78: 82: 85: 89] sts.
Change to 3¾mm (US 5) needles.
Join in yarn A.
Now work in patt in stripes as folls:
Row 1 (RS): Using yarn A, K to last 7 sts, (P1, K1) 3 times, K1.
Row 2: Using yarn A, (K1, P1) 3 times, K1, P to end.
These 2 rows set the sts – front opening edge 7 sts still in rib with all other sts now in st st.
Keeping sts correct as now set, cont as folls:
Using yarn A, work 8 rows, dec 1 st at beg of 7th of these rows.
66 [68: 70: 74: 77: 81: 84: 88] sts.
Using yarn B, work 10 rows.
These 20 rows form striped patt and beg side seam shaping.
Cont in striped patt, shaping side seam by dec 1 st at beg of 5th and 4 foll 16th rows.
61 [63: 65: 69: 72: 76: 79: 83] sts.
Cont straight until left front matches back to beg of armhole shaping, ending with RS facing for next row.
Shape armhole
Keeping patt correct, cast off 4 sts at beg of next row.
57 [59: 61: 65: 68: 72: 75: 79] sts.
Work 1 row.
Working all armhole decreases as set by back, dec 1 st at armhole edge of next and foll 4 alt rows. 52 [54: 56: 60: 63: 67: 70: 74] sts.
Cont straight until 24 [24: 24: 26: 26: 26: 28: 28] rows less have been worked than on back to beg of back neck shaping, ending with RS facing for next row.
Shape front neck
Next row (RS): Patt 33 [35: 37: 42: 44: 48: 52: 56] sts and turn, leaving rem 19 [19: 19: 18: 19: 19: 18: 18] sts on a holder.
Keeping stripes correct, dec 1 st at neck edge of next 6 rows, then on foll 4 [4: 4: 5: 5: 5: 6: 6] alt rows, then on 2 foll 4th rows.

21 [23: 25: 29: 31: 35: 38: 42] sts.
Work 3 rows, ending with RS facing for next row.
Shape shoulder
Cast off 7 [8: 8: 10: 10: 12: 13: 14] sts at beg of next and foll alt row.
Work 1 row.
Cast off rem 7 [7: 9: 9: 11: 11: 12: 14] sts.
Mark positions for 7 buttons along left front opening edge – first to come in row 33 (from cast-on edge), last to come just above neck shaping, and rem 5 buttons evenly spaced between.

RIGHT FRONT
Using 3mm (US 2/3) needles and yarn A cast on 68 [70: 72: 76: 78: 82: 86: 90] sts.
Break off yarn A and join in yarn B.
Row 1 (RS): K2, *P1, K1, rep from * to end.
Row 2: *P1, K1, rep from * to end.
These 2 rows form rib.
Work in rib for a further 8 rows, dec 1 [1: 1: 1: 0: 0: 1: 1] st at beg of last row and ending with RS facing for next row.
67 [69: 71: 75: 78: 82: 85: 89] sts.
Change to 3¾mm (US 5) needles.
Join in yarn A.
Now work in patt in stripes as folls:
Row 1 (RS): Using yarn A, K1, (K1, P1) 3 times, K to end.
Row 2: Using yarn A, P to last 7 sts, (K1, P1) 3 times, K1.
These 2 rows set the sts – front opening edge 7 sts still in rib with all other sts now in st st.
Keeping sts correct as now set, cont as folls:
Using yarn A, work 8 rows, dec 1 st at end of 7th of these rows.
66 [68: 70: 74: 77: 81: 84: 88] sts.
Using yarn B, work 10 rows.
Last 20 rows form striped patt and beg side seam shaping.
Work in striped patt for a further 2 rows, ending with RS facing for next row.
Row 33 (buttonhole row) (RS): Patt 3 sts, K2tog tbl, yfwd (to make a buttonhole), patt to end.
Making a further 5 buttonholes in this way to correspond with positions marked for buttons on left front, complete to match left front, reversing shapings and working first row of neck shaping as folls:
Shape front neck
Break yarn. Slip first 19 [19: 19: 18: 19: 19: 18: 18] sts onto a holder, rejoin appropriate yarn and patt to end.
33 [35: 37: 42: 44: 48: 52: 56] sts.

SLEEVES
Using 3mm (US 2/3) needles and yarn A cast on 57 [57: 59: 59: 61: 61: 63: 63] sts.

Break off yarn A and join in yarn B.
Work in rib as given for back for 6 rows, ending with RS facing for next row.
Change to 3¾mm (US 5) needles.
Join in yarn A.
Beg with a K row, now work in st st in stripes as folls:
Rows 1 to 6: Using yarn A and inc 1 st at each end of 3rd of these rows.
59 [59: 61: 61: 63: 63: 65: 65] sts.
Rows 7 to 12: Using yarn B and inc 1 st at each end of next and foll 4th row.
63 [63: 65: 65: 67: 67: 69: 69] sts.
These 12 rows form striped st st and beg sleeve shaping.
Cont in striped st st, shaping sides by inc 1 st at each end of 3rd and 0 [0: 1: 1: 3: 3: 6: 6] foll 4th rows, then on every foll 6th row until there are 97 [97: 101: 101: 105: 105: 109: 109] sts.
Cont straight until sleeve meas approx 42 [42: 43: 43: 44: 44: 44: 44] cm, ending after 2 rows using yarn A or B and with RS facing for next row.
Shape top
Keeping stripes correct, cast off 4 sts at beg of next 2 rows.
89 [89: 93: 93: 97: 97: 101: 101] sts.
Dec 1 st at each end of next and foll 3 alt rows, then on foll row, ending with RS facing for next row.
Cast off rem 79 [79: 83: 83: 87: 87: 91: 91] sts.

MAKING UP
Press as described on the information page.
Join both shoulder seams using back stitch, or mattress stitch if preferred.
Neckband
With RS facing, using 3mm (US 2/3) needles and yarn B, patt across 19 [19: 19: 18: 19: 19: 18: 18] sts on right front holder, pick up and knit 26 [26: 26: 28: 28: 28: 30: 30] sts up right side of neck, 55 [55: 55: 55: 57: 57: 57: 57] sts from back, and 26 [26: 26: 28: 28: 28: 30: 30] sts down left side of neck, then patt across 19 [19: 19: 18: 19: 19: 18: 18] sts on left front holder.
145 [145: 145: 147: 151: 151: 153: 153] sts.
Row 1 (WS): K1, *P1, K1, rep from * to end.
Row 2: K2, *P1, K1, rep from * to last st, K1.
These 2 rows form rib.
Work in rib for 1 row more, ending with RS facing for next row.
Row 4 (buttonhole row) (RS): Rib 3, K2tog tbl, yfwd (to make 7th buttonhole), rib to end.
Work in rib for a further 3 rows, ending with RS facing for next row.
Break off yarn B and join in yarn A.
Using yarn A, cast off in rib.
See information page for finishing instructions, setting in sleeves using the shallow set-in method.

ALLAY
LISA RICHARDSON

Main image page 72 & 73

YARN

	S	M	L	XL	XXL
To fit bust					
	81-86	91-97	102-107	112-117	122-127	cm
	32-34	36-38	40-42	44-46	48-50	in

Rowan Pima Cotton DK

5	6	7	8	8	x 50gm

(photographed in Leaf 072)

NEEDLES

1 pair 3¼mm (no 10) (US 3) needles
1 pair 4mm (no 8) (US 6) needles
3¼mm (no 10) (US 3) circular needles
3.25mm (no 10) (US D3) crochet hook
(optional)
Cable needle

TENSION

20 sts and 20 rows to 10 cm measured over patt using 4mm (US 6) needles.

SPECIAL ABBREVIATIONS

DC6B = (sl 1 purlwise, drop next 3 yrn) 6 times - 6 elongated sts now on right needle, slip last 3 of these sts onto cable needle and leave at back of work, slip other 3 sts back onto left needle, P3 from cable needle, P3.

CROCHET ABBREVIATIONS

ch = chain; **dc** = double crochet.

Pattern note: When working patt, the sts made by the (yrn) once or 3 times do **NOT** count as sts. On the row after these sts have been made, drop these sts by letting the yrn(s) fall off left needle, leaving elongated sts.

BACK

Using 3¼mm (US 3) needles cast on 93 [105: 117: 129: 141] sts.
Row 1 (RS) : K3, ★P3, K3, rep from ★ to end.
Row 2: P3, ★K3, P3, rep from ★ to end.
These 2 rows form rib.
Work in rib for a further 16 rows, dec 1 st at end of last row and ending with RS facing for next row. 92 [104: 116: 128: 140] sts.
Change to 4mm (US 6) needles.
Now work in patt as folls:
Row 1 (RS) : Purl
Row 2: Knit.
Row 3: Purl.
Row 4: P1, ★yrn, P1, rep from ★ to end.
Row 5: Purl (remembering to drop the yrns).
92 [104: 116: 128: 140] sts.

Rows 6 and 7: As rows 2 and 3.
Row 8: P1, ★(yrn) 3 times, P1, rep from ★ to last st, P1.
Row 9: P1, ★DC6B, rep from ★ to last st, P1.
Rows 10 and 11: As rows 2 and 3.
Row 12: As row 4.
These 12 rows form patt.
Cont in patt as folls:
Work 8 rows, dec 1 st at each end of 3rd of these rows and ending with RS facing for next row. 90 [102: 114: 126: 138] sts.
Row 21: P6, ★DC6B, rep from ★ to last 6 sts, P6.
Work 11 rows, dec 1 st at each end of 2nd and foll 8th row and ending with RS facing for next row. 86 [98: 110: 122: 134] sts.
Row 33: P4, ★DC6B, rep from ★ to last 4 sts, P4.
Work 11 rows, inc 1 st at each end of 10th row and ending with RS facing for next row. 88 [100: 112: 124: 136] sts.
Row 45: P5, ★DC6B, rep from ★ to last 5 sts, P5.
Work 11 rows, inc 1 st at each end of 6th row and ending with RS facing for next row. 90 [102: 114: 126: 138] sts.
Row 57: As row 21.
Work 13 rows, inc 1 st at each end of 2nd row, ending after patt row 10 and with RS facing for next row. 92 [104: 116: 128: 140] sts. (Back should meas 41 cm.)

Shape armholes

Keeping patt correct, dec 1 st at each end of next 3 rows, then on foll alt row. 84 [96: 108: 120: 132] sts.
Work 3 rows, ending with RS facing for the next row. ★★
Inc 1 st at each end of next and 7 [8: 8: 9: 9] foll 4th rows, taking inc sts into patt, ending after patt row 11 [3: 3: 7: 7] and with **WS** facing for next row.
100 [114: 126: 140: 152] sts.
Now beg with patt row 4 and repeating patt rows **4 to 7 only,** cont as folls:
Work 1 row, ending with RS facing for next row.

Shape back neck

Next row (RS): Patt 31 [38: 43: 50: 55] sts and turn, leaving rem sts on a holder.
Work each side of neck separately.
Keeping patt as now set correct, dec 1 st at neck edge of next 4 rows.
27 [34: 39: 46: 51] sts.
Work 1 row, ending with RS facing for next row.
Break yarn and leave right back shoulder sts on a holder.
With RS facing, rejoin yarn to rem sts, cast off centre 38 [38: 40: 40: 42] sts, patt to end.
Complete to match first side, reversing shapings.

FRONT

Work as given for back to ★★.
Inc 1 st at each end of next and 5 [6: 6: 7: 7] foll 4th rows, taking inc sts into patt and ending with **WS** facing for next row.
96 [110: 122: 136: 148] sts.
Now working in patt to match patt on back shoulder sections, cont as folls:
Work 3 rows, ending with RS facing for next row, ending after patt row 6 [10: 10: 2: 2] and with RS facing for next row.

Shape front neck

Next row (RS): Inc in first st, patt 30 [37: 42: 49: 54] sts and turn, leaving rem sts on a holder.
Work each side separately.
Keeping patt as now set correct, dec 1 st at neck edge of next 4 rows, then on foll 2 alt rows **and at same time** inc 1 st at armhole edge of 4th row. 27 [34: 39: 46: 51] sts.
Work 3 rows, ending with RS facing for next row.

Join shoulder seam

Holding RS of sts of left back shoulder seam against RS of sts on needle (left front shoulder seam), cast off both sets of sts tog by working one st of back shoulder tog with corresponding st of front shoulder.
With RS facing, rejoin yarn to rem sts, cast off centre 34[34: 36: 36: 38] sts, patt to end.

63 [65: 65: 67: 67] cm
(25 [25½: 25½: 26½: 26½] in)

46 [52: 58: 64: 70] cm
(18 [20½: 23: 25: 27½] in)

Complete to match first side, reversing shapings.

MAKING UP
Press as described on the information page.
Neckband
With RS facing and using 3¼mm (US 3) circular needle, pick up and knit 12 sts down left side of neck, 34 [34: 36: 36: 38] sts from front, 12 sts up right side of neck, then 48 [48: 50: 50: 52] sts from back. 106 [106: 110: 110: 114] sts.
Round 1 (RS): Purl.
Round 2 (eyelet round): sl 1, K1, psso, yfwd, K54 [54: 56: 56: 58], yfwd, K2tog, sl 1, K1, psso, yfwd, K44 [44: 46: 46: 48], yfwd, K2tog.
Cast off purlwise (on RS).
Armhole borders (both alike)
With RS facing and using 3¼mm (US 3) needles, pick up and knit 96 [102: 106: 110: 114] sts evenly all round armhole edge.
Row 1 (WS): Knit.
Row 2 (eyelet row): K46 [49: 51: 53: 55], yfwd, K2tog, sl 1, K1, psso, yfwd, K46 [49: 51: 53: 55].
Cast off knitwise (on **WS**).
See information page for finishing instructions.
Shoulder ties (make 2)
Using 3.25mm (US D3) crochet hook, make 2 ch and work 1 dc into 2nd ch from hook,

★1 dc into bar of yarn running up left side of dc just made, rep from ★ until tie is 50 cm long.
Fasten off.
Note: If you prefer, make twisted cords this length, rather than crochet ties.
Thread shoulder ties along each shoulder edge as in photograph – beg by threading tie through eyelet hole in armhole border, then thread tie in and out of elongated st row nearest shoulder and then through eyelet hole in neckband. Work along other side of shoulder seam in same way. Pull up ties to gather shoulder edge and tie ends in a bow.

SOOTHE
MARIE WALLIN
Main image page 74 & 75

YARN

S	M	L	XL	XXL	
To fit bust					
81-86	91-97	102-107	112-117	122-127	cm
32-34	36-38	40-42	44-46	48-50	in

Rowan Lenpur™ Linen

7	8	9	10	11	x 50gm

(photographed in Rye 572)

NEEDLES
1 pair 3¼mm (no 10) (US 3) needles
1 pair 4mm (no 8) (US 6) needles

TENSION
22 sts and 30 rows to 10 cm measured over patt using 4mm (US 6) needles.

BACK
Using 3¼mm (US 3) needles cast on 97 [107: 121: 135: 149] sts.
Work in g st for 12 rows, ending with RS facing for next row.
Change to 4mm (US 6) needles.
Now work in patt as folls:
Row 1 (RS): K10 [0: 0: 7: 0], P11 [4: 11: 11:

3], ★K11, P11, rep from ★ to last 10 [15: 0: 7: 14] sts, K10 [11: 0: 7: 11], P0 [4: 0: 0: 3].
Row 2: P10 [0: 0: 7: 0], K11 [4: 11: 11: 3], ★P11, K11, rep from ★ to last 10 [15: 0: 7: 14] sts, P10 [11: 0: 7: 11], K0 [4: 0: 0: 3].
Rows 3 to 22: As rows 1 and 2, 10 times.
Row 23: Purl.
Row 24: Knit.
Row 25: K8 [0: 2: 0: 0], P9 [4: 9: 0: 7], ★K9, P9, rep from ★ to last 8 [13: 2: 9: 16] sts, K8 [9: 2: 9: 9], P0 [4: 0: 0: 7].
Row 26: P8 [0: 2: 0: 0], K9 [4: 9: 0: 7], ★P9, K9, rep from ★ to last 8 [13: 2: 9: 16] sts, P8 [9: 2: 9: 9], K0 [4: 0: 0: 7].
Rows 27 to 42: As rows 25 and 26, 8 times.
Rows 43 and 44: As rows 23 and 24.
Beg and ending rows as indicated, working chart rows 1 to 38 **once only** and then repeating chart rows 39 to 50 **throughout**, now work in patt from chart as folls:
Work 2 [4: 8: 10: 14] rows, ending with RS facing for next row.
(Back should meas 18 [19: 20: 21: 22] cm.)
Shape for cap sleeves
Keeping patt correct, inc 1 st at each end of next and foll 4th row, then on foll 3 alt rows, then on foll 7 rows, ending with RS facing for next row. 121 [131: 145: 159: 173] sts.
Cast on 3 sts at beg of next 2 rows. 127 [137: 151: 165: 179] sts.
Place markers at both ends of last row to denote base of armhole openings.
Cont straight until work meas 22 [23: 24: 25: 26] cm from markers, ending with RS facing for next row.
Shape shoulders and neck
Next row (RS): Cast off 14 [15: 17: 20: 22] sts, patt until there are 33 [37: 41: 45: 49] sts on right needle and turn, leaving rem sts on a holder.
Work each side of neck separately.

Keeping patt correct, cast off 3 sts at beg of next row, 14 [15: 17: 20: 22] sts at beg of foll row, then 3 sts at beg of next row.
Cast off rem 13 [16: 18: 19: 21] sts.
With RS facing, rejoin yarn to rem sts, cast off centre 33 [33: 35: 35: 37] sts, patt to end.
Complete to match first side, reversing shapings.

FRONT
Using 4mm (US 6) needles cast on 141 [151: 165: 179: 193] sts.
Now work in patt as folls:
Work patt rows 1 to 23 as given for back.
Row 24: K4 [3: 3: 4: 4], K2tog, (K8 [9: 10: 11: 12], K2tog) 13 times, K5 [3: 4: 4: 5]. 127 [137: 151: 165: 179] sts.

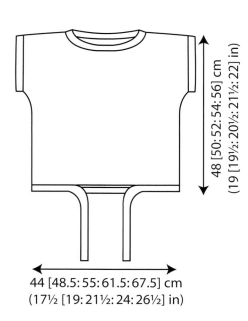

48 [50: 52: 54: 56] cm
(19 [19½: 20½: 21½: 22] in)

44 [48.5: 55: 61.5: 67.5] cm
(17½ [19: 21½: 24: 26½] in)

Row 25: K5 [0: 0: 6: 0], P9 [1: 8: 9: 4], *K9, P9, rep from * to last 5 [10: 17: 6: 13] sts, K5 [9: 9: 6: 9], P0 [1: 8: 0: 4].

Row 26: P5 [0: 0: 6: 0], K9 [1: 8: 9: 4], *P9, K9, rep from * to last 5 [10: 17: 6: 13] sts, P5 [9: 9: 6: 9], K0 [1: 8: 0: 4].

Rows 27 to 42: As rows 25 and 26, 8 times.

Row 43: Purl.

Row 44: K4 [2: 3: 3: 4], K2tog, (K7 [8: 9: 10: 11], K2tog) 13 times, K4 [3: 3: 4: 4:]. 113 [123: 137: 151: 165] sts.

Row 45: K4 [0: 2: 0: 2], P7 [2: 7: 2: 7], *K7, P7, rep from * to last 4 [9: 2: 9: 2] sts, K4 [7: 2: 7: 2], P0 [2: 0: 2: 0].

Row 46: P4 [0: 2: 0: 2], K7 [2: 7: 2: 7], *P7, K7, rep from * to last 4 [9: 2: 9: 2] sts, P4 [7: 2: 7: 2], K0 [2: 0: 2: 0].

These 2 rows form patt.

Keeping patt correct, cont as folls:

Work 0 [2: 6: 8: 12] rows, ending with RS facing for next row.

Sizes S, M, L and XL only

Inc 1 st at each end of next and 1 [1: 1: 0: -] foll 4th row, then on foll 3 [2: 0: 0: -] alt rows, then on foll 1 [0: 0: 0: -] row. 125 [131: 141: 153: -] sts.

Work 0 [1: 1: 3: -] rows, ending with RS facing for next row.

All sizes

Row 59 (RS): Inc in first st, P to last st, inc in last st. 127 [133: 143: 155: 167] sts.

Row 60: (Inc in first st) 1 [1: 0: 0: 0] times, K9 [4: 10: 9: 7], K2tog, (K5 [6: 6: 7: 8], K2tog) 15 times, K9 [5: 11: 9: 8], (inc in last st) 1 [1: 0: 0: 0] times. 113 [119: 127: 139: 151] sts.

Beg and ending rows as indicated and **starting with chart row 17,** working chart rows 17 to 38 **once only** and then repeating chart rows 39 to 50 **throughout,** now work in patt from chart as folls:

Inc 1 st at each end of next [next: next: next:

3rd] and foll 0 [0: 1: 2: 3] alt rows, then on foll 3 [5: 7: 7: 7] rows, ending with RS facing for next row. 121 [131: 145: 159: 173] sts.

Cast on 3 sts at beg of next 2 rows. 127 [137: 151: 165: 179] sts.

Place markers at both ends of last row to denote base of armhole openings.

Cont straight until 12 [12: 14: 14: 16] rows less have been worked than on back to beg of shoulder shaping, ending with RS facing for next row.

Shape neck

Next row (RS): Patt 47 [52: 59: 66: 73] sts and turn, leaving rem sts on a holder.

Work each side of neck separately.

Keeping patt correct, dec 1 st at neck edge of next 4 rows, then on foll 2 [2: 3: 3: 4] alt rows. 41 [46: 52: 59: 65] sts.

Work 3 rows, ending with RS facing for next row.

Shape shoulder

Cast off 14 [15: 17: 20: 22] sts at beg of next and foll alt row.

Work 1 row.

Cast off rem 13 [16: 18: 19: 21] sts.

With RS facing, rejoin yarn to rem sts, cast off centre 33 sts, patt to end.

Complete to match first side, reversing shapings.

MAKING UP

Press as described on the information page.

Join right shoulder seam using back stitch, or mattress stitch if preferred.

Neckband

With RS facing and using 3¼mm (US 3) needles, pick up and knit 12 [12: 14: 14: 16] sts down left side of neck, 33 sts from front, 12 [12: 14: 14: 16] sts up right side of neck, then 45 [45: 47: 47: 49] sts from back. 102 [102: 108: 108: 114] sts.

Work in g st for 6 rows, ending with **WS** facing for next row.

Cast off knitwise (on **WS**).

Join left shoulder and neckband seam.

Armhole borders (both alike)

With RS facing and using 3¼mm (US 3) needles, pick up and knit 96 [100: 104: 110: 114] sts evenly along armhole row-end edges between markers.

Work in g st for 6 rows, ending with **WS** facing for next row.

Cast off knitwise (on **WS**).

Hem pleat border

Mark points along front cast-on edge 46 [51: 58: 65: 72] sts in from both ends of row - there should be 49 sts between markers.

With RS facing and using 3¼mm (US 3) needles, pick up and knit 49 sts evenly along cast-on edge between markers.

Work in g st for 2 rows, ending with **WS** facing for next row.

Cast off knitwise (on **WS**).

Right front hem border and tie

With RS facing and using 3¼mm (US 3) needles, beg at side seam edge, pick up and knit 46 [51: 58: 65: 72] sts evenly along cast-on edge to hem pleat border, then 2 sts along row-end edge of hem pleat border, turn and cast on 80 sts. 128 [133: 140: 147: 154] sts.

Work in g st for 12 rows, ending with **WS** facing for next row.

Cast off knitwise (on **WS**).

Left front hem border and tie

With RS facing and using 3¼mm (US 3) needles, cast on 80 sts, turn and pick up and knit 2 sts along row-end edge of hem pleat border, then 46 [51: 58: 65: 72] sts evenly along cast-on edge to side seam. 128 [133: 140: 147: 154] sts.

Work in g st for 12 rows, ending with **WS** facing for next row.

Cast off knitwise (on **WS**).

See information page for finishing instructions.

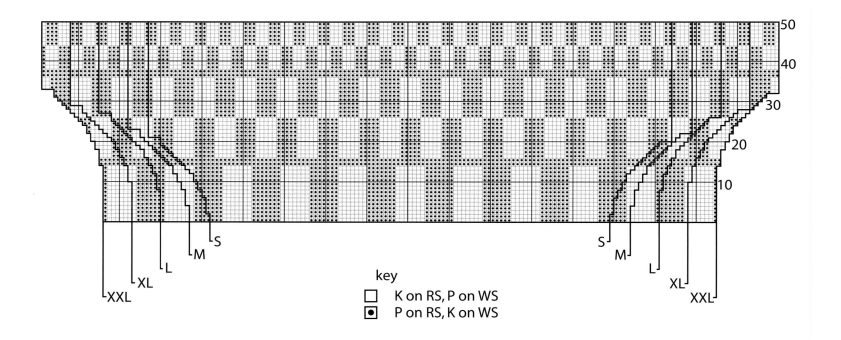

key

☐ K on RS, P on WS

⊡ P on RS, K on WS

FULFILL
LISA RICHARDSON

Main image page 66

YARN

	S	M	L	XL	XXL	
To fit bust						
	81-86	91-97	102-107	112-117	122-127	cm
	32-34	36-38	40-42	44-46	48-50	in

Rowan Purelife Revive

9	10	11	12	12	x 50gm

(photographed in Loam 472)

CROCHET HOOK

3.50mm (no 9) (US E4) crochet hook

TENSION

4 patt reps to 11 cm in width and 5 patt reps
(10 rows) to 12 cm measured over patt using
3.50mm (US E4) crochet hook.

CROCHET ABBREVIATIONS

ss = slip stitch; **ch** = chain; **dc** = double
crochet; **tr** = treble.

BODY (worked in one piece to armholes)
Using 3.50mm (US E4) hook make 336 [378:
420: 462: 504] ch.
Foundation row (RS): 2 tr into 3rd ch from
hook, *miss 3 ch, 1 dc into next ch**, 3 ch,
1 tr into each of next 3 ch, rep from * to end,
ending last rep at **, turn. 48 [54: 60: 66: 72]
patt reps.
Now work in patt as folls:
Row 1: 3 ch (counts as 1 tr), 2 tr into first dc,
*miss 3 tr, 1 dc into next ch, 3 ch, 1 tr into
each of next 2 ch, 1 tr into next dc, rep from *
to last 3 sts, miss 2 tr, 1 dc into top of 3 ch at
beg of previous row, turn.
Row 2: As row 1.
These 2 rows form patt.
Work in patt for a further 37 [39: 39: 41: 41]
rows, ending after patt row 1 and with RS
facing for next row. (Body should meas 48 [50:
50: 53: 53] cm.)
Divide for armholes
Next row (RS): 3 ch (counts as 1 tr), 2 tr into
first dc, (miss 3 tr, 1 dc into next ch, 3 ch, 1 tr
into each of next 2 ch, 1 tr into next dc)

14 [16: 18: 20: 22] times, miss 3 tr, 1 dc into
next ch and turn, leaving rem 33 [37: 41: 45:
49] patt reps unworked. 15 [17: 19: 21: 23] patt
reps.
Work on this set of sts only for right front.
Next row: Ss across (1 dc and 3 tr) and into
next ch, 3 ch (counts as 1 tr), 1 tr into each of
next 2 ch, 1 tr into next dc, patt to end, turn.
14 [16: 18: 20: 22] patt reps.
Work 1 row.
Rep last 2 rows 1 [1: 2: 2: 2] times more.
13 [15: 16: 18: 20] patt reps.
Work in patt for a further 13 [13: 13: 13: 15]
rows, ending after patt row 1 and with RS
facing for next row. (Armhole should meas
22 [22: 24: 24: 26] cm.)
Fasten off.
Shape back
With RS facing, return to last complete row
worked, miss (2 ch, 1 dc, 3 tr, 3 ch, 1 dc and
3 tr – 2 patt reps) after right front, attach yarn
to next ch and cont as folls:
Next row (RS): 3 ch (counts as 1 tr), 2 tr into
ch at base of 3 ch (this is ch where yarn was
rejoined), (miss 3 tr, 1 dc into next ch, 3 ch,
1 tr into each of next 2 ch, 1 tr into next dc)
13 [15: 17: 19: 21] times, miss 3 tr, 1 dc into
next ch and turn, leaving rem 17 [19: 21: 23:
25] patt reps unworked.
14 [16: 18: 20: 22] patt reps.
Work on this set of sts only for back.
Next row: Ss across (1 dc and 3 tr) and into
next ch, 3 ch (counts as 1 tr), 1 tr into each of
next 2 ch, 1 tr into next dc, patt to end, turn.
13 [15: 17: 19: 21] patt reps.

Rep last row 3 [3: 5: 5: 5] times more.
10 [12: 12: 14: 16] patt reps.
Work in patt for a further 13 [13: 13: 13: 15]
rows, ending after patt row 1 and with RS
facing for next row.
Fasten off, placing markers 2 [3: 2½: 3½: 4½]
patt reps in from each end of row to denote
back neck.
Shape left front
With RS facing, return to last complete row
worked, miss (2 ch, 1 dc, 3 tr, 3 ch, 1 dc and
3 tr – 2 patt reps) after back, attach yarn to
next ch and cont as folls:
Next row (RS): 3 ch (counts as 1 tr), 2 tr into
ch at base of 3 ch (this is ch where yarn was
rejoined), miss 3 tr, 1 dc into next ch, 3 ch, 1 tr
into each of next 2 ch, 1 tr into next dc, patt to
end, turn. 15 [17: 19: 21: 23] patt reps.
Work on this set of sts only for left front.
Work 1 row.
Next row: Ss across (1 dc and 3 tr) and into
next ch, 3 ch (counts as 1 tr), 1 tr into each of
next 2 ch, 1 tr into next dc, patt to end, turn.
14 [16: 18: 20: 22] patt reps.
Rep last 2 rows 1 [1: 2: 2: 2] times more.
13 [15: 16: 18: 20] patt reps.
Work in patt for a further 13 [13: 13: 13: 15]
rows, ending after patt row 1 and with RS
facing for next row.
Fasten off.

MAKING UP

Press as described on the information page.
Join shoulder seams.
See information page for finishing instructions.

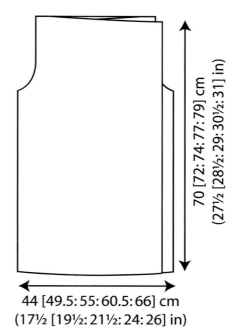

70 [72: 74: 77: 79] cm
(27½ [28½: 29: 30½: 31] in)

44 [49.5: 55: 60.5: 66] cm
(17½ [19½: 21½: 24: 26] in)

LAZY

MARIE WALLIN

Main image page 82 & 83

YARN

	S	M	L	XL	XXL	
To fit bust						
	81-86	91-97	102-107	112-117	122-127	cm
	32-34	36-38	40-42	44-46	48-50	in

Rowan Purelife Revive and Organic Cotton DK

A Rev Basalt 462						
	3	3	4	4	5	x 50gm
B Org Oak Apple 990						
	2	2	3	3	3	x 50gm
C Rev Pumice 461						
	3	3	3	4	4	x 50gm
D Org Light Brazilwood 997						
	2	2	2	2	2	x 50gm
E Rev Pink Granite 463						
	2	2	2	2	2	x 50gm
F Org Cherry Plum 989						
	1	1	1	1	1	x 50gm

NEEDLES

1 pair 3¾mm (no 9) (US 5) needles
1 pair 6mm (no 4) (US 10) needles

TENSION

11 sts and 20 rows to 10 cm measured over patt using 6mm (US 10) needles and Revive and Organic Cotton DK held together. (Over striped patt using combination of one and 2 strands of yarn, row tension is 24½ rows to 10 cm.)

Pattern note: The number of sts varies whilst working patt. Do **NOT** count sts on patt rows where only one strand of yarn is used. All st counts relate to the number of sts there would be on rows using 2 strands of yarn held together.

BACK

Using 6mm (US 10) needles and yarns A and B held together cast on 57 [63: 69: 75: 83] sts.
Now work in patt as folls:
Row 1 (RS): Purl.
Row 2: K1, *yfwd, K2tog, rep from * to end.
Row 3: Purl.
Row 4: *Sl 1, K1, psso, yfwd, rep from * to last st, K1.
These 4 rows form patt.
Work 12 rows, ending with RS facing for next row.
Break off yarn B and cont using yarn A only.
Change to 3¾mm (US 5) needles.
Row 17 (RS): *P twice into each st, working first into strand of yarn A and then into strand

of yarn B, rep from * to last st, P1. (There are now 113 [125: 137: 149: 165] sts on needle.)
Beg with patt row 2, work in patt for 7 rows.
Join in yarn B and cont using yarns A and B held together.
Change to 6mm (US 10) needles.
Row 25: *P2tog, rep from * to last st, P1.
(There are now 57 [63: 69: 75: 83] sts on needle.)
Beg with patt row 2, work in patt for 3 rows.
Break off yarns A and B and join in yarns C and D.
Work 8 rows.
Break off yarn D and cont using yarn C only.
Change to 3¾mm (US 5) needles.
Row 37 (RS): As row 17.
Beg with patt row 2, work in patt for 15 rows.
Join in yarn D and cont using yarns C and D held together.
Change to 6mm (US 10) needles.
Row 53: As row 25.
Beg with patt row 2, work in patt for 7 rows.
Break off yarns C and D and join in yarns A and B.
Work 4 rows.
Break off yarns A and B and join in yarns E and F.
Work 4 rows.
Break off yarn F and cont using yarn E only.
Change to 3¾mm (US 5) needles.
Row 69 (RS): As row 17.
Beg with patt row 2, work in patt for 7 rows.
Join in yarn F and cont using yarns E and F held together.
Change to 6mm (US 10) needles.
Row 77: As row 25.
Beg with patt row 2, work in patt for 3 rows.
Break off yarns E and F and join in yarns A and B.
Last 80 rows form striped patt.
Cont in striped patt until back meas 45 [46: 47: 48: 49] cm, ending with RS facing for next row.

Shape for cap sleeves

Keeping patt correct, inc 1 st at each end of next and foll 2 alt rows. 63 [69: 75: 81: 89] sts.
Place markers at both ends of last row to denote base of armhole openings.
Cont straight until all 80 striped patt rows have been completed twice.
Now working in patt using yarns A and B held together **only** for rest of back, cont as folls:
Cont straight until work meas 22 [23: 24: 25: 26] cm from markers, ending with RS facing for next row.

Shape shoulders and neck

Next row (RS): Cast off 8 [10: 11: 13: 14] sts, patt until there are 12 [13: 15: 16: 18] sts on right needle and turn, leaving rem sts on a holder.
Work each side of neck separately.
Cast off 3 sts at beg of next row.
Cast off rem 9 [10: 12: 13: 15] sts.
With RS facing, rejoin yarns to rem sts, cast off centre 23 [23: 23: 23: 25] sts, patt to end.
Complete to match first side, reversing shapings.

FRONT

Work as given for back until 14 [14: 16: 16: 18] rows less have been worked than on back to beg of shoulder shaping, ending with RS facing for next row.

Shape neck

Next row (RS): Patt 24 [27: 31: 34: 38] sts and turn, leaving rem sts on a holder.
Work each side of neck separately.
Keeping patt correct, dec 1 st at neck edge of next 4 rows, then on foll 3 [3: 4: 4: 5] alt rows.
17 [20: 23: 26: 29] sts.
Work 3 rows, ending with RS facing for next row.

Shape shoulder

Cast off 8 [10: 11: 13: 14] sts at beg of next row.
Work 1 row.

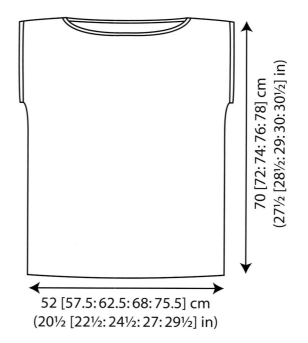

70 [72: 74: 76: 78] cm
(27½ [28½: 29: 30: 30½] in)

52 [57.5: 62.5: 68: 75.5] cm
(20½ [22½: 24½: 27: 29½] in)

Cast off rem 9 [10: 12: 13: 15] sts.
With RS facing, rejoin yarns to rem sts, cast off centre 15 [15: 13: 13: 13] sts, patt to end.
Complete to match first side, reversing shapings.

MAKING UP
Press as described on the information page.
Join right shoulder seam using back stitch, or mattress stitch if preferred.

Neckband
With RS facing, using 3¾mm (US 5) needles and yarn A, pick up and knit 21 [21: 24: 24: 27] sts down left side of neck, 30 [30: 26: 26: 26] sts from front, 21 [21: 24: 24: 27] sts up right side of neck, then 58 [58: 58: 58: 62] sts from back. 130 [130: 132: 132: 142] sts.
Work in g st for 2 rows, ending with **WS** facing for next row.
Cast off knitwise (on **WS**).

Join left shoulder and neckband seam.
Armhole borders (both alike)
With RS facing, using 3¾mm (US 5) needles and yarn A, pick up and knit 96 [100: 104: 110: 114] sts evenly along armhole row-end edges between markers.
Work in g st for 2 rows, ending with **WS** facing for next row.
Cast off knitwise (on **WS**).
See information page for finishing instructions.

RUSTIC
MARIE WALLIN

Main image page 78 & 81

YARN

	S-M	L-XL	XXL	
To fit bust				
	81-97	102-117	122-127	cm
	32-38	40-46	48-50	in

Rowan Summer Tweed

	5	7	8	x 50gm

(photographed in Raffia 515)

NEEDLES
1 pair 4½mm (no 7) (US 7) needles
1 pair 7mm (no 2) (US 10½) needles

TENSION
13 sts and 18 rows to 10cm measured over patt using 7mm (US 10½) needles.

Pattern note: The number of sts varies whilst working patt. Do **NOT** count sts after patt rows 1 to 3, or 8 to 10. The st counts given do **NOT** include any sts made on these rows but relate to the original number of sts.

BACK and FRONT (both alike)
Using 4½ mm (US 7) needles cast on 67 [81: 89] sts.
Row 1 (RS) : K1, *P1, K1, rep from * to end.
Row 2: P1, *K1, P1, rep from * to end.
These 2 rows form rib.
Work in rib for a further 25 rows, ending with **WS** facing for next row.
Row 28 (WS) : Rib 11 [8: 8], M1, (rib 22 [16:18], M1) 2 [4: 4] times, rib 12 [9: 9].

70 [86: 94] sts.
Change to 7mm (US 10½) needles.
Now work in patt as folls:
Row 1 (RS) : K1, *yfwd, K1, rep from * to last st, K1.
Row 2: K1, P to last st, K1.
Row 3: K1, *K2tog, rep from * to last st, K1.
Rows 4 and 5: K1, *yfwd, K2tog, rep from * to last st, K1.
Rows 6 and 7: Knit.
Rows 8 to 14: As rows 1 to 7.
These 14 rows form patt.
Cont in patt until work meas 43 [47: 49] cm, ending with RS facing for next row.
Shape shoulders and neck
Next row (RS): Cast off 6 [8: 10] sts, patt until there are 15 [20: 22] sts on right needle and turn, leaving rem sts on a holder.
Work each side of neck separately.
Keeping patt correct, dec 1 st at neck edge of next 3 rows, ending with RS facing for next row, **and at same time** cast off 6 [8: 10] sts at beg of 2nd of these rows.
Cast off rem 6 [9: 9] sts.
With RS facing, rejoin yarn to rem sts, cast off centre 28 [30: 30] sts, patt to end.
Complete to match first side, reversing shapings.

MAKING UP
Press as described on the information page.
Join right shoulder seam using back stitch, or mattress stitch if preferred.
Neckband
With RS facing and using 4½ mm (US 7) needles, pick up and knit with 5 sts down left of front neck, 34 [36:36] sts from front, 5 sts up right side of front neck, 5 sts down right side of back neck, 34 [36: 36] sts from back, then 5 sts up left side of back neck. 88 [92: 92] sts.
Beg with a P row, work in st st for 5 rows, ending with RS facing for next row.
Cast off.
Join left shoulder and neckband seam, reversing seam for st st roll of neckband. Mark points along side seam edges of front and back 24 [26: 27] cm either side of shoulder seams.
Armhole borders (both alike)
With RS facing and using 4½ mm (US 7) needles, pick up and knit 71 [77: 81] sts evenly along armhole edge between markers.
Beg with row 2, work in rib as given for back and front for 7 rows, ending with RS facing for next row.
Cast off in rib.
See information page for finishing instructions.

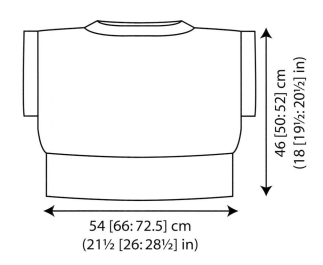

46 [50: 52] cm
(18 [19½: 20½] in)

54 [66: 72.5] cm
(21½ [26: 28½] in)

TEASE
GRACE MELVILLE

Main image page 77

● ● ●

YARN

8	10	12	14	16	18	

To fit bust

81	86	91	97	102	107	cm
32	34	36	38	40	42	in

Rowan Denim

9	10	10	11	11	12	x 50gm

(photographed in Tennessee 231)

NEEDLES

1 pair 3¾mm (no 9) (US 5) needles
1 pair 4mm (no 8) (US 6) needles
Cable needle

TENSION

Before washing: 20 sts and 28 rows to 10 cm
measured over st st, 24 sts and 32 rows to 10 cm
measured over bodice patt, both using 4mm
(US 6) needles.

After washing: 20 sts and 32 rows to 10 cm
measured over st st, 24½ sts and 35 rows to 10 cm
measured over bodice patt, both using 4mm
(US 6) needles.

Tension note: Denim will shrink when
washed for the first time. Allowances have been
made in the pattern for shrinkage (see size
diagram for after washing measurements).

SPECIAL ABBREVIATIONS

bind 4 = slip next 4 sts onto cable needle,
wrap yarn anti-clockwise 4 times round sts on
cable needle ending with yarn at back of work,
now slip these 4 sts onto right needle; **bind 6
=** slip next 6 sts onto cable needle, wrap yarn
anti-clockwise 4 times round sts on cable
ending with yarn at back of work, now slip
these 6 sts onto right needle; **bind 10 =** slip
next 10 sts onto cable needle, wrap yarn anti-
clockwise 4 times round sts on cable needle
ending with yarn at back of work, now slip
these 10 sts onto right needle.

Pattern note: The number of sts varies whilst
working bodice patt. All st counts given do NOT
include sts made whilst working patt but presume
there are 28 sts in each patt rep at all times.

BACK

Using 3¾mm (US 5) needles cast on 120 [126:
128: 136: 142: 146] sts.
Work in g st for 4 rows, ending with RS facing
for next row.
Change to 4mm (US 6) needles.

Now work pleats as folls:
Row 1 (RS): K21 [23: 23: 26: 28: 29], *place
marker on needle, sl 1, K5, P1, K10, P1, K5,
sl 1, place another marker on needle*, K30 [32:
34: 36: 38: 40], rep from * to * once more,
K21 [23: 23: 26: 28: 29].
Row 2: (P to marker, slip marker onto right
needle, P6, sl 1, P10, sl 1, P6, slip marker onto
right needle) twice, P to end.
Row 3: (K to marker, slip marker onto right
needle, sl 1, K5, P1, K10, P1, K5, sl 1, slip
marker onto right needle) twice, K to end.
Rows 4 and 5: As rows 2 and 3.
Row 6: As row 2.
Row 7: (K to marker, slip marker onto right
needle, sl 1, K3, sl 1, K1, psso, P1, K2tog, K6,
sl 1, K1, psso, P1, K2tog, K3, sl 1, slip marker
onto right needle) twice, K to end.
112 [118: 120: 128: 134: 138] sts.
Row 8: (P to marker, slip marker onto right
needle, P5, sl 1, P8, sl 1, P5, slip marker onto
right needle) twice, P to end.
Row 9: (K to marker, slip marker onto right
needle, sl 1, K4, P1, K8, P1, K4, sl 1, slip marker
onto right needle) twice, K to end.
Rows 10 and 11: As rows 8 and 9.
Row 12: As row 8.
Row 13: (K to marker, slip marker onto right
needle, sl 1, K2, sl 1, K1, psso, P1, K2tog, K4,
sl 1, K1, psso, P1, K2tog, K2, sl 1, slip marker
onto right needle) twice, K to end.
104 [110: 112: 120: 126: 130] sts.
Row 14: (P to marker, slip marker onto right
needle, P4, sl 1, P6, sl 1, P4, slip marker onto
right needle) twice, P to end.
Row 15: (K to marker, slip marker onto right
needle, sl 1, K3, P1, K6, P1, K3, sl 1, slip marker
onto right needle) twice, K to end.
Row 16: As row 14.
Row 17: (K to marker, slip marker onto right
needle, sl 1, K1, sl 1, K1, psso, P1, K2tog, K2,
sl 1, K1, psso, P1, K2tog, K1, sl 1, slip marker
onto right needle) twice, K to end.
96 [102: 104: 112: 118: 122] sts.
Row 18: (P to marker, slip marker onto right
needle, P3, sl 1, P4, sl 1, P3, slip marker onto
right needle) twice, P to end.
Row 19: (K to marker, slip marker onto right
needle, sl 1, K2, P1, K4, P1, K2, sl 1, slip marker

onto right needle) twice, K to end.
Row 20: As row 18.
Row 21: *K to marker, slip marker onto right
needle, sl 1, (sl 1, K1, psso, P1, K2tog) twice,
sl 1, slip marker onto right needle, rep from *
once more, K to end.
88 [94: 96: 104: 110: 114] sts.
Row 22: *P to marker, slip marker onto right
needle, (P2, sl 1) twice, P2, slip marker onto
right needle, rep from * once more, P to end.
Row 23: (K to marker, slip marker onto right
needle, sl 1, sl 1, K1, psso, K2, K2tog, sl 1, slip
marker onto right needle) twice, K to end.
84 [90: 92: 100: 106: 110] sts.
Row 24: (P to marker, slip marker onto right
needle, P6, slip marker onto right needle)
twice, P to end.
Row 25: (K to marker, slip marker onto right
needle, sl 1, sl 1, K1, psso, K2tog, sl 1, slip
marker onto right needle) twice, K to end.
80 [86: 88: 96: 102: 106] sts.
Row 26: (P to marker, slip marker onto right
needle, P4, slip marker onto right needle)
twice, P to end.
Row 27: (K to marker, slip marker onto right
needle, sl 1, K1, psso, K2tog, slip marker onto
right needle) twice, K to end.
76 [82: 84: 92: 98: 102] sts.
Remove markers.
Change to 3¾mm (US 5) needles.
Work in g st for 5 rows, ending with RS facing
for next row.
Next row (RS): K4 [7: 4: 8: 7: 5], M1, (K4,
M1) 17 [17: 19: 19: 21: 23] times, K4 [7: 4: 8:
7: 5].
94 [100: 104: 112: 120: 126] sts.
Change to 4mm (US 6) needles.
Next row: Purl.
Starting and ending rows as indicated, repeating
the 28 st patt rep 2 [2: 2: 3: 3: 3] times across
every row and repeating the 28 row patt rep
throughout, now work in patt from chart as folls:
(**Note:** For size 14 **only**, at beg of row 7,
replace "bind 6" with "K1, bind 4", and at end
of row replace "bind 6" with "bind 4, K1.")
Inc 1 st at each end of 13th and 3 foll 10th
rows, taking inc sts into st st.
102 [108: 112: 120: 128: 134] sts.
Cont straight until back meas 31 [31: 30: 33.5:

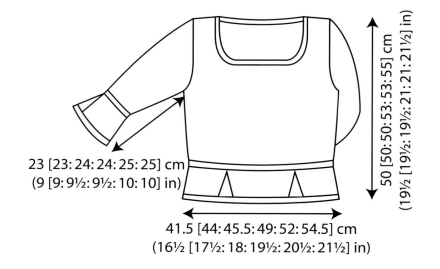

23 [23: 24: 24: 25: 25] cm
(9 [9: 9½: 9½: 10: 10] in)

41.5 [44: 45.5: 49: 52: 54.5] cm
(16½ [17½: 18: 19½: 20½: 21½] in)

50 [50: 50: 53: 53: 55] cm
(19½ [19½: 19½: 21: 21: 21½] in)

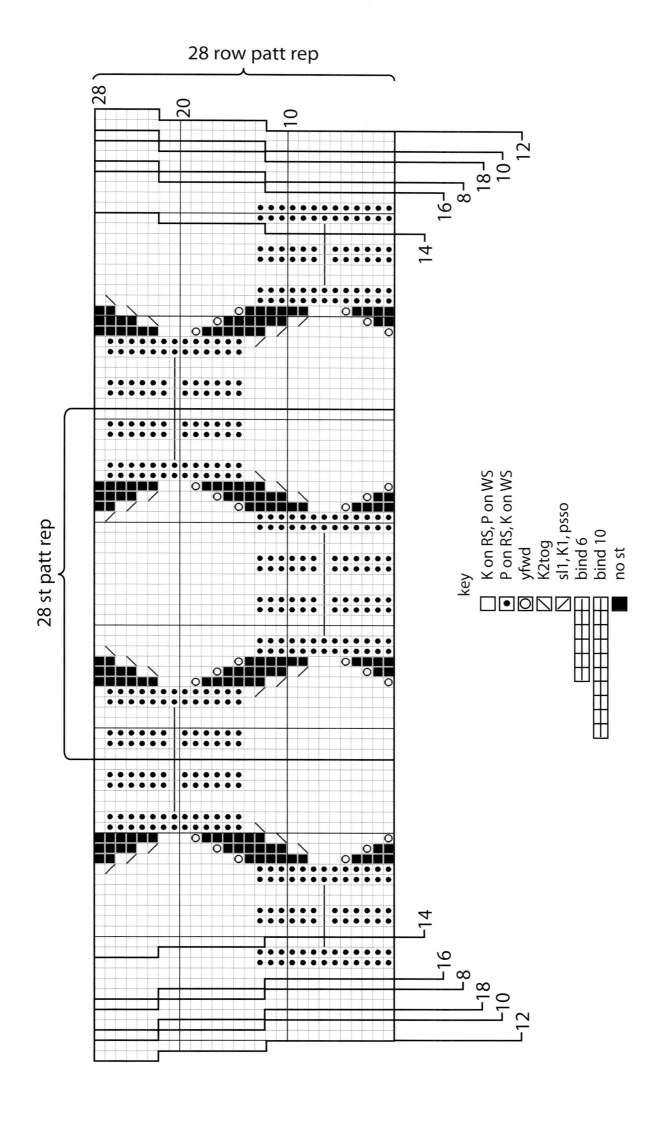

28 row patt rep

28 st patt rep

key

K on RS, P on WS
P on RS, K on WS
yfwd
K2tog
sl1, K1, psso
bind 6
bind 10
no st

143

32.5: 34.5] cm, ending with RS facing for next row.

Shape armholes

Keeping patt correct, cast off 3 [4: 4: 5: 5: 6] sts at beg of next 2 rows.
96 [100: 104: 110: 118: 122] sts.
Dec 1 st at each end of next 5 [5: 7: 7: 9: 9] rows, then on foll 3 [3: 2: 3: 3: 4] alt rows.
80 [84: 86: 90: 94: 96] sts.
Cont straight until armhole meas 22 [22: 23: 23: 24: 24] cm, ending with RS facing for next row.

Shape shoulders and back neck

Next row (RS): Cast off 5 [6: 6: 7: 7: 7] sts, patt until there are 16 [17: 18: 19: 20: 21] sts on right needle and turn, leaving rem sts on a holder.
Work each side of neck separately.
Cast off 3 sts at beg of next row, then 5 [6: 6: 7: 7: 7] sts at beg of foll row, and 3 sts at beg of next row.
Cast off rem 5 [5: 6: 6: 7: 8] sts.
With RS facing, rejoin yarn to rem sts, cast off centre 38 [38: 38: 38: 40: 40] sts, patt to end.
Complete to match first side, reversing shapings.

FRONT

Work as given for back until 28 [28: 28: 32: 32: 32] rows less have been worked than on back to beg of shoulder shaping, ending with RS facing for next row.

Shape front neck

Next row (RS): Patt 29 [31: 32: 35: 36: 37] sts and turn, leaving rem sts on a holder.
Work each side of neck separately.
Keeping patt correct, dec 1 st at neck edge of next 8 rows, then on foll 4 alt rows, then on 2 [2: 2: 3: 3: 3] foll 4th rows.
15 [17: 18: 20: 21: 22] sts.
Work 3 rows, ending with RS facing for next row.

Shape shoulder

Cast off 5 [6: 6: 7: 7: 7] sts at beg of next and foll alt row.
Work 1 row.
Cast off rem 5 [5: 6: 6: 7: 8] sts.
With RS facing, rejoin yarn to rem sts, cast off centre 22 [22: 22: 20: 22: 22] sts, patt to end.
Complete to match first side, reversing shapings.

SLEEVES

Using 3¾mm (US 5) needles cast on 74 [74:

76: 76: 78: 78] sts.
Work in g st for 4 rows, ending with RS facing for next row.
Change to 4mm (US 6) needles.
Row 1 (RS): K27 [27: 28: 28: 29: 29], place marker on needle, sl 1, K4, P1, K8, P1, K4, sl 1, place another marker on needle, K27 [27: 28: 28: 29: 29].
Row 2: P to marker, slip marker onto right needle, P5, sl 1, P8, sl 1, P5, slip marker onto needle, P to end.
Row 3: K to marker, slip marker onto right needle, sl 1, K4, P1, K8, P1, K4, sl 1, slip marker onto right needle, P to end.
Row 4: As row 2.
Row 5: K to marker, slip marker onto right needle, sl 1, K2, sl 1, K1, psso, P1, K2tog, K4, sl 1, K1, psso, P1, K2tog, K2, sl 1, slip marker onto right needle, K to end.
70 [70: 72: 72: 74: 74] sts.
Row 6: P to marker, slip marker onto right needle, P4, sl 1, P6, sl 1, P4, slip marker onto right needle, P to end.
Row 7: K to marker, slip marker onto right needle, sl 1, K3, P1, K6, P1, K3, sl 1, slip marker onto right needle, K to end.
Row 8: As row 6.
Row 9: K to marker, slip marker onto right needle, sl 1, K1, sl 1, K1 psso, P1, K2tog, K2, sl 1, K1, psso, P1, K2tog, K1, sl 1, slip marker onto right needle, K to end.
66 [66: 68: 68: 70: 70] sts.
Row 10: P to marker, slip marker onto right needle, P3, sl 1, P4, sl 1, P3, slip marker onto right needle, P to end.
Row 11: K to marker, slip marker onto right needle, sl 1, K2, P1, K4, P1, K2, sl 1, slip marker onto right needle, K to end.
Row 12: As row 10.
Row 13: K to marker, slip marker onto right needle, sl 1, (sl 1, K1, psso, P1, K2tog) twice, sl 1, slip marker onto right needle, K to end.
62 [62: 64: 64: 66: 66] sts.
Row 14: P to marker, slip marker onto right needle, (P2, sl 1) twice, P2, slip marker onto right needle, P to end.
Row 15: K to marker, slip marker onto right needle, sl 1, sl 1, K1, psso, K2, K2tog, sl 1, slip marker onto right needle, K to end.
60 [60: 62: 62: 64: 64] sts.
Row 16: P to marker, slip marker onto right needle, P6, slip marker onto right needle, P to end.
Row 17: K to marker, slip marker onto right

needle, sl 1, sl 1, K1, psso, K2tog, sl 1, slip marker onto right needle, K to end.
58 [58: 60: 60: 62: 62] sts.
Row 18: P to marker, slip marker onto right needle, P4, slip marker onto right needle, P to end.
Row 19: K to marker, slip marker onto right needle, sl 1, K1, psso, K2tog, slip marker onto right needle, K to end.
56 [56: 58: 58: 60: 60] sts.
Remove markers.
Change to 3¾mm (US 5) needles.
Work in g st for 5 rows, ending with RS facing for next row.
Change to 4mm (US 6) needles.
Beg with a K row, work in st st, shaping sides by in 1 st at each end of 3rd [next: next: next: next: next] and foll 0 [1: 0: 2: 0: 2] alt rows, then on every foll 4th row until there are 74 [76: 78: 80: 82: 84] sts.
Cont straight until sleeve meas 26.5 [26.5: 27.5: 27.5: 28.5: 28.5] cm, ending with RS facing for next row.

Shape top

Cast off 3 [4: 4: 5: 5: 6] sts at beg of next 2 rows.
68 [68: 70: 70: 72: 72] sts.
Dec 1 st at each end of next 5 rows, then on foll 2 alt rows, then on 3 foll 4th rows.
48 [48: 50: 50: 52: 52] sts.
Work 1 row.
Dec 1 st at each end of next and every foll alt row to 40 sts, then on foll 11 rows, ending with RS facing for next row.
Cast off rem 18 sts.

MAKING UP

Do NOT press.
Join right shoulder seam using back stitch, or mattress stitch if preferred.

Neckband

With RS facing and using 3¾mm (US 5) needles, pick up and knit 26 [26: 26: 29: 29: 29] sts down left side of neck, 22 [22: 22: 20: 22: 22] sts from front, 26 [26: 26: 29: 29: 29] sts up right side of neck, then 50 [50: 50: 50: 52: 52] sts from back. 124 [124: 124: 128: 132: 132] sts.
Work in g st for 4 rows, ending with **WS** facing for next row.
Cast off knitwise (on **WS**).
Machine wash all pieces before completing sewing together.
See information page for finishing instructions, setting in sleeves using the set-in method.

CHARM
ERIKA KNIGHT

Main image page 24 & 25

● ● ●

YARN

S	M	L	XL	XXL

To fit bust
81-86 91-97 102-107 112-117 122-127 cm
32-34 36-38 40-42   44-46   48-50   in

Rowan Fine Milk Cotton
6   6   7   7   8   x 50 gm
(photographed in Ardour 508)

CROCHET HOOK

2.50mm (no 11) (US C2) crochet hook

TENSION

4 patt reps to 16 cm in width and 2 patt reps (8 rows) to 9 cm measured over patt using 2.50mm (US C2) crochet hook.

CROCHET ABBREVIATIONS

ss = slip stitch; **ch** = chain; **dc** = double crochet; **tr** = treble.

BODY (worked in one piece)
Right front
Using 2.50mm (US C2) hook work foundation row as folls:
Foundation row (RS): 7 ch, ★ss into 4th ch from hook, 3 ch, (2 tr, 3 ch, 1 ss, 3 ch and 2 tr) into loop just formed – this is first base flower unit★★, 10 ch, rep from ★ until there are 7 [8: 9: 10: 11] base flower units in total, ending last rep at ★★, turn work, keeping RS facing but so that you can work back across upper (straight) edge of this row.
Now work in patt as folls:
Row 1 (RS): ★3 ch, 1 ss into ring at centre of flower, 3 ch, (2 tr, 3 ch, 1 ss - centre petal completed, 3 ch and 2 tr) into centre of same flower, miss 2 ch connecting flowers, 1 ss into next ch★★, 7 ch, miss 2 ch, 1 ss into next ch, rep from ★ to end, ending last rep at ★★, turn. 7 [8: 9: 10: 11] patt reps – each flower forms a patt rep and has 4 petals.
Row 2: 11 ch, 1 ss into 4th ch from hook, 3 ch, 2 tr into ring just formed, 3 ch, 1 ss into top of 3 ch at end of centre petal of last complete flower, ★10 ch, 1 ss into 4th ch from hook, 3 ch, 2 tr into ring just made, 1 ss into 4th of 7-ch connecting flowers, 3 ch, (1 ss, 3 ch

and 2 tr) into same ring as last 2 tr, 3 ch, 1 ss into top of 3 ch of centre petal of next flower, rep from ★ to end.
Row 3: 9 ch, miss (1 ss and 2 ch) at end of previous row, 1 ss into next ch, ★3 ch★★, (1 ss, 3 ch, 2 tr, 3 ch, 1 ss, 3 ch and 2 tr) into ring at centre of next flower, miss 2 ch, 1 ss into next ch, 7 ch, miss (3 ch, 1 ss and 2 ch), 1 ss into next ch, rep from ★ to end, ending last rep at ★★, (1 ss, 3 ch and 2 tr) into centre of last flower, turn.
Row 4: ★10 ch, 1 ss into 4th ch from hook, 3 ch, 2 tr into ring just formed, 1 ss into 4th of 7-ch connecting flowers, 3 ch, (1 ss, 3 ch and 2 tr) into same ring as last 2 tr★★, 3 ch, 1 ss into top of 3 ch of centre petal of next flower, rep from ★ to end, ending last rep at ★★, turn.
These 4 rows form patt.
Work in patt for a further 19 [23: 19: 19: 23] rows, ending after patt row 3 but do **NOT** turn at end of last row. (Right front should meas 27 [32: 27: 27: 32] cm.)★★★
Now, keeping RS facing, work edging row down row-end edge of right front as folls:
Edging row (RS): ★3 ch, (1 ss, 3 ch, 2 tr, 3 ch, 1 ss, 3 ch and 2 tr) into centre of edge flower, miss 3 ch of 7-ch connecting rows, 1 ss into next ch★★, 6 ch, 1 ss into last ch before centre petal of next edge flower, rep from ★ to end, ending last rep at ★★.
Fasten off. (You should now have a panel 7 [8: 9: 10: 11] flowers wide and 12 [14: 12: 12: 14] flowers deep.)
Shape cap sleeve
Next row (RS): 7 ch, ★1 ss into 4th ch from hook, 3 ch, (2 tr, 3 ch, 1 ss, 3 ch and 2 tr) into loop just formed – this is first base flower unit★★, 10 ch, rep from ★ once more, then from ★ to ★★ again – 3 new base flower units completed, 3 ch, 1 ss into first of 3-ch at beg of edging row, patt to end across top of last row of right front section, turn.
10 [11: 12: 13: 14] patt reps.
Cont in patt across all sts for a further 15 [15: 19: 19: 19] rows, ending after patt row 3.

Fasten off.
Left front
Work as given for right front to ★★★.
Next row (WS): Turn work and patt until ss at end of first petal of last flower has been completed, 3 ch, 2 tr into ring at centre of last flower of this row, now make 3 extra base flower units as folls: ★10 ch, 1 ss into 4th ch from hook, 3 ch, (2 tr, 3 ch, 1 ss, 3 ch and 2 tr) into loop just formed, turn.
10 [11: 12: 13: 14] patt reps.
Cont in patt across all sts for a further 14 [14: 18: 18: 18] rows, ending after patt row 3.
Join sections
Next row (WS): Patt across all 10 [11: 12: 13: 14] flowers of left front, then patt across all 10 [11: 12: 13: 14] flowers of right front, turn.
20 [22: 24: 26: 28] patt reps.
Cont in patt across all sts for a further 7 [7: 11: 11: 11] rows, ending after patt row 3 but do **NOT** turn at end of last row.
Now, keeping RS facing, work edging row down row-end edge of right cap sleeve.
Fasten off.
With **WS** facing, miss last 3 flowers of last complete row worked, rejoin yarn to top of 3 ch at end of centre petal of next flower, work 14 [16: 18: 20: 22] patt reps and turn, leaving rem 3 flowers unworked.
Cont in patt on these 14 [16: 18: 20: 22] patt reps for a further 23 [27: 23: 23: 27] rows, ending after patt row 3 but do **NOT** turn at end of last row.
Now, keeping RS facing, work edging row down row-end edge of right back side seam.
Fasten off.

MAKING UP

Press as described on the information page. Attach yarn at top of left front opening edge and work edging row down left front opening edge.
Fasten off.
Join side and sleeve seams.
See information page for finishing instructions.

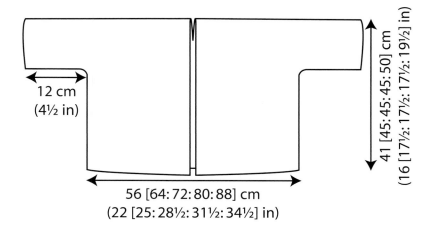

12 cm (4½ in)

56 [64: 72: 80: 88] cm (22 [25: 28½: 31½: 34½] in)

41 [45: 45: 45: 50] cm (16 [17½: 17½: 17½: 19½] in)

BEGUILE
LISA RICHARDSON
Main image page 8 & 9

●●

YARN

	S	M	L	XL	XXL	
To fit bust						
	81-86	91-97	102-107	112-117	122-127	cm
	32-34	36-38	40-42	44-46	48-50	in

Rowan Kidsilk Haze and Fine Milk Cotton

A	KSH Pearl 590					
	4	4	5	5	5	x 25gm
B	FMC Opaque 506					
	2	2	2	2	3	x 50gm

CROCHET HOOK

2.50mm (no 11) (US C2) crochet hook

TENSION

7½ patt reps and 13 rows to 10 cm measured over patt using 2.50mm (US C2) hook and yarn A.

CROCHET ABBREVIATIONS

ss = slip stitch; **ch** = chain; **dc** = double crochet; **tr** = treble; **sp(s)** = space(s); **dc2tog** = (insert hook as indicated, yoh and draw loop though) twice, yoh and draw through all 3 loops; **yoh** = yarn over hook.

BACK

Using 2.50mm (US C2) hook and yarn B make 74 [82: 90: 100: 110] ch.
Row 1 (RS): 1 dc into 2nd ch from hook, 1 dc into each ch to end, turn.
73 [81: 89: 99: 109] sts.
Row 2: 1 ch (does NOT count as st), 1 dc into each dc to end, turn.
Rep last row 8 times more, ending with RS facing for next row.
Row 11: 1 ch (does NOT count as st), (1 dc, 3 ch and 1 tr) into first dc, *miss 1 dc, (1 dc, 3 ch and 1 tr) into next dc, rep from * to last 2 dc, miss 1 dc, 1 dc into last dc, turn.
36 [40: 44: 49: 54] patt reps.
Break off yarn B and join in yarn A.
Now work in patt as folls:
Row 1 (WS): 3 ch (counts as 1 tr), miss dc at base of 3 ch, *(1 dc, 3 ch and 1 tr) into next ch sp, rep from * to end, working tr at end of last rep into dc at beg of previous row, turn.
Row 2: 1 ch (does NOT count as st), 1 dc into tr at end of previous row, 3 ch, 1 tr into first ch sp, *(1 dc, 3 ch and 1 tr) into next ch sp, rep from * to last st, 1 dc into top of 3 ch at beg of previous row, turn.
These 2 rows form patt.

Cont in patt until back meas approx 34 [35: 36: 37: 38] cm, ending with RS facing for next row.
Shape for cap sleeves
Next row (RS): 1 ch (does NOT count as st), (1 dc, 3 ch and 1 tr) into tr at end of previous row – 1 patt rep increased, (1 dc, 3 ch and 1 tr) into first ch sp, *(1 dc, 3 ch and 1 tr) into next ch sp, rep from * to last st, (1 dc, 3 ch, 1 tr and 1 dc) into top of 3 ch at beg of previous row – 1 patt rep increased, turn.
38 [42: 46: 51: 56] patt reps.
Work 1 row.
Rep last 2 rows 4 times more, then first of these rows (the inc row) again.
48 [52: 56: 61: 66] patt reps.
Place markers at both ends of last row to denote base of armhole openings.
Cont straight until work meas 18 [19: 20: 21: 22] cm from markers, ending with RS facing for next row.
Shape back neck
Next row (RS): 1 ch (does NOT count as st), 1 dc into tr at end of previous row, 3 ch, 1 tr into first ch sp, *(1 dc, 3 ch and 1 tr) into next ch sp, rep from * 15 [17: 18: 20: 22] times more, miss 1 dc, 1 dc into next tr and turn, leaving rem sts unworked.
Work on this set of 17 [19: 20: 22: 24] patt reps only for first side of neck.
Next row: Ss across and into first ch sp, 3 ch (counts as 1 tr), *(1 dc, 3 ch and 1 tr) into next ch sp, rep from * to end, working tr at end of last rep into dc at beg of previous row, turn.
16 [18: 19: 21: 23] patt reps.
Next row: 1 ch (does NOT count as st), 1 dc into tr at end of previous row, 3 ch, 1 tr into first ch sp, *(1 dc, 3 ch and 1 tr) into next ch sp, rep from * 13 [15: 16: 18: 20] times more, miss 1 dc, 1 dc into next tr, turn.
15 [17: 18: 20: 22] patt reps.
Next row: Ss across and into first ch sp, 3 ch (counts as 1 tr), *(1 dc, 3 ch and 1 tr) into next ch sp, rep from * to end, working tr at end of last rep into dc at beg of previous row.

14 [16: 17: 19: 21] patt reps.
Fasten off.
Return to last complete row worked, miss centre 14 [14: 16: 17: 18] ch sps, rejoin yarn to tr before next ch sp, 1 ch (does NOT count as st), 1 dc into tr where yarn was rejoined, 3 ch, 1 tr into next ch sp, patt to end, turn.
17 [19: 20: 22: 24] patt reps.
Next row: Patt to last-but-one ch sp, 1 dc into last-but-one ch sp, 3 ch, 1 tr into next dc, turn.
16 [18: 19: 21: 23] patt reps.
Next row: Ss into first ch sp, 3 ch (does NOT count as st), (1 dc, 3 ch and 1 tr) into next ch sp, patt to end, turn.
15 [17: 18: 20: 22] patt reps.
Next row: Patt to last-but-one ch sp, 1 dc into last-but-one ch sp, 3 ch, 1 tr into next dc.
14 [16: 17: 19: 21] patt reps.
Fasten off.

FRONT

Work as given for back until 2 rows less have been worked than on back to beg of back neck shaping, ending with RS facing for next row.
Shape front neck
Next row (RS): 1 ch (does NOT count as st), 1 dc into tr at end of previous row, 3 ch, 1 tr into first ch sp, *(1 dc, 3 ch and 1 tr) into next ch sp, rep from * 15 [17: 18: 20: 22] times more, miss 1 dc, 1 dc into next tr and turn, leaving rem sts unworked.
Work on this set of 17 [19: 20: 22: 24] patt reps only for first side of neck.
Next row: Ss across and into first ch sp, 3 ch (counts as 1 tr), *(1 dc, 3 ch and 1 tr) into next ch sp, rep from * to end, working tr at end of last rep into dc at beg of previous row, turn.
16 [18: 19: 21: 23] patt reps.
Next row: 1 ch (does NOT count as st), 1 dc into tr at end of previous row, 3 ch, 1 tr into first ch sp, *(1 dc, 3 ch and 1 tr) into next ch sp, rep from * 13 [15: 16: 18: 20] times more, miss 1 dc, 1 dc into next tr, turn.
15 [17: 18: 20: 22] patt reps.
Next row: Ss across and into first ch sp, 3 ch

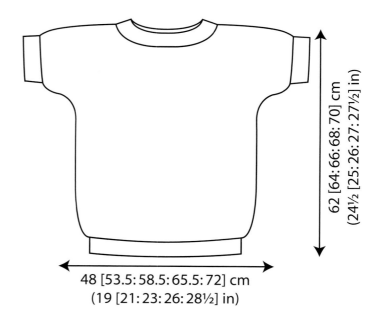

62 [64: 66: 68: 70] cm
(24½ [25: 26: 27: 27½] in)

48 [53.5: 58.5: 65.5: 72] cm
(19 [21: 23: 26: 28½] in)

(counts as 1 tr), ★(1 dc, 3 ch and 1 tr) into next ch sp, rep from ★ to end, working tr at end of last rep into dc at beg of previous row, turn. 14 [16: 17: 19: 21] patt reps.
Work 2 rows.
Fasten off.
Return to last complete row worked, miss centre 14 [14: 16: 17: 18] ch sps, rejoin yarn to tr before next ch sp, 1 ch (does NOT count as st), 1 dc into tr where yarn was rejoined, 3 ch, 1 tr into next ch sp, patt to end, turn. 17 [19: 20: 22: 24] patt reps.
Next row: Patt to last-but-one ch sp, 1 dc into last-but-one ch sp, 3 ch, 1 tr into next dc, turn. 16 [18: 19: 21: 23] patt reps.
Next row: Ss into first ch sp, 3 ch (does NOT count as st), (1 dc, 3 ch and 1 tr) into next ch sp, patt to end, turn. 15 [17: 18: 20: 22] patt reps.

Next row: Patt to last-but-one ch sp, 1 dc into last-but-one ch sp, 3 ch, 1 tr into next dc, turn. 14 [16: 17: 19: 21] patt reps.
Work 2 rows.
Fasten off.

MAKING UP
Press as described on the information page.
Join both shoulder seams.
Neckband
With RS facing, using 2.50mm (US C2) hook and yarn B, attach yarn at neck edge of left shoulder seam, 1 ch (does NOT count as st), work 1 round of dc evenly around entire neck edge, ending with ss to first dc, turn.
Next round: 1 ch (does NOT count as st), 1 dc into each dc to end, working (dc2tog) as required to ensure neckband lays flat and ending with ss to first dc, turn.

Rep last round 8 times more.
Fasten off.
Join side/underarm seams below markers.
Armhole borders (both alike)
With RS facing, using 2.50mm (US C2) hook and yarn B, attach yarn at top of side/underarm seam, 1 ch (does NOT count as st), work 1 round of dc evenly around entire armhole edge, ensuring number of dc worked is divisible by 4 and ending with ss to first dc, turn.
Next round: 1 ch (does NOT count as st), ★1 dc into next dc, dc2tog over next 2 dc, 1 dc into next dc, rep from ★ to end, ss to first dc, turn.
Next round: 1 ch (does NOT count as st), 1 dc into each dc to end, ss to first dc, turn.
Rep last round 7 times more.
Fasten off.
See information page for finishing instructions.

FANTASY
● ● ●
MARIE WALLIN
Main image page 4, 6 & 7

YARN

	S	M	L	XL	XXL
To fit bust					
	81-86	91-97	102-107	112-117	122-127	cm
	32-34	36-38	40-42	44-46	48-50	in

Rowan Purelife Organic Cotton 4 ply

9	9	10	11	11	x 50gm

(photographed in Rhubarb 760)

CROCHET HOOK
2.50mm (no 11) (US C2) crochet hook

TENSION
2 patt reps to 14 cm in width and 2 patt reps (16 rows) to 16.5 cm measured over patt using 2.50mm (US C2) crochet hook.

CROCHET ABBREVIATIONS
ss = slip stitch; **ch** = chain; **dc** = double crochet; **tr** = treble; **dtr** = double treble; **qtr** = quadruple treble; **sp(s)** = space(s); **SK** = Solomon's knot worked as folls: lengthen

loop on hook to approx 1.5 cm, yarn over hook and draw loop through (thereby making one long loose ch st), 1 dc under back loop of ch just made.

BACK
Using 2.50mm (US C2) hook make 146 [162: 178: 194: 210] ch **loosely.**
Foundation row (RS): 1 dc into 2nd ch from hook, ★1 SK, miss 3 ch, 1 dtr into next ch, 1 SK, miss 3 ch, 1 qtr into next ch, 1

SK, miss 3 ch, 1 dtr into next ch, 1 SK, miss 3 ch, 1 dc into next ch, rep from ★ to end, turn. 9 [10: 11: 12: 13] patt reps.
Now work in patt as folls:
Row 1: 3 ch, 1 dc into 2nd ch from hook, ★1 SK, miss 1 SK, 1 tr into next st, rep from ★ to end, turn.
Row 2: 6 ch, 1 dc into 2nd ch from hook, ★1 SK, miss 1 SK, 1 dtr into next st, 1 SK, miss 1 SK, 1 dc into next st, 1 SK, miss 1

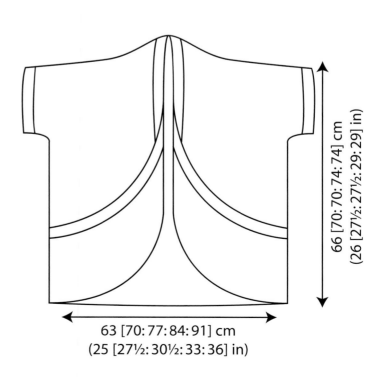

66 [70: 70: 74: 74] cm
(26 [27½: 27½: 29: 29] in)

63 [70: 77: 84: 91] cm
(25 [27½: 30½: 33: 36] in)

SK, 1 dtr into next st, 1 SK, miss 1 SK, 1 qtr into next st, rep
from * to end, turn.

Row 3 and 4: As row 1 and 2.

Row 5: As row 1.

Row 6: 1 ch, 1 dc into first st, *1 SK, miss 1 SK, 1 dtr into next st, 1 SK, miss 1 SK, 1 qtr into next st, 1 SK, miss 1 SK, 1 dtr into next st, 1 SK, miss 1 SK, 1 dc into next st, rep from * to end, turn.

Row 7: As row 1.

Row 8: As row 6.

These 8 rows form patt.

Work in patt for a further 35 [39: 35: 39: 43] rows, ending after patt row 3 [7: 3: 7: 3] and with RS facing for next row. (Back should meas 45 [50: 45: 50: 54] cm.)

Shape cap sleeves

Using 2.50mm (US C2) hook and spare ball of yarn, make 8 ch **loosely** and attach with a ss to dc at beg of last row worked.

Fasten off and cut off yarn.

Sizes S, L and XXL only

Next row (RS): 9 ch, 1 dc into 2nd ch from hook, 1 SK, miss 3 ch, 1 dtr into next ch, 1 SK, miss 3 ch, 1 qtr into st at end of previous row – ½ patt rep increased, patt until qtr has been worked into st where length of ch was attached, now work across 8 ch attached to beg of previous row as folls: 1 SK, miss 3 ch, 1 dtr into next ch, 1 SK, miss 3 ch, 1 dc into last ch – ½ patt rep increased, turn. 10 [–: 12: –: 14] patt reps.

Sizes M and XL only

Next row (RS): 13 ch, 1 dc into 2nd ch from hook, 1 SK, miss 8 ch, 1 dtr into next ch, 1 SK, miss 3 ch, 1 dc into st at end of previous row – ½ patt rep increased, patt until dc has been worked into st where length of ch was attached, now work across 8 ch attached to beg of previous row as folls: 1 SK, miss 3 ch, 1 dtr into next ch, 1 SK, miss 3 ch, 1 qtr into last ch ½ patt rep increased, turn. - [11: -: 13: -] patt reps.

All sizes

Beg with patt row 1 [5: 1: 5: 1], cont in patt for a further 19 [19: 23: 23: 23] rows, ending after patt row 3 [7: 7: 3: 7]. (Armhole should meas 21 [21: 25: 25: 25] cm.)

Fasten off, placing markers either side of centre

3 patt reps to denote back neck.

LEFT FRONT

Using 2.50mm (US C2) hook make 98 [114: 114: 130: 130] ch **loosely**.

Work foundation row as given for back. 6 [7: 7: 8: 8] patt reps. Now work in patt as given for back for 43 [47: 43: 47: 51] rows, ending after patt row 3 [7: 3: 7: 3] and with RS facing for next row.

Shape cap sleeve

Inc ½ patt rep at beg of next row in same way as inc was worked on back. 6½ [7½: 7½: 8½: 8½] patt reps. Cont in patt as now set for a further 19 [19: 23: 23: 23] rows, ending after a rep of patt row 1.

Fasten off.

Shape collar extension

Miss first 3½ [4: 4½: 5: 5½] patt reps of next row, rejoin yarn to st at end of last missed patt rep, make appropriate ch for beg of row and patt to end, turn.

Work a further 11 rows on these 3 [3½: 3: 3½: 3] patt reps **only** for back collar extension.

Fasten off.

RIGHT FRONT

Using 2.50mm (US C2) hook make 98 [114: 114: 130: 130] ch **loosely**.

Work foundation row as given for back. 6 [7: 7: 8: 8] patt reps. Now work in patt as given for back for 43 [47: 43: 47: 51] rows, ending after patt row 3 [7: 3: 7: 3] and with RS facing for next row.

Shape cap sleeve

Inc ½ patt rep at end of next row in same way as inc was worked on back. 6½ [7½: 7½: 8½: 8½] patt reps. Cont in patt as now set for a further 19 [19: 23: 23: 23] rows, ending after a rep of patt row 1.

Shape collar extension

Next row: Work 3 [3½: 3: 3½: 3] patt reps and turn, leaving rem 3½ [4: 4½: 5: 5½] patt reps unworked.

Work a further 11 rows on these 3 [3½: 3: 3½: 3] patt reps **only** for back collar extension.

Fasten off.

MAKING UP

Press as described on the information page.

Join shoulder seams. Join tops of last rows of back collar extensions, then sew one edge to back neck (between markers), easing in slight fullness.

Front edging

With **WS** facing and using 2.50mm (US C2) hook, attach yarn at base of left front opening edge and work 1 row of dc evenly up entire left front opening edge, then down entire right front opening edge to base of right front opening edge, working a multiple of 12 sts plus one, turn.

Row 1 (WS of edging, RS of garment): 1 ch (does NOT count as st), 1 dc into first dc, *(5 ch, miss 4 dc, 1 dc into next dc) twice**, (5 ch, 1 dc into next dc) twice, rep from * to end, ending last rep at **, turn.

Row 2: 6 ch (counts as 1 tr and 3 ch), 1 dc into first ch sp, *3 ch, 1 dc into next ch sp, rep from * until dc has been worked into last ch sp, 3 ch, 1 tr into dc at beg of previous row, turn.

Row 3: 1 ch (does NOT count as st), 1 dc into first tr, 5 ch, miss first ch sp, *(1 dc, 5 ch, 1 dc, 5 ch and 1 dc) into next ch sp, 5 ch**, miss 1 ch sp, 1 dc into next ch sp, 5 ch, miss 1 ch sp, rep from * to end, ending last rep at **, 1 dc into last ch sp, turn.

Row 4: As row 2.

Row 5: 1 ch (does NOT count as st), 1 dc into tr at end of previous row, 5 ch, miss first 2 ch sps, *1 dc into next ch sp, 5 ch, miss 1 ch sp, (1 dc, 5 ch, 1 dc, 5 ch and 1 dc) into next ch sp, 5 ch, miss 1 ch sp, rep from * to end.

Fasten off.

Cuff edgings (both alike)

Work along row-end edges of cap sleeve extensions as given for front edging.

Mark points along lower edges of fronts 15 [17: 17: 19: 19] cm in from base of side seam, then mark another point 12 [15: 15: 18: 18] cm away from first, measuring towards front opening edge. Fold lower edge so that marked points meet, forming a pleat along lower edge of each front. Now fold each front diagonally so that lower edge of front matches side seam edge. Stitch lower edge to side seam edge, securing pleat in place. Join side and underarm seams, securing pleat in seams.

See information page for finishing instructions.

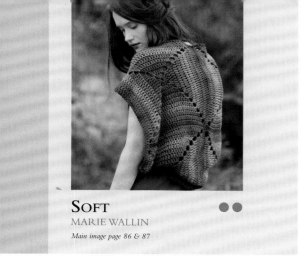

SOFT
MARIE WALLIN
Main image page 86 & 87

●●

YARN

	S-M	L-XL	
To fit bust			
	81-97	102-117	cm
	32-38	40-46	in

Rowan Lenpur™ Linen

A Incense 568
| | 2 | 3 | x 50gm |

B Cocoa 573
| | 2 | 3 | x 50gm |

C Jungle 569
| | 2 | 3 | x 50gm |

D Creek 567
| | | 3 | 4 | x 50gm |

CROCHET HOOK
6.00mm (no 4) (US J10) crochet hook

TENSION
One completed motif measures 30 cm square using 6.00mm (US J10) crochet hook and yarn DOUBLE.

CROCHET ABBREVIATIONS
ss = slip stitch; **ch** = chain; **dc** = double crochet; **tr** = treble; **sp(s)** = space(s).

MOTIFS (make 4 [6])
Using 6.00mm (US J10) crochet hook and yarn A DOUBLE make 4 ch and join with a ss to form a ring.
Round 1 (RS): 5 ch (counts as 1 tr and 2 ch), (3 tr into ring, 2 ch) 3 times, 2 tr into ring, ss to 3rd of 5 ch at beg of round.
Round 2: Ss into next ch, 7 ch (counts as 1 tr and 4 ch),2 tr into first ch sp, *1 tr into each of next 3 tr**, (2 tr, 4 ch and 2 tr) into corner ch sp, rep from * to end, ending last rep at **, 1 tr into ch sp used at beg of round, ss to 3rd of 7 ch at beg of round.
Round 3: Ss into next ch, 7 ch (counts as 1 tr and 4 ch),2 tr into first ch sp, *1 tr into each of next 7 tr**, (2 tr, 4 ch and 2 tr) into corner ch sp, rep from * to end, ending last rep at **, 1 tr into ch sp used at beg of round, ss to 3rd of 7 ch at beg of round.
Break off yarn A and join in yarn B DOUBLE.
Round 4: Ss into next ch, 7 ch (counts as 1 tr and 4 ch),2 tr into first ch sp, *1 tr into each of next 11 tr**, (2 tr, 4 ch and 2 tr) into corner ch sp, rep from * to end, ending last rep at **, 1 tr into ch sp used at beg of round, ss to 3rd

of 7 ch at beg of round.
Round 5: Ss into next ch, 7 ch (counts as 1 tr and 4 ch),2 tr into first ch sp, *1 tr into each of next 15 tr**, (2 tr, 4 ch and 2 tr) into corner ch sp, rep from * to end, ending last rep at **, 1 tr into ch sp used at beg of round, ss to 3rd of 7 ch at beg of round.
Break off yarn B and join in yarn C DOUBLE.
Round 6: Ss into next ch, 7 ch (counts as 1 tr and 4 ch),2 tr into first ch sp, *1 tr into each of next 19 tr**, (2 tr, 4 ch and 2 tr) into corner ch sp, rep from * to end, ending last rep at **, 1 tr into ch sp used at beg of round, ss to 3rd of 7 ch at beg of round.
Round 7: Ss into next ch, 7 ch (counts as 1 tr and 4 ch),2 tr into first ch sp, *1 tr into each of next 23 tr**, (2 tr, 4 ch and 2 tr) into corner ch sp, rep from * to end, ending last rep at **, 1 tr into ch sp used at beg of round, ss to 3rd of 7 ch at beg of round.
Break off yarn C and join in yarn D DOUBLE.
Round 8: Ss into next ch, 7 ch (counts as 1 tr and 4 ch),2 tr into first ch sp, *1 tr into each of next 27 tr**, (2 tr, 4 ch and 2 tr) into corner ch sp, rep from * to end, ending last rep at **, 1 tr into ch sp used at beg of round, ss to 3rd of 7 ch at beg of round.
Round 9: Ss into next ch, 7 ch (counts as 1 tr and 4 ch),2 tr into first ch sp, *1 tr into each of next 31 tr**, (2 tr, 4 ch and 2 tr) into corner ch sp, rep from * to end, ending last rep at **, 1 tr into ch sp used at beg of round, ss to 3rd of 7 ch at beg of round.
Fasten off.
Motif is a square - in each corner there is a 4-ch sp and along each side there are 35 tr.

BODY
With RS facing, using 6.00mm (US J10) crochet hook and yarn A DOUBLE attach yarn to one corner 4-ch sp of a motif and work along one side as folls: 3 ch (counts as first tr), 1 tr into same ch sp, 1 tr into each of next 35 tr, 2 tr into next corner ch sp, turn.
Holding motifs RS together, now attach next motif to this motif as folls: 1 ch (does NOT count as st), 1 dc into corner ch sp of next

motif **and** top of last tr on first motif, 1 dc into same ch sp of next motif **and** top of next tr on first motif, (1 dc into next tr of next motif **and** top of next tr on first motif) 35 times, 1 dc into next corner ch sp of next motif **and** top of next tr on first motif, 1 dc into same ch sp of next motif **and** top of 3 ch at beg of previous row on first motif.
Fasten off.
Cont to join motifs in this way to form a rectangle 2 motifs wide and 2 [3] motifs long - these (longer) edges forms upper and lower edges. When joining motifs across edges that have already been joined, work 3 sts into ends of joining rows.

MAKING UP
Press as described on the information page.
Upper and lower edgings (both alike)
With RS facing, using 6.00mm (US J10) crochet hook and yarn A DOUBLE attach yarn to one corner 4-ch sp of joined motifs and work along upper (or lower) edge as folls: 3 ch (counts as first tr), 1 tr into same ch sp, (1 tr into each of next 35 tr, 2 tr into next corner ch sp, 3 tr into joining row-ends, 2 tr into next corner ch sp) 1 [2] times, 1 tr into each of next 35 tr, 2 tr into last corner ch sp.
Fasten off.
Armhole borders (both alike)
Fold joined section RS facing so that top of upper and lower edgings match.
With RS facing, using 6.00mm (US J10) crochet hook and yarn A DOUBLE attach yarn to 5th tr in from end of edging row and cont as folls: 1 ch (does NOT count as st), working through trs of both edges, work 1 dc into each of next 5 tr (to join underarm seam).
Now work around armhole edge as folls: 3 ch (counts as 1 tr), 2 tr into first edging row-end edge, 2 tr into next corner ch sp, 1 tr into each of next 35 tr, 2 tr into next corner ch sp, 3 tr into joining row-ends, 2 tr into next corner ch sp, 1 tr into each of next 35 tr, 2 tr into next corner ch sp, 2 tr into other edging row-end edge, ss to top of 3 ch at beg of round.
Fasten off.

See information page for finishing instructions.

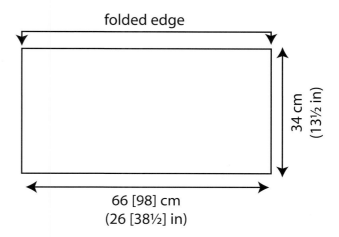

folded edge

34 cm
(13½ in)

66 [98] cm
(26 [38½] in)

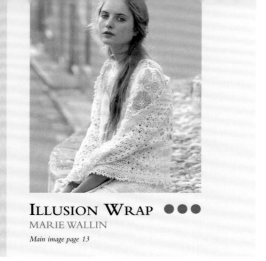

ILLUSION WRAP ●●●
MARIE WALLIN
Main image page 13

YARN
Rowan Purelife Organic Cotton 4 ply
     10   x 50gm
(photographed in Natural 751)

CROCHET HOOK
2.50mm (no 12) (US C2) crochet hook

TENSION
Motif measures 12.5 cm square using 2.50mm
(US C2) crochet hook.

FINISHED SIZE
Completed wrap measures 170 cm (67 ins)
long and 44 cm (17½ ins) wide.

CROCHET ABBREVIATIONS
ss = slip stitch; **ch** = chain; **dc** = double
crochet; **htr** = half treble; **tr** = treble; **qttr** =
(yoh) 5 times, insert hook as indicated, yoh and
draw loop through, (yoh and draw through 2
loops) 6 times; **str** = (yoh) 6 times, insert hook
as indicated, yoh and draw loop through, (yoh
and draw through 2 loops) 7 times; **tr2tog** =
*yoh and insert hook as indicated, yoh and
draw loop through, yoh and draw through 2
loops, rep from * once more, yoh and draw
through all 3 loops on hook; **ttr2tog** = *(yoh)
3 times, insert hook as indicated, yoh and draw
loop through, (yoh and draw through 2 loops)
3 times, rep from * once more, yoh and draw
through all 3 loops on hook; **yoh** = yarn over
hook.

MAIN PANELS (make 6)
Motif
Using 2.50mm (US C2) hook make 16 ch and
join with a ss to form a ring.
Round 1 (RS): 1 ch (does NOT count as st),
24 dc into ring, ss to first dc. 24 sts.
Round 2: 1 ch (does NOT count as st), 1 dc
into first dc, *4 ch, ttr2tog over next 2 dc,
(8 ch, 1 qttr, 7 ch, 1 dc, 8 ch, 1 str, 8 ch, 1 dc,
7 ch, 1 qttr, 7 ch and 1 ss) into top of ttr2tog
just worked (to form group of 3 leaves), 4 ch,
1 dc into next dc of round 1, 7 ch, miss 2 dc,
1 dc into next dc, rep from * to end, replacing
dc at end of last rep with ss to first dc.
Fasten off. (There should be 4 groups of
3 leaves around outer edge of work.)
With RS facing, attach yarn to 8th ch at beg
of centre leaf of one group of 3 leaves and cont
as folls:
Round 3: 1 ch (does NOT count as st), 1 dc

into ch where yarn was rejoined, *2 ch, miss
1 str, 1 dc into next ch, 5 ch, miss (7 ch, 1 dc
and 6 ch), 1 dc into next ch, miss 1 qttr, 1 dc
into next ch, 4 ch, 1 qttr into next ch sp of
round 2, 4 ch, miss first 7 ch of first leaf of next
group of 3 leaves, 1 dc into 8th ch, miss 1 qttr,
1 dc into next ch, 5 ch, miss (6 ch, 1 dc and
7 ch), 1 dc into next ch, rep from * to end,
replacing dc at end of last rep with ss to
first dc.
Round 4: 1 ch (does NOT count as st), 1 dc
into st at base of 1 ch, *3 dc into corner 2-ch
sp, 1 dc into next dc, 1 dc into each of next
5 ch, 1 dc into each of next 2 dc, 1 dc into
each of next 4 ch, 1 dc into next qttr, 1 dc into
each of next 4 ch, 1 dc into each of next 2 dc,
1 dc into each of next 5 ch, 1 dc into next dc,
rep from * to end, replacing dc at end of last
rep with ss to first dc. 112 sts.
Round 5: Ss across and into 3rd dc (this is
centre dc of group of 3 dc worked into corner
ch sp), 4 ch (counts as 1 tr and 1 ch), (3 tr,
1 ch and 1 tr) into dc at base of 4 ch, *(1 ch,
miss 1 dc, 1 tr into next dc) 13 times, 1 ch, miss
1 dc**, (1 tr, 1 ch, 3 tr, 1 ch and 1 tr) into next
(corner) dc, rep from * to end, ending last rep
at **, ss to 3rd of 4 ch at beg of round.
Round 6: Ss into first ch sp, 4 ch (counts as
1 tr and 1 ch), *miss 1 tr, 3 tr into next
(corner) tr**, (1 ch, miss 1 tr, 1 tr into next ch
sp) 16 times, 1 ch, rep from * to end, ending
last rep at **, (1 ch, miss 1 tr, 1 tr into next ch
sp) 15 times, 1 ch, 1 ss into 3rd of 4 ch at beg
of round. 144 sts.
Fasten off.

First side section
With RS facing, attach yarn to one corner tr of
motif, 1 ch (does NOT count as st), 1 dc into
place where yarn was rejoined, 1 dc into each
of next 36 sts (last st should be next corner tr),
turn. 37 sts.
Now work in patt as folls:
Row 1 (WS): 3 ch (counts as first tr), miss dc
at base of 3 ch, 1 tr into next tr, (3 ch, miss
3 dc, 1 tr into each of next 3 dc) 5 times, 3 ch,
miss 3 dc, 1 tr into each of last 2 dc, turn.
Row 2: 2 ch (counts as first htr), miss tr at base
of 2 ch, *1 dc into next tr, 5 ch, miss 3 ch, 1 dc
into next tr**, 2 ch, miss 1 tr, 1 dc into next tr,
rep from * to end, ending last rep at **, 1 htr
into top of 3 ch at beg of previous row, turn.
Row 3: 1 ch (does NOT count as st), 1 dc
into htr at base of 1 ch, *miss 1 dc, 5 tr into
next ch sp, miss 1 dc, 1 dc into next ch sp, rep
from * to end, working dc at end of last rep
into top of 2 ch at beg of previous row, turn.
Row 4: 4 ch (counts as 1 tr and 1 ch), miss first
dc and next tr, *1 dc into next tr, 2 ch, miss
1 tr, 1 dc into next tr**, 4 ch, miss (1 tr, 1 dc
and 1 tr), rep from * to end, ending last rep at
**, 1 ch, miss 1 tr, 1 tr into last dc, turn.
Row 5: 3 ch (counts as first tr), miss tr at base
of 3 ch, 1 tr into next ch sp, *3 ch, miss (1 dc,
1 ch and 1 dc)**, 3 tr into next ch sp, rep from
* to end, ending last rep at **, 1 tr into next ch
sp, 1 tr into 3rd of 4 ch at beg of previous row,
turn.
Rep rows 2 to 5, twice more, then rows 2 to
4 again.
Fasten off.

Second side section
With RS facing, attach yarn to next corner tr of
same motif, 1 ch (does NOT count as st),
1 dc into place where yarn was rejoined, now
working along opposite side of motif used for
first side section work 1 dc into each of next 36
sts (last st should be final corner tr), turn. 37 sts.
Now work in patt as folls:
Row 1 (WS): 3 ch (counts as first tr), 2 tr into
dc at base of 3 ch, *miss 2 dc, 1 tr into next dc,
miss 2 dc**, 5 tr into next dc, rep from * to
end, ending last rep at **, 3 tr into last dc, turn.
Row 2: 4 ch (counts as 1 tr and 1 ch), 1 tr
into tr at base of 4 ch, *miss 2 tr, 1 tr into next
tr, miss 2 tr**, (1 tr, 2 ch and 1 tr) into next tr,
rep from * to end, ending last rep at **, (1 tr,
1 ch and 1 tr) into top of 3 ch at beg of
previous row, turn.
Row 3: 4 ch (counts as 1 tr and 1 ch), 1 tr
into first ch sp, *miss 1 tr, 1 tr into next tr, miss
1 tr**, (1 tr, 2 ch and 1 tr) into next ch sp, rep
from * to end, ending last rep at **, 1 tr into
last ch sp, 1 ch, 1 tr into 3rd of 4 ch at beg of
previous row, turn.
Row 4: 3 ch (counts as 1 tr), miss tr at base
of 3 ch, 2 tr into first ch sp, *miss 1 tr, 1 tr into
next tr, miss 1 tr**, 5 tr into next ch sp, rep
from * to end, ending last rep at **, 2 tr into
last ch sp, 1 tr into 3rd of 4 ch at beg of
previous row, turn.
Rep rows 2 to 4, 4 times more, then row 2
again, ending with RS facing for next row.***
Do NOT fasten off.

Joining panel
With RS facing and now working down row-
end edge of second side section, across side of
motif, then up row-end edge of first side
section, cont as folls: 1 ch (does NOT count as
st), work 109 dc evenly along edge, turn.
Foundation row (WS): 4 ch (counts as 1 htr
and 2 ch), miss st at base of 6 ch and next dc,
1 dc into next dc, *miss 3 dc, 1 tr into next dc,
(2 ch and 1 tr) 3 times into same ch sp as last
tr, miss 3 dc, 1 dc into next dc**, 5 ch, miss
3 dc, 1 dc into next dc, rep from * to end,
ending last rep at **, 2 ch, miss 1 dc, 1 htr into
next dc, turn. 9 patt reps.
Now work in patt as folls:
Row 1: 3 ch (counts as 1 htr and 1 ch), 1 dc
into first ch sp, *3 tr into next ch sp, (2 ch,
3 tr into next ch sp) twice**, (1 dc, 3 ch and
1 dc) into next ch sp, rep from * to end, ending
last rep at **, 1 dc into last ch sp, 1 ch, 1 htr
into 2nd of 4 ch at beg of previous row, turn.
Row 2: 4 ch (counts as 1 tr and 1 ch), miss htr
at end of previous row, (1 tr, 2 ch and 1 tr) into
first ch sp, *1 dc into next ch sp, 5 ch, 1 dc into
next ch sp, 1 tr into next ch sp**, (2 ch and
1 tr) 3 times into same ch sp as last tr, rep from
* to end, ending last rep at **, 2 ch, 1 tr into
same ch sp as last tr, 1 ch, 1 tr into 2nd of 3 ch
at beg of previous row, turn.
Row 3: 3 ch (counts as 1 tr), 1 tr into first ch
sp, 2 ch, 3 tr into next ch sp, *(1 dc, 3 ch and
1 dc) into next ch sp, 3 tr into next ch sp**,
(2 ch, 3 tr into next ch sp) twice, rep from * to
end, ending last rep at **, 2 ch, 1 tr into next
ch sp, 1 tr into 3rd of 4 ch at beg of previous
row, turn.
Row 4: 4 ch (counts as 1 htr and 2 ch), miss

2 tr at end of previous row, 1 dc into next ch sp, ★1 tr into next ch sp, (2 ch and 1 tr) 3 times into same ch sp as last tr, 1 dc into next ch sp★★, 5 ch, 1 dc into next ch sp, rep from ★ to end, ending last rep at ★★, 2 ch, 1 htr into top of 3 ch at beg of previous row, turn.
These 4 rows form patt.
Work in patt for a further 9 rows, ending after patt row 1 and with **WS** facing for next row.
Next row (WS): 3 ch (counts as 1 tr), miss htr at end of previous row, 1 tr into first ch sp, ★2 ch, 1 dc into next ch sp, 3 ch, 1 dc into next ch sp, 2 ch★★, 3 tr into next ch sp, rep from ★ to end, ending last rep at ★★, 1 tr into last ch sp, 1 tr into 2nd of 3 ch at beg of previous row.
Fasten off.

END PANEL
Work as given for main panel to ★★★.
Fasten off.

MAKING UP
Press as described on the information page.

Using photograph as a guide, join main panels together to form one long strip - attach top of last row of one main panel to free motif edge of next panel. Complete strip of panels by attaching end panel to one end of strip so that there are motifs at both ends of joined strip.

End borders (both alike)
With RS facing, attach yarn to one corner of joined panels and work across end of panel as folls: 1 ch (does NOT count as st), work 103 dc evenly across end of strip, turn. 103 sts.
Row 1 (WS): 1 ch (does NOT count as st), 1 dc into each dc to end, turn.
Row 2: 1 ch (does NOT count as st), 1 dc into first dc, ★2 ch, miss 2 dc, 1 dc into next dc★★, miss 2 dc, 5 tr into next dc, miss 2 dc, 1 dc into next dc, rep from ★ to end, ending last rep at ★★, turn. 9 patt reps.
Row 3: 1 ch (does NOT count as st), 1 dc into first dc, 2 ch, miss (2 ch and 1 dc), ★1 tr into next tr, (1 ch, 1 tr into next tr) 4 times★★, miss 1 dc, 1 dc into next ch sp, miss 1 dc, rep from ★ to end, ending last rep at ★★, 2 ch, miss

(1 dc and 2 ch), 1 dc into last dc, turn.
Row 4: 3 ch (does NOT count as st), miss (1 dc and 2 ch), 1 tr into next tr, ★(2 ch, miss 1 ch, 1 tr into next tr) 3 times, 2 ch, miss 1 ch, tr2tog over next 2 tr omitting dc between these 2 tr, rep from ★ to end, working tr2tog at end of last rep into last tr and dc at beg of previous row and omitting 2 ch between these 2 sts, turn.
Row 5: 1 ch (does NOT count as st), 1 dc into tr2tog at end of previous row, ★3 dc into next ch sp★★, 7 ch, rep from ★ to end, ending last rep at ★★, 1 dc into tr at beg of previous row.
Fasten off.

Side borders (both alike)
With RS facing, attach yarn to one corner of joined panels and work along edge of joined sections as folls: 1 ch (does NOT count as st), work 454 dc evenly across end of strip, turn. 454 sts.
Work rows 1 to 5 as given for end borders, noting that there will be 50 patt reps.
Fasten off.
See information page for finishing instructions.

UNWIND WRAP
KAFFE FASSETT
Main image page 88 & 89

YARN
Rowan Summer Tweed and Kidsilk Haze

A	KSH	Anthracite 639	1	x 25gm
B	KSH	Trance 582	1	x 25gm
C	STw	Harbour 549	2	x 50gm
D	KSH	Heavenly 592	1	x 25gm
E	STw	Toast 530	1	x 50gm
F	KSH	Majestic 589	2	x 25gm
G	STw	Reed 514	1	x 50gm
H	KSH	Dewberry 600	1	x 25gm
I	STw	Blueberry 525	1	x 50gm
K	STw	Sweet Pea 543	1	x 50gm

NEEDLES
6mm (no 4) (US 10) circular needle, 120 cm long

TENSION
18 sts and 26 rows to 10 cm measured over patt using 6 mm (US 10) needles.

FINISHED SIZE
Completed wrap measures 150 cm (59 ins) long (excluding fringe) and 40 cm (15½ ins) wide.

Pattern note: Fringe is formed by knotting together ends of yarns used for stripes. When joining in and cutting off yarns, leave an end of approx 25 cm - this will form the fringe.

WRAP
Using 6mm (US 10) circular needle and yarn C cast on 270 sts.
Work in g st for 2 rows, ending with RS facing for next row.
Joining in and cutting off colours as required (see pattern note) and beg with a K row, now work in st st in stripes as folls:
Rows 1 and 2: Using yarn F.
Row 3: Using yarn B.
Row 4: Using yarn G.
Row 5: Using yarn B.
Row 6: Using yarn H.
Row 7: Using yarn F.
Row 8: Using yarn A.
Row 9: Using yarn I.
Row 10: Using yarn B.
Row 11: Using yarn A.

Row 12: Using yarn K.
Rows 13 and 14: Using yarn B.
Row 15: Using yarn D.
Row 16: Using yarn F.
Row 17: Using yarn G.
Row 18: Using yarn A.
Row 19: Using yarn F
Row 20: Using yarn H.
Row 21: Using yarn C.
Row 22: Using yarn B.
Row 23: Using yarn H.
Row 24: Using yarn F.
Row 25: Using yarn B.
Row 26: Using yarn E.
Rows 27 and 28: Using yarn A.
Row 29: Using yarn H.
Row 30: Using yarn I.
Rows 31 and 32: Using yarn F.
Row 33: Using yarn B.
Row 34: Using yarn H.
Row 35: Using yarn G.
Row 36: Using yarn H.
Rows 37 and 38: Using yarn F.
Row 39: Using yarn K.
Row 40: Using yarn A.
Row 41: Using yarn B.
Rows 42 and 43: Using yarn D.
Row 44: Using yarn E.
Row 45: Using yarn F.
Row 46: Using yarn B.
Row 47: Using yarn H.
Row 48: Using yarn C.

Row 49: Using yarn H.
Row 50: Using yarn F.
Row 51: Using yarn I
Row 52: Using yarn A.
Rows 53 and 54: Using yarn F.
Row 55: Using yarn D.
Row 56: Using yarn G
Row 57: Using yarn F.
Row 58: Using yarn B.
Row 59: Using yarn H.
Row 60: Using yarn E.
Row 61: Using yarn H.
Row 62: Using yarn A.
Row 63: Using yarn D.
Row 64: Using yarn F.
Row 65: Using yarn K.
Row 66: Using yarn B.

Rows 67 and 68: Using yarn F.
Row 69: Using yarn C.
Row 70: Using yarn A.
Rows 71 and 72: Using yarn H.
Row 73: Using yarn F.
Row 74: Using yarn G.
Row 75: Using yarn A
Rows 76 and 77: Using yarn F.
Row 78: Using yarn A.
Row 79: Using yarn G.
Row 80: Using yarn F.
Rows 81 and 82: Using yarn H.
Row 83: Using yarn A.
Row 84: Using yarn C.
Rows 85 and 86: Using yarn F.
Row 87: Using yarn B.
Row 88: Using yarn K.

Row 89: Using yarn F.
Row 90: Using yarn D.
Row 91: Using yarn A.
Row 92: Using yarn H.
Row 93: Using yarn E.
Row 94: Using yarn H.
Row 95: Using yarn B.
Row 96: Using yarn F.
Row 97: Using yarn G.
Row 98: Using yarn D.
Rows 99 and 100: Using yarn F.
Using yarn C, work in g st for 2 rows.
Cast off.

MAKING UP
For fringe, knot together groups of 3-4 ends along both row-end edges. Trim fringe level.

WHOLESOME
JENNIE ATKINSON

Main image page 68 & 69

YARN

S	M	L	XL	XXL

To fit bust
81-86 91-97 102-107 112-117 122-127 cm
32-34 36-38 40-42 44-46 48-50 in

Rowan Denim and Pima Cotton DK
A DenimMemphis 229

11	12	13	14	15	x 50gm

1 x 50 g ball of Pima Cotton in each of 3
colours for embroidery (B – Dijon 071,
C – Verdigris 074 and D – Clay 075)

NEEDLES
1 pair 3¼mm (no 10) (US 3) needles
1 pair 3¾mm (no 9) (US 5) needles
1 pair 4mm (no 8) (US 6) needles

BUTTONS – 5 x BN1028, from Bedecked.
Please see information page for contact details.

TENSION
Before washing: 20 sts and 28 rows to 10 cm
measured over st st, 20 sts and 25½ rows to
10 cm measured over patt, both using 4mm
(US 6) needles.

After washing: 20 sts and 32 rows to 10 cm
measured over st st, 21 sts and 28½ rows to
10 cm measured over patt, both using 4mm
(US 6) needles.

Tension note: Denim will shrink when
washed for the first time. Allowances have been
made in the pattern for shrinkage (see size
diagram for after washing measurements).

Pattern note: The number of sts varies whilst
working patt. Do **NOT** count sts after patt
rows 8 or 15. All st counts given refer to the
original number of sts and do **NOT** include sts
made on patt rows 8 or 15.

BACK
Using 3¼mm (US 3) needles and yarn A cast
on 91 [103: 115: 127: 139] sts.

★★Beg with a K row, work in st st for 6 rows,
ending with RS facing for next row.
Row 7 (picot row) (RS): K1, ★yfwd, K2tog,
rep from ★ to end.
Change to 4mm (US 6) needles.
Beg with a P row, work in st st for 7 rows,
ending with RS facing for next row and inc
1 st at end of last row.★★
92 [104: 116: 128: 140] sts.
Now work in patt as folls:
Rows 1 and 2: Knit.
Row 3 (RS): K1, ★K2tog, yfwd, rep from
★ to last st, K1.
Rows 4 and 5: Knit.
Row 6: Purl.
Row 7: Knit.
Row 8: K1, ★K2tog, rep from ★ to last st, K1.
Row 9: K1, ★K1, pick up loop lying between
needles and K into front of this loop, rep from

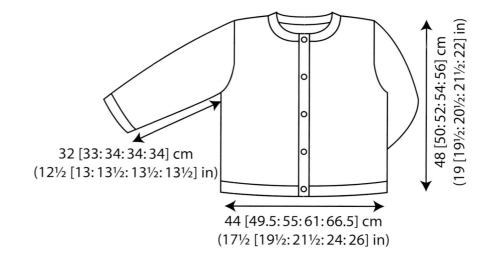

32 [33: 34: 34: 34] cm
(12½ [13: 13½: 13½: 13½] in)

44 [49.5: 55: 61: 66.5] cm
(17½ [19½: 21½: 24: 26] in)

48 [50: 52: 54: 56] cm
(19 [19½: 20½: 21½: 22] in)

* to last st, K1.
Row 10: Purl.
Row 11: Knit.
Rows 12 and 13: As rows 10 and 11.
Row 14: Knit.
Row 15: K1, *(yfwd) twice, K1, rep from * to end.
Row 16: K1, *drop double yfwd, K1, rep from * to end.
Row 17: K1, *(sl 1) 3 times, K2tog, pass 3 slipped sts over, (K1, P1, K1, P1, K1) all into next st, rep from * to last st, K1.
Rows 18 and 19: Knit.
Row 20: Purl.
These 20 rows form patt.
Cont in patt until back meas 29 [30: 31.5: 32.5: 33.5] cm **from picot row**, ending with RS facing for next row.

Shape armholes
Keeping patt correct, cast off 4 [5: 6: 7: 8] sts at beg of next 2 rows. 84 [94: 104: 114: 124] sts.
Dec 1 st at each end of next 3 [5: 7: 9: 11] rows, then on foll 3 [4: 4: 4: 3] alt rows. 72 [76: 82: 88: 96] sts.
Cont straight until armhole meas 22.5 [23.5: 24.5: 25.5: 27] cm, ending with RS facing for next row.

Shape shoulders and back neck
Next row (RS): Cast off 6 [6: 7: 8: 9] sts, patt until there are 17 [19: 20: 22: 24] sts on right needle and turn, leaving rem sts on a holder.
Work each side of neck separately.
Cast off 3 sts at beg of next row, then 6 [6: 7: 8: 9] sts at beg of foll row, and 3 sts at beg of next row.
Cast off rem 5 [7: 7: 8: 9] sts.
With RS facing, rejoin yarn to rem sts, cast off centre 26 [26: 28: 28: 30] sts, patt to end.
Complete to match first side, reversing shapings.

LEFT FRONT
Using 3¼mm (US 3) needles and yarn A cast on 43 [49: 55: 61: 67] sts.
Work as given for back from ** to **. 44 [50: 56: 62: 68] sts.
Now work in patt as given for back until left front matches back to beg of armhole shaping, ending with RS facing for next row.

Shape armhole
Keeping patt correct, cast off 4 [5: 6: 7: 8] sts at beg of next row. 40 [45: 50: 55: 60] sts.
Work 1 row.
Dec 1 st at armhole edge of next 3 [5: 7: 9: 11] rows, then on foll 3 [4: 4: 4: 3] alt rows. 34 [36: 39: 42: 46] sts.
Cont straight until 23 [23: 25: 25: 27] rows less have been worked than on back to beg of shoulder shaping, ending with **WS** facing for next row.

Shape front neck
Keeping patt correct, cast off 7 sts at beg of next row. 27 [29: 32: 35: 39] sts.
Dec 1 st at neck edge of next 5 rows, then on foll 3 [3: 4: 4: 5] alt rows, then on 2 foll 4th rows. 17 [19: 21: 24: 27] sts.

Work 3 rows, ending with RS facing for next row.
Shape shoulder
Cast off 6 [6: 7: 8: 9] sts at beg of next and foll alt row.
Work 1 row.
Cast off rem 5 [7: 7: 8: 9] sts.

RIGHT FRONT
Work as given for left front, reversing all shapings.

SLEEVES
Using 3¼mm (US 3) needles and yarn A cast on 49 [51: 53: 55: 57] sts.
Beg with a K row, work in st st for 6 rows, ending with RS facing for next row.
Row 7 (picot row) (RS): K1, *yfwd, K2tog, rep from * to end.
Change to 4mm (US 6) needles.
Beg with a P row, work in st st for 7 rows, ending with RS facing for next row and inc 1 st at end of last row. 50 [52: 54: 56: 58] sts.
Now work in patt as folls:
Rows 1 and 2: Knit.
Row 3 (RS): Inc in first st, *K2tog, yfwd, rep from * to last st, inc in last st. 52 [54: 56: 58: 60] sts.
Rows 4 and 5: Knit.
Row 6: Purl.
Row 7: Inc in first st, K to last st, inc in last st. 54 [56: 58: 60: 62] sts.
Row 8: K1, *K2tog, rep from * to last st, K1.
Row 9: K1, *K1, pick up loop lying between needles and K into front of this loop, rep from * to last st, K1.
Row 10: Purl.
Row 11: As row 7. 56 [58: 60: 62: 64] sts.
Row 12: Purl.
Rows 13 and 14: Knit.
Row 15: Inc in first st, *(yfwd) twice, K1, rep from * to last st, (yfwd) twice, inc in last st. 58 [60: 62: 64: 66] sts.
Row 16: K2, *drop double yfwd, K1, rep from * to last st, K1.
Row 17: K2 [3: 1: 2: 3], *(sl 1) 3 times, K2tog, pass 3 slipped sts over, (K1, P1, K1, P1, K1) all into next st, rep from * to last 2 [3: 1: 2: 3] sts, K2 [3: 1: 2: 3].
Row 18: Knit.
Row 19: As row 7. 60 [62: 64: 66: 68] sts.
Row 20: Purl.
These 20 rows form patt and beg sleeve shaping.
Cont in patt, shaping sides by inc 1 st at each end of 3rd and every foll 4th row to 68 [74: 80: 88: 96] sts, then on every foll 6th [6th: 6th: 6th: -] row until there are 80 [84: 88: 92: -] sts, taking inc sts into patt.
Cont straight until sleeve meas 36 [37: 38: 38: 38] cm **from picot row**, ending with RS facing for next row.

Shape top
Keeping patt correct, cast off 4 [5: 6: 7: 8] sts at beg of next 2 rows. 72 [74: 76: 78: 80] sts.
Dec 1 st at each end of next 3 rows, then on foll 3 alt rows, then on 2 foll 4th rows.

56 [58: 60: 62: 64] sts.
Work 1 row.
Dec 1 st at each end of next and every foll alt row to 44 sts, then on foll 9 rows, ending with RS facing for next row. 26 sts.
Cast off 4 sts at beg of next 2 rows.
Cast off rem 18 sts.

MAKING UP
Do NOT press.
Join both shoulder seams using back stitch, or mattress stitch if preferred.
Neckband
With RS facing, using 3¾mm (US 5) needles and yarn A, pick up and knit 28 [28: 30: 30: 32] sts up right side of neck, 39 [39: 41: 41: 43] sts from back, then 28 [28: 30: 30: 32] sts down left side of neck. 95 [95: 101: 101: 107] sts.
Beg with a P row, work in st st for 5 rows, ending with RS facing for next row.
Row 6 (picot row) (RS): K1, *yfwd, K2tog, rep from * to end.
Change to 3¼mm (US 3) needles.
Beg with a P row, work in st st for 5 rows, ending with RS facing for next row.
Cast off.
Button band
With RS facing, using 3¾mm (US 5) needles and yarn A, pick up and knit 81 [83: 87: 91: 93] sts evenly down left front opening edge, between picot row of neckband and picot row at lower edge.
Beg with a P row, work in st st for 5 rows, ending with RS facing for next row.
Row 6 (picot row) (RS): K1, *yfwd, K2tog, rep from * to end.
Change to 3¼mm (US 3) needles.
Beg with a P row, work in st st for 5 rows, ending with RS facing for next row.
Cast off.
Buttonhole band
Work as given for button band, picking up sts up right front opening edge and with the addition of 5 buttonholes worked in rows 2 and 10 as folls:
Buttonhole row (RS): K4 [3: 3: 3: 4], *yfwd, K2tog (to make a buttonhole), K16 [17: 18: 19: 19], rep from * 3 times more, yfwd, K2tog (to make 5th buttonhole), K3 [2: 2: 2: 3].
Machine wash all pieces before completing sewing together.
See information page for finishing instructions, setting in sleeves using the set-in method. Fold lower edges of sleeves and body to inside along picot rows and slip stitch in place. Fold neckband to inside along picot row and slip stitch in place. Fold front bands to inside along picot rows and slip stitch in place.
Embroidery
Using photograph as a guide, embroider back, fronts and sleeves as folls:
Using yarn B, work a row of cross stitches over patt rows 5 to 7. Using yarn C, work a line of herringbone stitch over rows 10 to 13. Using yarn D, work a row of cross stitches over patt rows 19 to 1.

INFORMATION

TENSION

Obtaining the correct tension is perhaps the single factor which can make the difference between a successful garment and a disastrous one. It controls both the shape and size of an article, so any variation, however slight, can distort the finished garment. Different designers feature in our books and it is **their** tension, given at the **start** of each pattern, which you must match. We recommend that you knit a square in pattern and/or stocking stitch (depending on the pattern instructions) of perhaps 5 - 10 more stitches and 5 - 10 more rows than those given in the tension note. Mark out the central 10cm square with pins. If you have too many stitches to 10cm try again using thicker needles, if you have too few stitches to 10cm try again using finer needles. Once you have achieved the correct tension your garment will be knitted to the measurements indicated in the size diagram shown at the end of the pattern.

SIZING & SIZE DIAGRAM NOTE

The instructions are given for the smallest size. Where they vary, work the figures in brackets for the larger sizes. **One set of figures refers to all sizes.** Included with most patterns in this magazine is a **'size diagram'**, of the finished garment and its dimensions. The measurement shown at the bottom of each **'size diagram'** shows the garment width 2.5cm below the armhole shaping. To help you choose the size of garment to knit please refer to the sizing guide on page 98.

CHART NOTE

Many of the patterns in the book are worked from charts. Each square on a chart represents a stitch and each line of squares a row of knitting. Each colour used is given a different letter and these are shown in the **materials** section, or in the **key** alongside the chart of each pattern. When working from the charts, read odd rows (K) from right to left and even rows (P) from left to right, unless otherwise

stated. When working lace from a chart it is important to note that all but the largest size may have to alter the first and last few stitches in order not to lose or gain stitches over the row.

WORKING A LACE PATTERN

When working a lace pattern it is important to remember that if you are unable to work both the increase and corresponding decrease and vica versa, the stitches should be worked in stocking stitch.

KNITTING WITH COLOUR

There are two main methods of working colour into a knitted fabric: **Intarsia** and **Fairisle** techniques. The first method produces a single thickness of fabric and is usually used where a colour is only required in a particular area of a row and does not form a repeating pattern across the row, as in the fairisle technique.

Fairisle type knitting: When two or three colours are worked repeatedly across a row, strand the yarn **not** in use loosely behind the stitches being worked. If you are working with more than two colours, treat the "floating" yarns as if they were one yarn and always spread the stitches to their correct width to keep them elastic. It is advisable not to carry the stranded or "floating" yarns over more than three stitches at a time, but to weave them under and over the colour you are working. The "floating" yarns are therefore caught at the back of the work.

FINISHING INSTRUCTIONS

After working for hours knitting a garment, it seems a great pity that many garments are spoiled because such little care is taken in the pressing and finishing process. Follow the text below for a truly professional-looking garment.

PRESSING

Block out each piece of knitting and following the instructions on the ball band press the garment pieces, omitting the ribs. Tip: Take special care to press the edges, as this will make sewing up both

easier and neater. If the ball band indicates that the fabric is not to be pressed, then covering the blocked out fabric with a damp white cotton cloth and leaving it to stand will have the desired effect. Darn in all ends neatly along the selvage edge or a colour join, as appropriate.

STITCHING

When stitching the pieces together, remember to match areas of colour and texture very carefully where they meet. Use a seam stitch such as back stitch or mattress stitch for all main knitting seams and join all ribs and neckband with mattress stitch, unless otherwise stated.

CONSTRUCTION

Having completed the pattern instructions, join left shoulder and neckband seams as detailed above. Sew the top of the sleeve to the body of the garment using the method detailed in the pattern, referring to the appropriate guide:

Straight cast-off sleeves: Place centre of cast-off edge of sleeve to shoulder seam. Sew top of sleeve to body, using markers as guidelines where applicable.

Square set-in sleeves: Place centre of cast-off edge of sleeve to shoulder seam. Set sleeve head into armhole, the straight sides at top of sleeve to form a neat right-angle to cast-off sts at armhole on back and front.

Shallow set-in sleeves: Place centre of cast off edge of sleeve to shoulder seam. Match decreases at beg of armhole shaping to decreases at top of sleeve. Sew sleeve head into armhole, easing in shapings.

Set- in sleeves: Place centre of cast-off edge of sleeve to shoulder seam. Set in sleeve, easing sleeve head into armhole.

Join side and sleeve seams.
Slip stitch pocket edgings and linings into place. Sew on buttons to correspond with buttonholes. Ribbed welts and neckbands and any areas of garter stitch should not be pressed.

ABBREVIATIONS

K	knit
P	purl
st(s)	stitch(es)
inc	increas(e)(ing)
dec	decreas(e)(ing)
st st	stocking stitch (1 row K , 1 row P)
g st	garter stitch (K every row)
beg	begin(ning)
foll	following
rem	remain(ing)
rev st st	reverse stocking stitch (1 row K , 1 row P)
rep	repeat
alt	alternate
cont	continue
patt	pattern
tog	together
mm	millimetres
cm	centimetres
in(s)	inch(es)
RS	right side
WS	wrong side
sl 1	slip one stitch
psso	pass slipped stitch over
p2sso	pass 2 slipped stitches over
tbl	through back of loop
M1	make one stitch by picking up horizontal loop before next stitch and knitting into back of it
M1P	make one stitch by picking up horizontal loop before next stitch and purling into back of it
yfwd	yarn forward
yrn	yarn round needle
meas	measures
0	no stitches, times or rows
–	no stitches, times or rows for that size
yon	yarn over needle
yfrn	yarn forward round needle
wyib	with yarn at back

CROCHET TERMS

UK crochet terms and abbreviations have been used throughout. The list below gives the US equivalent where they vary.

ABBREV.	UK	US
dc	double crochet	single crochet
htr	half treble	half double crochet
tr	treble	double crochet
dtr	double treble	treble

EXPERIENCE RATING

● = Easy, straight forward knitting

● ● = Suitable for the average knitter

● ● ● = For the more experienced knitter

BUTTONS AND RIBBONS USED IN THIS MAGAZINE ARE SOURCED FROM:

Bedecked Limited, 1 Castle Wall, Back Fold, Hay-on-Wye, Via Hereford, HR3 5EQ

www.bedecked.co.uk
Shop tel: 01497 822769
Email: thegirls@bedecked.co.uk

WASH CARE INFORMATION

You may have noticed over the last season that the wash care symbols on our ball bands and shade cards have changed. This is to bring the symbols we use up to date and hopefully help you to care for your knitting and crochet more easily. Below are the symbols you are likely to see and a brief explanation of each.

MACHINE WASH SYMBOLS

Machine Wash, Cold — Machine Wash, Cold, Gentle — Machine Wash, Warm — Machine Wash, Warm, Gentle

HAND WASH SYMBOLS

Do Not Wash — Hand Wash, Normal — Hand Wash, Cold — Hand Wash, Warm

DRY CLEAN SYMBOLS

Do Not Dry Clean — Dry Clean — Dry Clean, in Certain Solvents, Consult Cleaner — Dry Clean, Any Solvent

IRONING SYMBOLS

Do Not Iron — Iron Low Heat — Iron Medium Heat

DO NOT BLEACH SYMBOL

Do Not Bleach

DRYING SYMBOLS

Do Not Tumble Dry — Tumble Dry, Gentle, Low Heat — Dry Flat in Shade — Dry Flat — Do Not Wring

ROWAN OVERSEAS STOCKISTS

For more information on overseas stockists and Mail Order details please contact the
Rowan distributor / agent listed under each country. 'ROWAN AT ....' stockists carry a large range of Rowan Yarns.

AUSTRALIA

Melbourne	Australian Country Spinners Pty Ltd (Dist)	Level 7, 409 St. Kilda Road	tkohut@auspinners.com.au	3004	(03) 9380 3830	
Albert Park	Wool Baa	124 Bridport Street	sales@woolbaa.com	3206	(03) 9690 6633	www.woolbaa.com
Berry	Sew & Tell	Shop 2, 133 Queens St		2535	(02) 4464 2428	
Hornsby	Hornsby Wool & Craft Nook	Shop 3-3A, 5-31 Florence St		2077	(02) 9482 4924	hornsbywool_craft@bigpond.com
Macquarie	Cassidys Dept Store	Jamison Centre		2614	(02) 6251 1911	cassidys@dragnet.com.au
Melbourne	Clegs	60 Elizabeth St		3000	(03) 9654 7677	
Melbourne	**Sunspun (Rowan At)**	**185 Canterbury Road**	shop@sunspun.com.au	**3126**	**(03) 9830 1609**	**www.sunspun.com.au**
Moonah	Tasmanian Wool Suppliers	58 Main Road		7009	(03) 6278 1800	woolsuppliers@bigpond.com
Mosman Park	Calico and Ivy	1 Glyde Street	info@calicoandivy.com,	6012	(08) 9383 3794	www.calicohouse.com.au
Mount Eliza	Windmills & Roses	36-38 Ranelagh Drive		3930	(03) 9787 4949	
Sydney	Tapestry Craft	50 York Street		2000	(02) 929 8588	
Wembley	Woolly Latte's	46-48 Grantham Street		6014	(08) 9287 1492	

AUSTRIA

Baden	Stick + Strick	Hauptplatz 8	susanne.hasieber@stickundstrick.at	2500	0043/2252/49570	www.stickundstrick.at
Feldkirch	**Zum Schwarzen Schaf (Rowan At)**	**Schlossergasse 1**	wolle@zumschwarzenschaf.at	**6800**	**0043/552281072**	**www.zumschwarzenschaf.at**
Hornstein	ROWAN AT Wollerei	Mühlgasse 5	shop@wollerei.at	7053	0043/2689/42528	www.wollerei.at
Innsbruck	Kogler Anton	Museumstr. 6		6020	0043/512584186	
Kitzbuehel	Kitzbuehel Handarbeiten	Im Gries Nr. 23		6370	0043/535672646	
Kolsass	Wolle + Staune (Sabine Kahn)	Auweg 2a	kahn@wolleundstaune.at	6114	0043/664/2629093	www.wolleundstaune.at
Salzburg	Graf Robert	Schrannengasse 2		5020	0043/662876038	
Wels	Zimmermann & Kroboth Gesmbh	Salzburgerstrasse 140		4600	0043/724241291	
Wien	Cadek Maria	Schultergasse 2		1010	0043/1/5354412	
Wien	**Zwei Glatt Zwei Verkehrt (Rowan At)**	**Josefstaeddter Str. 14**	wolle@zweiglattzweiverkehrt.at	**1080**	**0043/1/4035736**	**www.zweiglattzweiverkehrt.at**
Wien	Stick + Strick	Simmeringer Haupstrasse 86	susanne.hasieber@stickundstrick.at	1110	0043/1/7494268	www.stickundstrick.at
Wien	Wolle fuer Mode Fleischmann	Neubaugasse 59/3		1070	0043/1/5233394	
Wien	Wollstube Beck	Kalvarienbergasse 32		1170	0043/1/4037211	
Wien	Wollboutique Pinguin	Alserstrasse 21		1080	0043/1/4080010	

BELGIUM

Aalter	Angela's Wolboetiek	Stationstraat 40	angela.vercruysse@telenet.be	9880	09 / 374 27 28	
Antwerpen	**ROWAN AT Lana**	**Anselmostraat 92**	info@lana-antwerpen.be	**2018**	**03/ 238 70 17**	**www.lana-antwerpen.be**
Arlon	Brin De Soie	Rue des Faubourg 19		6700	063/ 445 680	
Brugge	Vonck Kaat	Walweinstraat 3		8000	050/340345	www.stikkestek@telenet.be
Brussel	Art et Fil	25, Rue du Baillie		1000	02/ 647 64 51	
Eeklo	Hobbyfarm	Pastoor Bontestraat, 37		9900	09/3786664	
Gent	Stoffenidee	Burgstraat 38 A		9000		annemarie_dw@yahoo.co.uk
Geraardsbergen	Maxime's Hobby	Guilleminlaan 237		9500	054/411145	
Hamme	Guy's Naaicentrum	Roodkruisstraat 98	info@guysnaaicentrum.be	9220	052/ 47 18 05	www.guysnaaicentrum.be
Ieper	Origami	Jules Capronstraat 10		8900	057/21.60.22	hobbyshop-origami@skynet.be
Jemeppe	Boite a fils	Rue Joseph Wettinck, 40		4101	04/2338710	
Kortrijk	Alle steken op een rij	Grote Kring 14		8500		
Kortrijk	Filati	Steenpoort 11		8500	056/210513	filatie-kortrijk@skynet.be
Leuven	t Wolwinkeltje	Parijsstraat 25		3000	016 22 75 48	deforcerosemie@hotmail.com
Lokeren	De Wolkamer	Gentsesteenweg 477		9160	09/355 20 55	
Mere	De Breinaald	Nieuwstraat 10		9420	0475/480234	
Merelbeke	t Wolhuisje	Oude Gaversesteenweg 45		9820	0497/80 61 71	
Sint Truiden	Govaerts	Van Mechelen, Markt 61			011/682288	
Torhout	Lana Exclusif	Oostenstraat 88A		8820	050/21.36.32	www.lana-exclusief.be
Tournai	Paprika Cotton	rue Saint-Martin 62		7500	069/23.53.83	www.paprikacotton.be
Vilvoorde	Tegendraads	Leuvensestraat 110		1800	02/2537484	
Virton	La Compagnie des Laines	Grand Rue 56	ornellaf@skynet.be	6760	0474 675047	
Wilsele	D.Yarns	P Van Langendoncklaan 17	d_van_nueten@hotmail.com	3012	(016) 20 13 81	

CANADA

South Carolina	Greer	Westminster Fibers (Distributor)	8 Shelter Drive		29650	www.westminsterfibers.com
Alberta	**Calgary**	**Pudding Yarns (Rowan At)**	**1516-6th St, SW**		**T2R 0Z8**	**403 244 2996**
Alberta	Edmonton	River City Yarns	3438 99th St	rivercityyarns@shaw.ca	T6E 5X5	780 477-9276
British Columbia	Victoria	Beehive Wool Shop	1700 Douglas Street	beehivewoolshop@telus.net	V8W 2G7	250 385 2727
British Columbia	Port Moody	Black Sheep Yarns	88 Clarke St		V3H 0B6	778 355-9665
British Columbia	Vancouver	Three Bags Full	4458 Main St		V5V 3R3	604 874 9665
British Columbia	**North Vancouver**	**Urban Yarns (Rowan At)**	**3111 Highland Boulevard**	knitting@urbanyarns.ca	**V7R 2X5**	**604 984 2214 www.urbanyarns.ca**
British Columbia	**Vancouver**	**Urban Yarns (Rowan At)**	**4437 West 10th Ave**	urbanyarns@telus.net	**V6R 2H8**	**604 228 1122 www.urbanyarns.ca**
British Columbia	Richmond	Wool and Wicker	120-12051 2nd Ave			604 275 1239
Ontario	Perth	Janie H Knits	528 Glen Tay Rd	info@janiehknits.com	K7H 3C3	613 326-0626 www.janiehknits.com
Ontario	Barrie	Knit & Quilt.com	79 Anne Street South		L4N 2E2	705 737 4422
Ontario	Milton	Main St.Yarns	15 Martin St, Unit AM8	info@mainstyarns.com	L9T 2R1	905 693-4299 www.mainstyarns.com
Ontario	**Toronto**	**Romni Wools Ltd (Rowan At)**	**658 Queen St West**		**M6J 1E5**	**416 703 0202**
Ontario	**Ancaster**	**The Needle Emporium (Rowan At)**	**420 Wilson St. East**	gisele@woolnthings.com	**L9G 2C3**	**800 667-9167 www.needleemporium.com**
Ontario	**Ottawa**	**Wool NThings (Rowan At)**	**1439 Youville Drive, Unit 20**	gisele@woolnthings.com	**K1C 4M8**	**613 841 8689 www.woolnthings.com**
Quebec	**Montreal**	**Effiloche (Rowan At)**	**6252 Saint Hubert**	ginette@effiloche.com	**H2S 2M2**	**514 276-2547**
Quebec	Montreal	Mouline Yarns	2657 Notre-Dame West	svetlana@moulineyarns.com	H3J 1N9	514 935-4401 www.moulineyarns.com

CHINA

Shanghai	Coats Shanghai Ltd. (Distributor)	No. 9 Building, Baosheng Road, Songjiang Industrial Zone	victor.li@coats.com		86 21 5774 3733
Beijing	Sanli Knitting Fashion Co., Ltd.	ROOM 204, Yunding Center, Block 2 Xiluoyuan, Fengtai.	zka@sina.com		+86--(0)10-88893570; 88865049
Shanghai	Shanghai Yujun Co. Ltd	Room 2404, World Trade Tower No.500 Guandong Road	jessechang@vip.163.com	200002	+86--(0)21-60529096; 60529097; 60529098

DENMARK

Copenhagen	Coats HP A/S (Distributor)	Tagensvej 85C, St.tv		9000	45 35 86 90 49	
Ålborg	Rowan AT Design Vaerkstedet	Boulevarden 9	butik@design-vaerkstedet.dk	9000	45 98 12 07 13	
Århus	Rowan AT Inger`s	Volden 19	design.club@mail.dk	8000	45 86 19 40 44	www.design-club.dk
Blåvand	Rowan AT Ho Strik	Hovej 21	info@hostrik.dk	6857	45 75 27 54 03	www.hostrik.dk
Farum	Fingerbollet	Farum Hovedgade 83	fingerboellet@gmail.com	3520	45 44 95 70 01	
Fredriksberg	Wilfert's	Gammel Kongevej 102	britta@wilferts.dk	1850	45 33 22 54 90	www.wilferts.dk
Gilleleje	Gilleje Stof og Garn	Stationsvej 1		3250	45 48 30 31 10	
Helsinge	Uldgalleriet	Østergade 2	gitte@uldgalleriet.dk	3200	45 48 79 71 36	
Hornslet	Filt	Tingvej 7B	fischer-filt@mail.dk	8543	45 86 97 51 33	www.fischer-filt.dk
Horsens	**Rowan AT Strikkekunsten**	**Søndergade 41 B**	kontakt@strikkekunsten.dk	**8700**	**45 75 65 16 54**	**www.strikkekunsten.dk**
Hørsholm	Engle Stof	Usserød Kongevej 10 A	englestof@mail.dk	2970	45 45 86 33 78	
København	**Rowan AT Sommerfuglen**	**Vandkunsten 3, Kbh.K**	mail@sommerfuglen.dk	**1467**	**45 33 32 82 90**	**www.sommerfuglen.dk**
København	ROWAN AT Uldstedet	Fiolstræde 13, Kbh.K	uldstedet@uldstedet.dk	1171	45 33 91 17 71	www.uldstedet.dk
Kolding	Martha	Sondergade 4	martha-garn@webspeed.dk	6600	45 75 52 48 08	
Lyngby	**Rowan AT Uldstedet**	**Gl. Jernbanevej 7**	uldstedet@uldstedet.dk	**2800**	**45 45 88 10 88**	**www.uldstedet.dk**
Nyborg	Ulrikka	Nørregade 13	ulrikkagarn@yahoo.dk	5800	45 65 30 22 80	www.ulrikkagarn.dk
Randers	Uldma	Rosengade 2	salg@uldma.dk	8900	45 86 46 64 66	www.uldma.dk
Ribe	Ribes Broderi & Garn	Dagmarsgade 4	symaskineland@symaskineland.dk	6760		
Roskilde	**Rowan AT Garnhøkeren**	**Karen Olsdatterstræde 9**		**4000**	**45 46 37 20 63**	
Skanderborg	Rowan AT Stof & Sy	Adelgade 123	info@stofogsy.dk	8660	45 86 52 02 45	www.stofogsy.dk
Slangerup	Rowan AT Paradisets Bamser, Tøj og Brugskunst	Kvinderupvej 17	pia.freck@mail.tele.dk	3550	45 47 33 58 66	www.butikparadiset.dk
Svendborg	Ulrikka	Gerritsgade 2	ulrikkagarn@yahoo.dk	5700	45 62 22 21 17	www.ulrikkagarn.dk
Tarm	Uldgården	Fjerbækvej 12, Vodstrup	uldgaarden@uldgaarden.dk	6880	45 97 37 42 71	www.uldgaarden.dk
Thisted	**Rowan AT Strikkefeen**	**Vestergade 18 C**	strikkefeen@hotmail.com	**7700**	**45 97 92 12 33**	**www.strikkefeenthisted.dk**
Varde	Cotton Wear	Smedegade 9	cccsejunge@hotmail.com	6800	45 75 22 33 00	www.cottonwear.dk
Vejle	**Rowan AT Garn & Design Arne S. Hansen**	**Vestergade 45**	garn-design@mail.dk	**7100**	**45 75 82 02 49**	**www.garn-design.dk**
Viborg	Mathilde	St. Sct. Mikkelsgade 37		8800	45 86 61 50 22	

FAERO ISLANDS

Klaksvik	Fa Búnin	N.P. Gøta 20, Postrum 282		F-700	00298 455210
Torshavn	Igloo SP/F Spuni	Sverresgøta 19, Postbox 181		F-110	00298 315264

FINLAND

Kerava	Coats Opti Crafts Oy (Distributor)	Ketjutie 3	coatsopti.sales@coats.com	04220	(358) 9 274871	www.coatscrafts.fi

City	Name	Address	Email	Postal	Phone	Website
Angers	Maison Marot	12 rue Champeronniere		49100	02 41 88 37 66	
Bordeaux	La Lainerie	22 rue des Ayres		33000	05 56 81 43 92	
Colmar	Ambiance Laine	5 rue des Pretres	info@ambiance-laine.fr	68000	03 89 41 87 71	
Dijon	Planete Laines	20 rue du Chateau		21000	03 80 30 37 96	
Joigny	Lady Laine	47 bis rue Gambetta	ladylaine.joigny@wanadoo.fr	89300	03 86 62 21 21	
Le Havre	Mercerie Zip	81 rue de Paris		76600	02 35 21 61 73	
Le Plessis Robinson	La Mercerie Carrée	8 place François Spoerry	www.la-mercerie-carree.fr	92350	01 46 32 61 74	www.lestrouvaillesdamandine.com/boutique
Levallois-Perret	Laines en Vogue	36 rue Gabriel Peri	contact@millemilliersdemailles.fr	923000	01 47 57 58 64	www.millemilliersdemailles.
Lognes	Les Trouvailles d'Amandine	3 Grande Allée Le Nôtre	contact@lestrouvaillesdamandine.com	77185	09 50 37 93 95	www.ambiance-laine.fr
Montpellier	Anne Ouvrages	28 rue Paul Brousse		34000	04 67 92 50 92	
Moret sur Loing	La Patte de l'Ours	32 rue de l'Eglise	lapattedelours@orange.fr	77250	01.60.70.15.17	www.la-patte-de-lours.blogspot.com
Nancy	2 Aiguilles dans la Cafetière	5 rue Gustave Simon		54000	03 83 39 46 70	
Nantes	Laines, Fil et blablala	6 rue du Chapeau Rouge, .	benedicte.mosser@orange.fr	44000	02 40 80 58 24,	www.laine-fil-et-blablabla.com
Orléans	Au Fil d'Emma	79 Bvd A Martin		45000	09 50 14 85 84	www.aufildemma.com
Osmoy	So ! Fil	6 chemin du moutier	tricothe.sofil@gmail.com,	78910	01.34.87.29.15	http://tricothe.jimdo.com
Paris (16)	Le Grenier du Ranelagh - Elle Tricote	7 rue Duban		75016	01 45 20 11 80	
Paris (7)	Le Bon Marche	115 rue du Bac		75007	01 44 39 80 00	
Paris (9)	Le Comptoir	26 rue Cadet		75009	01 42 46 20 72	http://lecomptoir.canalblog.com
Poitiers	La Mercerie	4 rue Magenta		86000	05 49 52 59 22	
Rennes	LTM	11 rue Poullain Duparc		35000	02 99 78 20 60	
Strasbourg	Elle Tricote	8 rue du coq		67000	03 88 23 03 13	
Thonon Les Bains	Au Vieux Rouet	7 rue Ferdinand Dubouloz		74200	04 50 71 07 33	
Tours	La Boîte à Laine	37, rue du Grand Marché		37000	02 47 37 76 47	

City	Name	Address	Email	Postal	Phone	Website
Ahlen	Agnes Schubert	Gemmericher Str 39		59229	02382 - 72712	
Ammersbek	Angelika Lehmann	Schwarzerweg 21		22949	04532/4641	
Arnstein	Jutta Heurung	Marktstr. 8		97450	09363/6975	
Au a. Inn	Helga Holzner	Steinbach 1	bachmair-helga@t-online.de	83546	08073-916666	
Backnang	Wollstube Wollin	Marktstr. 28	info@wolle-backnang.de	71522	07191/902828	www.wolle-backnang.com
Bad Neuenahr-Ahrweiler	Dat Lädche	Niederhutstr. 17	dat-laedche_adams@t-online.de	53474	02641/4464	
Bad Soden	Beate Schilb	Hasselstr. 19		65812	06196/644113	
Bamberg	Friedericke Pfund	Promenadestr. 18	wollstudio@fritzi.pfund.de	96047	0951-202173	www.home.t-online.de/home/fritzi.pfund
Bayreuth	Strickart	Kirchplatz 7	strickwerk@gmx.de	95444	0921/5304870	www.strickart-cafe.de
Berlin	Claudia Thees	Bahnhofstr. 3		12555	030 /6562697	
Berlin	Holz & Wolle	Warnemünder Str. 29		14199	030/83222762	
Berlin	idee.Creativmarkt Berlin	Tauentzienstr. 21-24		10789	030/21230	
Berlin	Loops	Wörther Str. 19		10405	030/44054934	
Berlin	Jolanta Schulze	Aßmannstr. 40		12587	030-65484239	
Berlin	Kerstin Hering	Helene-Weigl-Platz 13		12681	030 66 30 80 55	
Berlin	Birgit Küttner	Teltower Damm 34		14169	030-8026500	
Biberach	Regina Kreuzer-Krause	Gymnasiumstr. 14		88400	07351/1889980	
Bielefeld	WollZauber	Vilsendorferstr. 45		33739	05206/2992	
Bielefeld	Kercan	Friedrich-Ebert-Strasse 2		33602	0521/60296	
Bielefeld	Granellino	Gotenstrasse 16		33647	0521/444425	
Bochum	Britta Bödecker	Grabenstr. 38		44787	0234/6408990	
Bonn-Duisdorf	Petra Klein	Rochusstr. 245		53123	0228-39047787	www.atelier-rosenbaum.de
Braunschweig	Susanne Wenke	Lange Str. 35		38100	0177/3447082	www.stil-bluete.net
Bremen	Wollstube A. Heyn	Brüggeweg 40-42		28309	0421/413869	
Bühl	Jasmin Radel	Hauptstr. l 70	mail@veilchenschoen-wollhandel.de	77815	07223/8010743	www.veilchenschoen-wollhandel.de
Coburg	Ramona Heinrichs	Kirchgasse 7	zuerdelsocke@aol.com	96450	09561/6752544	
Dachau	Barbara Reischl	Konrad-Adenauer-Str. 20	info@cotton-club-dachau.com	85221	08131-736859	www.cotton-club-dachau.com
Dannenberg	Annette Gierow	Lange Str. 32		29451	05861/976050	
Darmstadt	G.u.B.Bachmann	Gute Gartenstr.36		64291	06151/372680	
Detmold	Handarbeitsgeschäft Müller	Krummestr. 19	info@handarbeitenmueller.de	32756	05231/28216	www.handarbeitenmueller.de
Dornhan	Regina Temelkoski	Roßgartenstr. 14		72175	07455/2785	
Dresden	Strick und Faden	Rothenburger Str. 14	nachstrickundfaden@web.de	1099	0351/8104086	
Düsseldorf	Woll Duo	Scharnhorststr. 16		40477	0211/467776	
Elmshorn	Wollmond	Kirchenstr. 8		25335	04121-2611751	
Erlangen	Christa Peters-Keller,	Hauptstr. 115	shop@wollkontor-erlangen.de	91054	09131/204327	www.wollkontor-erlangen.de
Erlangen	Joana Leyer	Gundstr. 13	info@joana-leyer.de	91054	09131/6873290	www.joana-leyer.de
Esslingen	Sigrid Weyers-Bäuerle	Apothekergasse 13		73728	0711/354402	
Fallingbostel	Dagmar Ohlsen	Walsroder Str. 5		29683	05162/909320	
Felsberg	Wollstube	Untergasse 30		34587	05662-3741	
Finningen	Claudia Hager	Bergstr. 3	HagerClaudia@aol.com	89435	09074-921008,	www.handbags-and-more.de
Flensburg	Claus Greve	Dorotheenstrasse 24		24937	0177-1972315	
Frankfurt	Lana	Große Bockenheimer Str.35		60313	069/281758	
Frankfurt	Wolle-Boutique	Eckenheimer Landstr. 34		60318	069/59792080	
Frankfurt a.M.	Heidi Reuthlingshöfer	Marburger Str. 4		60487	069-71588980	
Freiburg	Welt der Handarbeit	Salzstr.37-39		79098	0761/2172135	
Freudenberg	Gabriele Rosler	Mittelstrasse 2		57258	02734/436999	
Friedrichsdorf	Claudia Hahn	Hugenottenstr. 85a		61381	06172/72498	
Gauting	Dr. Melanie Graeb	Grubmühlerfeldstr. 25	mgraeb@aol.com	82131	089-89357858	www.bonifaktur.de
Geretsried	Spinnrad-Handarbeiten	Drosselweg 1	spinnrad-handarbeiten@web.de	82538	08171/649100	
Göttingen	Wollzauber	Kurze Geismarstr. 40		37073	0551/486117	
Günzburg	Nähzentrum Fuchs	Augsburger Str. 28	Naehzentrum-Fuchs@gmx.de	89312	08221-1059,	
Hamburg	Hand-Werk	Im Mühlenkamp 44		22303	040/2798254	
Hamburg	Koch-Mühler	Hudtwalckerstr. 22		22299	040/47195680	
Hamburg	Pur-Pur-Wolle	Heußweg 41b,	info@purpurwolle.de	20255	040/4904579	www.purpurwolle.de
Hamburg	Wollboutique	Wandsbeker Chaussee 315	service@wollboutique.de	22089	040/2007620	
Hamburg	Wollvik	Ratsmühlendamm 26	wollvik@web.de	22335	040/41543767	
Hannover	Zeier-Möller Sophie	Sallstr. 81		30171	0511/3009622	
Heilbronn	Wollke	Am Kieselmarkt 2	wollke@t-online.de	74072	07131/629357	
Heppenheim	Alpaka	Friedrichstr. 23		64646	06252/2889	
Hilden	Ellen Klaft	Worrington Platz 28		40721	02103-298249	
Hohenhameln-Soßnar	Next Systems	Kleine Sackstr. 2	info@wollfactory.de	31249	05128/4091366	www.wollfactory.de
Homburg	Filatum	Saarbrücker Str.3	Ibeyersdorf@t-online.de	66424	06841/171300	
Ibbenbüren	Pottmeier	Unterer Markt 4		49477	05451/936411	
Kamp-Lintfort	Elfi's Wollwelt	Mörser Strasse 270		47475	02842/10 226	
Karlsruhe	Gabriele Bodesohn	Marienstr. 77-79		76137	0721/7597840	
Kassel	Christina Geyer	Friedrich-Ebert-Str. 147		34117	0561/710029	
Kelkheim	Kelkheimer Masche	Höchster Str. 8,		65779	06195/975678	
Kiel	Dörte Dietrich	Damaschkeweg 50a		24113	0431/2405493	www.wollwerkstatt-kiel.de
Kirchlengern	Corinna Schumacher	Lübbecker Str 5		32278	05223-9859721	
Koblenz	Birgit Reich	An der Liebfrauenkirche 11		56068	0261-9733224	
Köln	Maschenkunst	Christophstr. 9-11	info@maschenkunst.de	50670	0221/2783489	www.maschenkunst.de
Köln	Rapp	Goltsteinstr. 96		50568	0221-16906088	
Landsberg	Christel Sellwig	Herkom.Passage 111		86899	08191/21245	
Landshut	Barbara Zeilhofer	Kirchgasse 247		84028	0871/2764217	
Langgöns	Simone Junker	Breitgasse 12		35428	06403-940665	
Leutenbach	Astrid Bauchrowitz	Am Pfarrgarten 3		91359	09199-695460	
Leutkirch	Brigitta Schwarz-Frehner	Marktstr. 30	info@diezweigstelle.de	88299	07561-9834566	
Mainz	Andrea Seufert	Fuststr. 2		55166	06131-2407196	
Marburg	Saskia Krieger	Frauenbergstr. 13		35039	06421-34230	
Meckenheim	Heidrun Bergau	Neuer Markt 17		53340	02225-887969	
Melle	Freya Hoffknecht			49326	05428/927877	
Mönchengladbach	Gertrud Huppertz GmbH	Lüripperstr. 373 – 375		41065	373 – 375, 41065	
Moritzburg	Wollwunderland Schulze	Schlossallee 29	salonrokoko@web.de	01468	03520/799395	www.salon-rokoko.de
München	Brigitte Kreische	Nordendstr. 17	info@strickeria-muenchen.de	80799	089/88904532	www.strickeria-muenchen.de
Münster	Lacatus	Hörster Strasse 56	lacatusch@web.de	48143	0170/4733337	
Norderney	Patchwork-Stübchen	Jann-Berghaus-Str.13		26548	04932/927160	
Nürnberg	Anita Hammel	Weinmarkt 10	mail@tollewolle-online.de	90403	0911-209497	www.tollewolle-online.de
Oberasbach	Chic In Strick	Am Rathaus 14		90522	0911/697592	
Oberursel	Daniela Queißer	Rathausplatz 6		61440	06171/586555	
Oppenheim	Wolle in der Villa	Friedrich-Ebert Str.83	wolle-seufert@t-online.de	55276	06133/2131	
Osnabrück	Woll-Perle	Hakenstr. 3		49074	0541/258561	
Paderborn	Nicole Kersek-Meilwes	Kürassierweg 8		33104	05254-10126	
Plauen	Heike Bromnitz	Stresemannstr. 6		08523	03741 221316	www.naehstuebl-bromnitz.de
Potsdam	Rosmarie Adler	Friedrich-Ebert-Str. 27		14467	0331-2800609	
Ratingen	Wollkörbchen (Frau Szczygielski)	Turmstr. 30		40878	02102-80844	
Regensburg	Birgit Birner	Am Peterstor 1	Strickeria@gmx.net	93047	0941-58612300	
Reutlingen	Wolle und Mehr	Metzgerstr. 64		72764	07121/310488	
Salzhausen	Wollart Ute Rudat	Eyendorfer Str. 3		21376	04172-969123	
Schlüchtern	Dagmar Marburger	Obertorstr.8		36381	06661-1337	

GERMANY (cont)

Sindelfingen	Hilde´s Stricklädle	Obere Vorstadt 26		71063	07031/688183	
Soest	Der Faden	Potsdamer Platz 1		59494	02921/3192277	
Solingen	Sabine Ziel	Grünewalderstr. 1		42657	0212-2437886	
Stadtlohn	Wolle und Design	Görkeskamp 6	info@wolleunddesign.de	48703	02563/98208	www.wolleunddesign.de
Suhl	Steffi Hengelhaupt	Friedrich-König-Str. 5		98527	03681-723704	
Titisee-Neustadt	Ingeborg Steiert	Scheuerlenstr. 24		79822	07651/7218	
Troisdorf	Olga Wanner	Kölner Str. 83		53840	02241-72974	
Übach-Palenberg	Ute Ströbel	Von-Liebig-Str. 42		52531	02451/909205	
Ulm	Wolle & Ideen	Pfauengasse 17	Heike@Redlinghaus.de	89073	0731/619491	
Undorf	Roswitha Baierl	Hofmarktr. 38	rosis_wollstube@yahoo.de	93152	09404-6410341	
Vincenzbronn	Anita Krehn	Vincenzbronner Hauptstr. 26		90613	09105/9319	
Waghäusl-Wiesental	Petra Holzer	Mannheimer Str. 7		68753	07254-7799741	www.Bastelstubediesunddas.de
Wedel	Wolland	Rollberg 3		22880	04103/180455	
Weimar	Steffi Hengelhaupt	Eisfeld 3		99423	03643/901748	
Weinheim	Heide Fabian	Giselherstr. 19		69469	06201/256910	
Westerkappeln	Mode- und Wollpalette	Bahnhofstrasse 6		49492	05404/899939	
Wetter-Volmarstein	Christiane A. Struck	Osterfeldstrasse 11		58300	02335/8451940	
Wiesbaden	Fil a Fil Der Woll-Laden	Rathausstr. 61		65203	0611-66969	
Wuppertal	Strick und Stick	Auer Schulstrasse 5	d.teege-schitthelm@hotmail.de	42103	0202/4292104	

HOLLAND

Almere-Haven	Het Spoeltje	Meerstraat 52	handwerkzaak@hetspoeltje.nl	1353 AZ	036-5216817	www.hetspoeltje.nl
Amersfoort	H.W. Mur	Langestraat 13		3811 AA	033 461 7837	www.happytown.nl
Amsterdam	**ROWAN AT de Afstap (Lonnie Bussink)**	**Oude Leliestraat 12**	**info@afstap.nl**	**1015 AW**	**020-6231445**	**www.afstap.nl**
Bergen	**ROWAN AT Finlandia**	**Kleine Dorpsstraat 26**		**1861 KN**	**0725 894642**	
Dalen	**ROWAN AT Breiweb**	**Hoofdstraat 44**	**info@breiweb.nl**	**7751 GD**	**052 4551597**	**www.breiweb.nl**
De Rijp	Sylka Mode	Rechtestraat, 118		1483 BG	031/299674548	
Eindhoven	**ROWAN AT Breimode Brigitte**	**Ouverture 212**	**info@brigitte-handwerken.nl**	**5629 PX**	**040-2435576**	**www.brigitte-handwerken.nl**
Etten-Leur	De Wolboetiek	Bisschopsmolenstraat 169		4876 AL	076-5022597	
Groningen	Sajet	Guldenstraat 6	sales@sajet.com	9712 CE	050/314 09 00	www.sajet.com
Heerlen	Ut Bolke	Benzenraderweg 92		6417 SV	045 /571 64 51	
Hoorn	FA Schouten	Grote Noord, 120		1621 KM	031/229215682	
Joure	Ajoure	Pastorielaan 2	www.ajoure.nl	8501 EZ	051/3413344	
Kampen	Pingouin wol & handwerken	Oudestraat 20	pingouinkampen@uwnet.nl	8261 CP	038-3322811	
Leiden	**ROWAN AT Ribbels**	**Pieterskerk-Choorsteeg 18**	**christa.kroon@ribbels.nl**	**2311 TR**	**071 5133126**	**www.ribbels.nl**
Nieuwpoort	**ROWAN AT De Schapekop**	**Hoogstraat 30**	**info@deschapekop.nl**	**2965 AL**	**0184-602678**	**www.deschapekop.nl**
Oldenzaal	**ROWAN AT Lohuis**	**Steenstraat 26**	**t.lohuis@planet.nl**	**7571 BK**	**05415-12626**	**www.lohuis-tijhuis.nl**
Roden	Spinnewiel	Raadhuisstraat 2		9301 AB	050/5018893	
Rotterdam	Lydialaine	Goudsesingel 231 A		3031 EK	010/4136697	
Sittard	Wollstreet	Rijksweg Noord 61	info@wollstreet.nl	6131 CJ	0464-586330	
Someren	Het Weverke	Molenstraat 24		5711EW	0493-492092	
Utrecht	**ROWAN AT Modilaine**	**Lijnmarkt 22**	**Johannes.aikema@orange.nl**	**3511 KH**	**030-2328911**	
Voorburg	De Breikorf	Koningin Julianalaan 274	info@debreikorf.nl	2274 JR	070 3871286	www.breikorf.nl
Wapenveld	Klaziens Kreatie	Stationsweg 20		8191 AH	038/447 05 74	www.klazienskreatie.nl
Woudsend	Hannah Tricotage	Carmelieterstraat, 6		8551 RJ	031/514592343	
Zuidlaren	**ROWAN AT Ryahuis**	**Telefoonstraat 26**		**9471 EN**	**050-4092618**	
Zwolle	Rits-in	Assendorperstraat 105		8012 DH	0031/38421261	
	Ryahuis te Zuidlaren		info@ryahuis.nl			www.ryahuis.nl
	Rits-in te Zwolle		ritsin@planet.nl			www.ritsin.nl

HONG KONG

East Unity Company Ltd.	Unit B2, 7/F., Block B, Kailey Industrial Centre, 12 Fung Yip Street, Chai Wan, Hong Kong		eastunityco@yahoo.com.hk	(852)2869 7110

ICELAND

Reykjavik	*Rowan At Storkurinn (Dist)*	*Laugavegur 59*	*storkurinn@simnet.is*	*101*	*551 8258*	*www.storkurinn.is*

ITALY

Milano	*Coats cucirini srl (Distributor)*	*Viale sarca n° 223*		*20126*

JAPAN

Kobe	Hyogo	Union Wool	1-30-22 Kitanagasadori, Chuouku		650-0012	81-078-331-8854	
Oosaka	Oosaka	Masuzakiya	4-5-4 Kawaramachi, Chuouku		541-0048	81-06-6222-1110	
Tokyo	Tokyo	Mitsubaya	1-1-1 Minamiaoyama, Minatoku		107-0062	81-03-3404-1677	
Tokyo	Tokyo	Mitsukoshi Department Store	Hobby & Craft Salon 8F Mitsukoshi New Bild. 1-4-1 Nihonbashi Chuouku		103-8001	81-03-3273-6500	
Chiba	Chiba	Mitsukoshi Department Store	6F Mitsukoshi Bild. 2-6-1 Fujimi Cyuouku		260-8631	81-043-221-0515	
Kitakyusyu	Hukuoka	Izutsuya Department Store	2-4 igashiko, Kokurakitaku		803-0802	81-093-522-2729	
Oosaka	Oosaka	Hankyu Department Store	8-7 kakudacho, Kitaku		530-8350	81-06-6313-8938	
Tokyo	Tokyo	Puppy Shimokitazawa	2-26-4 Kitazawa, Setagayaku		155-0031	81-03-3468-0581	
Hiroshima	Hiroshima	Puppy Hiroshima	8-16 kamihacchoubori, nakaku		730-0031	81-082-222-0537	
Osaka	Japan	room amie	3-11-8-109Yamate-cho, Suita-city	info@roomamie.jp	564-0073	06-6821-3717	http://roomamie.jp
KOBE	HYOGO	Union Wool Co., Ltd.	1-30-22, Kitanagasadori Chuou-ku	union@smile.ocn.ne.jp	650-0012	078-331-8854	
Kobe	Hyogo	Union Wool	1-30-22 Kitanagasadori, Chuouku		650-0012	81-078-331-8854	
Oosaka	Oosaka	Masuzakiya	4-5-4 Kawaramachi, Chuouku		541-0048	81-06-6222-1110	
Tokyo	Tokyo	Mitsubaya	1-1-1 Minamiaoyama, Minatoku		107-0062	81-03-3404-1677	

KOREA

Seoul	*Seocho-Gu*	*Coats Korea Co. Lt (Distributor)*	*5F Eyeon B/D, 935-40 Bangbae-Dong*	*rozenpark@coats.com*	*137-060*	*82-2-521-6262*	*www.coatskorea.co.kr*
Seoul	Jongno-Gu	Danju	1F, 35-3 Sogyeok-Dong	jade@danju.co.kr	110-200	82-2-720-1127	www.danju.co.kr
Seoul	Jongno-Gu	My Knit Studio	3F, 144 Kwanhoon-Dong	myknit@mykint.com	110-300	82-2-722-0006	www.myknit.com

LEBANON

Beirut		y.knot	Saifi Village, Mkhalissiya Street 162	y.knot@cyberia.net.lb	(961) 1 992211	Coming soon under construction.

LUXEMBOURG

Luxembourg	Luxembourg	Bastel Kiste	Rue Du Fort Elisabeth 17-19		1463	00352/40 05 06
Luxembourg	Luxembourg	Ouvrages Elisabeth	Rue S. Bolivar 29, Esch/Alzette		4037	

MALTA

MALTA	Msida	John Gregory Ltd	8 Ta'Xbiex Sea Front	raygreg@onvol.net	MSD 1512	+356 2133 0202

NEW ZEALAND

Christchurch	*ACS New Zealand (Distributor)*	*1 March Plac, Belfast*		*64-3-323-6665*
Auckland	Alterknitives	PO Box 47961		64 9) 376 0337
Christchurch	Knit World	189 Peterborough St		03 379 2300
Dunedin	Knit World	139 Stuart Street		03 477 0400
Hamilton	Knit World	55 London Street		07 838 3868
Taupo	Fabryx	Unit 5a, 29 Totara Street		07 376 7494
Wellington	Knit World	Shop 210b, Left Bank, Cuba Mall		04 385 1918
	Knit World Mail Order	PO Box 30 645	info@knitting.co.nz,	04 586 4530

www.knitworldstudio.co.nz

NORWAY

Arendal	Blad Trad	Harebakksenteret,	blatrad@online.no	4846	37 03 64 33	
Asker	Garnstua Asker	Knud Askersvei	wesselel@online.no	1383	66 78 19 86	www.garnstua.no
Bergen	Coats Knappehuset AS	Pb 100, Ulset		5873	55 53 93 00	
Bryne	Idestova a/s Bryne	Arne Garborgs veg 15	anny@idestova.no	4370	99 29 30 03	www.idestova.no
Dombås	Tusenogen Tråd	Dombås Senter		2660	61 24 16 50	
Drammen	Ulla Garn & Broderi	Sankt Olavsgate 2	butikk@ullagarn.no	3018	32 89 00 58	www.ullagarn.no
Ejve	Garn & Lysstua A/S	Nils Hegelandsveg	bdovla@online.no	4735	37 93 06 46	
Grimstad	Broderihjørnet Huslidstua	Storgata 32	Husflidstua@live.no	4876	37 04 89 14	
Horten	Flittig Lise Horten	Apotekergaten 16	flittiglise@c2i.net	3187	33 04 60 55	
Kongsberg	Strikkestua Kongsberg	Kongsberg	tkolseth@online.no	3616	32 73 23 12	
Kragero	Strikk Inom	Sannidalsv. 196		3770	35 98 03 40	www.strikkinom.no
Kristiansand	Langfeldt Garn	H.Wergwlandsgt. 21-23	karin.pedersen@yahoo.no	4612	38 02 20 29	
Laksevåg	Pinnsvin Design	Lyngboveien 160	kontakt@pinnsvinsdesign.no	5164	99 37 09 12	www.pinnsvinsdesign.no

City	Store	Address	Email	Postcode	Phone	Website
Oslo	Ariadne Garn	Lilleakervn 16		283	22 73 06 20	
Oslo	Bentes Boutique	Chr. Michelsengt 1	garnbente@gmail.com	0568	22 37 44 86	
Oslo	Bentes Boutique	Gjovikgt. 1		0470	22 18 26 39	
Oslo	Linderud Garn og Hobby	Linderud Senter		0594	22 64 49 94	
Oslo	Strikkeriet	Stilla Senter	iren@strikkeriet.no	0491	22 95 78 13	www.strikkeriet.no
Oslo	Tjorven Garn og Gaver	Valkyriegt. 17	tina@tjorven.no	0366	22 69 33 60	www.tjorven.no
Oslo	Nøstet Mitt	Tveita Senter		0671	22 75 50 65	
Oslo	Nøstet Mitt	Lambertseter Senter		1150	23 38 22 20	
Sandnes	Kreaaktiv	Kvadrat Kjøpesenter	kreaktiv-kvadrat@quiltebutikken.com	4301	33 06 33 31	
Sarpsborg	Sarpsborg Garn og Broderi	Jernbanegaten 16	post@sarpsborggarnogbroderi.com	1706	69 15 27 60	
Ski	Trine Sv og Strikk	Idretsveien 6	post@trinestrikk.no	3018	64 87 25 68	
Skien	Strikkepinnen Skien	Ulefossveien 26	opgons@online.no	3730	35 52 72 21	

PORTUGAL

City	Store	Address	Email	Postcode	Phone	Website
Vila Nova de Gaia	Coats & Clark (Distributor)	Quinta de Cravel, Apartado 444		4431-968	223770700	www.coatscrafts.com.pt
Funchal	Eduardo G. Luiz & Fº (Coats & Clark agent in Madeira)	Av. De Zarco, 22, Cx. Postal 155		9002	291201990	
Ponta Delgada	Eduardo J. Moura (Coats & Clark agent in Azores)	R. Arcanjo Lar, 11 Cave, Apartado 182		9500	296284341	
Porto	Ovelha Negra	Rua da Conceição, 100		4050-214	+351 220935847	

SINGAPORE

Singapore	Golden Dragon Store (Distributor)	101 Upper Cross St. #02-51, People's Park Centre	gdscraft@hotmail.com	058357	(65) 65358454 /65358234

SOUTH AFRICA

Johannesburg	Arthur Bales Ltd (Distributor)	62 Fourth Avenue, Linden	arthurb@new.co.za	2195	(27) 118 882 401	www.arthurbales.co.za

SPAIN

City	Store	Address	Email	Postcode	Phone	Website
Barcelona	Coats Fabra, SA (Distributor)	Sant Adrià, 20	atencion.clientes@coats.com	8030	(34) 93 290 84 00	www.coatscrafts.es
Álava	Log Cabin	C/ Manuel Iradier, Pza. Iglesia del Carmen, Vitoria-Gasteiz		1005	(+34) 945142430	logcabin.vitoria@gmail.com
Barcelona	Oyambre	Roger de Lluria n. 92		8006	(34) 93 4872672	
Barcelona	Club de la Aguja	Ganduxer 72		8021	(34) 93 4143815	
Barcelona	Montserrat Mata	Maria Cristina 11, Badalona		8912	(34) 93 3832657	
Barcelona	Lanas Rodríguez	Providencia 130		8024	(34) 93 2196970	
Barcelona	Mercería Santana	Avda. Portal de l'Angel, 26		8002	(34) 933020948	
Barcelona	El Corte Inglés Barcelona	Plaza Catalunya 14		8002		
Barcelona	Iulia Komarova	Enric Granados 153, Vilassar De Mar				www.lanadeioulia.com
Barcelona	Dona Punt de Creu	Provenza 258		8008	(34) 934882784	
Bilbao	El Corte Inglés Bilbao	Gran Via 9		48001		
Eibar	Artile	Bidebarrieta 18, Guipuzcoa		20600	(34) 94 3207227	www.artilepunto.com
La Coruña	El Corte Inglés Coruña	Ramón y Cajal SN		15006		
Madrid	El Corte Inglés Madrid Castellana	Raimundo Fernandez Villaverde 79		28003	(34) 91 418 88 00	
Madrid	El Corte Inglés Madrid Preciados	Calle Preciados n°3		28013	(34) 91 3798000	
Madrid	El club de labores	Infanta Ma Teresa 11		28016	(+34) 913441068	www.clubdelabores.com
Madrid	Inke Labores S.L.	Don Ramón de la Cruz, 47		28001	915762847	
Madrid	Isabel Prieto	Pº Alcobendas, 10 (C.C. Bulevar), Alcobendas		28109		
Palma de Mallorca	El Corte Inglés Palma Mallorca - Roselló Alexandre Roselló 12 (suc.23)			7002	(34) 971770177	
Pamplona	La Chica de las lanas	San Miguel, 5		31001	(34) 948221684	
Zaragoza	El Corte Inglés Zaragoza	Pº Sagasta 3		50008	(34) 976211121	
	Tira del ovillo				(34) 686361083	www.tiradelovillo.com

SWEDEN

City	Store	Address	Email	Postcode	Phone	Website
Goteborg	Coats Expotex AB (Distributor)	JA Wettergrensgata 7, Göteborg, Västra Frölunda		421 30	(46) 33 720 79 00	
Älvsjö	ZigZag	Långsjövägen 25	bergqvist.katarina@telia.com	125 30	070-5713309	
Bollebygd	Nedergården	Stationsvägen 12	nedergardensgarn@telia.com	517 35	(033) 28 94 28	www.nedergardens.com
Boras	Stickat och Klart	Hallbergsgatan 2	kristina.karlson@hotmail.com	503 30	(033) 10 32 38	
Degerberga	Hemslojdsboden i Degerberga	Tingsvagen 23	lina@hemslojdsboden.com	297 31	(044) 350262	www.hemslojdsboden.com
Falkenberg	Sticka Latt	Brogatan 2		311 31	(0346) 17166	www.stickalatt.se
Gårdsjö	Garntorpet	Håhult 1	ingrid@garntorpet.se	547 74	(0523)44 005	www.garntorpet.se
Goteborg	2 Knit	Bondegatan 7	info@2knit.se	416 65	(031) 199080	www.2knit.se
Goteborg	Strikk	Vallgatan 23	info@strikkdesign.com	411 16	(031) 711 37 99	www.strikkdesign.com
Haljarp	Hedenskougs Garnhorna	Olofstorpsvagen 25		261 72	(0418) 430485	
Helsingborg	Tant Thea AB	Möllegränden 15	info@tantthea.se	252 23	(042)135153	www.tantthea.se
Hörby	Garnverandan	Gamla Torg 5	info@garnverandan.se	242 31	(0415)-311 300	www.garnverandan.se
Kristianstad	Helylle Hantverk	Vastra Storgatan 510	eva.martinsson@helylle.se	291 31	(044) 353250	www.helylle.se
Linkoping	Garnverket	Storgatan 54	maya@garnverket.com	582 28	(013)13 59 09	www.garnverket.com
Lund	Slandan	Lilla Fiskaregatan 1	slandan@telia.com	222 22	046 128077	www.slandaninlund.se
Malmo	Irmas Hus	Kalendegatan 13	annkarin@irmashus.se	211 35	(040) 611 08 00	www.irmashus.se
Orebro	Trend Tyg & Garn	Oscar C Kopmangatan 9	trend-tyg-garn@hotmail.com	702 10	019 103055	
Stockholm	Garnverket	Hantverkargatan 14	lena@garnverket.se	112 21	(08) 651 78 08	www.garnverket.com
Stockholm	NK Tyg & Sy	Hamngatan 18-20	sidencarlson@swipnet.se	111 47	(08) 762 88 50	
Stockholm	**Rowan At Wincent**	**Norrtullsgatan 27**	wincent@ownit.nu	113 27	(08) 33 70 60	**www.wincentgarner.se or wincentyarn.com**
Stockholm	Sticka by Marie Viktoria	Osterlanggatan 20	marievictoria@glocalnet.net	111 31	(08)21 18 31	www.knitting.se
Stockholm	**Wincent (Rowan At)**	**Norrtullsgatan 27**	butik.wincent@gmail.com	113 27	(08) 33 70 60	**www.wincentgarner.se or wincentyarn.com**
Sundsvall	Garnkorgen	Klackvagen 17	info@garnkorgen.se	856 53	(060) 124 501	www.garnkorgen.se
Taby	Trasselgarn & Broderi	Stationsvagen 16	info@trassel.se	187 30	(08) 638 00 59	www.trassel.se
Torslanda	Karma Garn	Gamla Flygplatsvagen 38	info@karmagarn.se	423 37	(031)92 00 98	www.karmagarn.se
Umea	Hemflit	Kungsgatan 51	eva@hemflit.com	903 26	(090) 77 03 84	www.hemflit.se
Uppsala	Yll & Tyll	Bredgrand 7c	info@yllotyll.com	753 20	(018) 10 51 90	www.yllotyll.com
Vasteras	Upplings Garn	Kungsgatan 2	info@upplings.se	722 11	(021) 13 00 94	
Vaxjo	Umbra	Batmanstorget 2	info@umbra.nu	352 80	(0470) 777901	

SWITZERLAND

Turgi (AG)	Coats Stroppel AG (Distributor)			CH-5300	056 298 12 20	
Aarau	Mode + Wolle	Graben 30	bpeter@mode-wolle.ch	5000	0041/628246611	
Aigle	Brin de Laine	Mme Sylviane Mosimann, Rue du Bourg 12		1860	024 466 61 84	
Arlesheim	Lana Moda	Obere Holle 25	tschanz.verena@intergga.ch	4144	0041/61 703 92 59	
Basel	MILLE FILI	Frau R. Sollberger, Thiersteinerallee 95		4053	061 331 16 80	
Basel	Zum Roten Faden	Steinenring 41		4051	079 919 71 87	
Bern	**Rowan at WollWirrWare**	**Astrid Balli, Wylestrasse 53**	info@wollwirrware.ch	3014	0041/31332 06 33	**www.wollwirrware.ch**
Buchs	WOLLIG-ANSTALT	Ingrid Näscher, Grünaustr. 17		9470	081/ 756 36 19	
Erlinsbach	Fadegrad	Cécile Blattner, Hauptstr. 12	info@collection-cecile.ch	5018	062/844 05 40	www.collection-cecile.ch
Fribourg	Aiguilles à malices	Marthe Fontana, Grand-Rue 53		1700	026 321 27 12	
Genève 28	Elna SA Centre Balexert	Av. Louis-Casai 27		1211	022 884 86 66	
Grabs	RTK Fashion	Mühlebachstr. 9		9472	079 646 78 81	
Hölstein	Wullestübli Hölstein	Dora Huber, Hauptstr. 19		4434	061 951 19 53	
Klosters	Mystitch Strickcafe	Aeussere Bahnhofstrasse 1		7250	081 420 28 24	
Lausanne	Boutique la Mercerie	rue Mercerie 3		1003	021 312 07 44	
Liestal	WOLLARE	Frau Trüssel-Küng, Rathausstrasse 65		4410	061/922 22 27	
Luzern	Naturel	Müller A. Habsburgerstr. 33		6003	041/210 65 41	
Muri	Stoff-und Wullehuesli	Markstrasse 17		5630	056 664 41 20	
Romanshorn	Strick-IN	Aleestrasse 44		8590	071 463 68 18	
Schoeftland	Mercerie	Vontobel Maya, Dorfstrasse 19		5040	062 721 00 80	
Sirnach	Wullwerk	Fischingerstr. 26		8370	071 960 06 90	
St. Gallen	Wolligx	Engelgasse 8		9000	071 223 20 30	
Signy-Centre	Passe – Present	Centre Commercial Signy		1274	022 361 18 45	
Steffisburg	Hinkel Pinkel Folmer Winkel	Thunstr. 57		3612	033/437 08 80	
Teufen	Presto-Lana	Sammelbuehldtrasse 10		9053	071 335 75 55	
Uster	Fallmasche GmbH	Poststrasse 6		8610	044 942 38 58	
Visp	Web and Wollstube	Kantonsstrasse 14		3930	027 946 47 06	
Weinfelden	Wollring	Rathausstrasse 14		8570	071 622 19 27	
Wettingen	Lana Luna…mehr als Wolle	Landstrasse 28		5430	056 430 00 26	
Zofingen	Blum Handarbeiten	Rathausgasse 17		4800	062 751 36 04	
Zurich	Hand-Art	Neumarkt 10		8001	044 251 57 57	
Zurich	**Rowan At Vilfil**	Kreuzstrasse 39, Beim Kreuzplatz	office@vilfil.com	8032	0041/443839903	www.vilfil.com

TAIWAN

Taiwan, R.O.C.	Taipei	Cactus Quality Co. Ltd (Distributor)	7FL-2, No. 140, Sec.2 Roosevelt Rd	cqcl@ms17.hinet.net	10084	00886-2-23656527	www.excelcraft.com.tw

THAILAND

Bangkok	Global Wide Trading (Distributor)	10 Lad Prao Soi 88	TheNeedleWorld@yahoo.com	10310	00 662 933 9019	global.wide@yahoo.com

State	City	Shop	Address	Email/Zip	Zip	Phone	Website
South Carolina	Greer	Westminster Fibers (Distributor)	8 Shelter Drive	info@westminsterfibers.com	29650	(800) 445-9276	www.westminsterfibers.com
Alabama	Birmingham	In The Making	3108 Heights Village		35243	(205) 298 1309	
Alaska	Anchorage	Far North Yarn Co. (Rowan At)	2636 Spenard Road, Ste 6		99503	(907) 258 5648	
Arizona	Scottsdale	Arizona Knitting & Needlepoint	3617 North Goldwater Blvd		85251	(480) 945 7455	www.arizonaknittingandneedlepoint.com
Arizona	Scottsdale	Jessica Knits	10401 East McDowell Mountain Ranch Road #7		85255	(480) 515 4454	www.jessicaknits.com
Arkansas	Fayetteville	Hand Held- A Knitting Gallery	15 North Block Ave		72701	(479)582-2910	
California	Anaheim Hills	Velona Needlecraft	5701 M Santa Ana Canyon Road		92807	800-972-1570	
California	Grayeagle	Woolly Notions	7580 Highway 89, House#118		96103	530-836-1680	
California	La Jolla	Knitting in La Jolla	909 Prospect Street		92037	800-956-5648	
California	Laguna Hills	Yarn Lady (Rowan At)	23052 Lake Forest Dr C-1		92653	949-421-8605	
California	Long Beach	Alamitos Bay Yarn Co (Rowan At)	174 Marina Dr		90803	562-799-8484	www.yarncompany.com
California	Los Altos	Uncommon Threads (Rowan At)	293 State Street		94022	650-941-1815	www.uncommonthreadsyarn.com
California	Los Angeles	Knit Culture Studio	8118 West Third St		90048	323-655-6487	www.knitculture.com
California	Los Gatos	Yarndogs (Rowan At)	151 East Main St		95030	408-399-1909	
California	Napa	Yarns on First	1305 First Street		94559	707-257-1363	
California	Oakland	Article Pract	5010 Telegraph Ave		94609	510-595-7875	
California	Pacific grove	Monarch Knitting & Quliting (Rowan At)	529 Central Avenue, Ste3		93950	831-647-9276	www.monarchknitting.com
California	Pasadena	Skein	1101 East Walnut St		91106	626-577-2035	
California	Petaluma	Knitterly (Rowan At)	1 Fourth St		94952	707-762-9276	
California	Rocklin	Filati Yarns (Rowan At)	4810 Granite Dr, Ste A-1		95677	800-398-9043	
California	Sacramento	Rumpelstiltskin	1021 R Street		95811	916-442-9225	
California	San Clemente	Strands Knitting Studio	111 Ave Granada		92672	(949)496-4021	
California	San Francisco	Imagiknit (Rowan At)	3897 18th Street		94114	415-621-6642	www.imagiknit.com
California	Santa Barabara	Cardigan's (Rowan At)	3030 State Street, Ste A		93105	805-569-0531	
California	Santa Monica	Compatto Yarn Salon	2112 Wilshire Blvd		90403	310-453-2130	
California	Santa Monica	Wildfiber	1453 14th Street, Ste E		90404	310-458-2748	www.wildfiber.com
California	Sunnyvale	Purlescence	586 South Murphy Ave		94086	408-735-9276	
California	Three Rivers	Creekside Yarns	41721 Sierra Drive		93271	559-561-4518	
California	Ventura	Anacapa Fine Yarns	4572 Telephone Road #909		93003	805-654-9500	
Colorado	Colorado Springs	Green Valley Weavers & Knitters	2115 W Colorado Ave		80904	(719)448-9963	
Colorado	Denver	Lamb Shoppe	3512 E 12th Ave		80206	(303) 322-2223	
Colorado	Fort Collins	Lambspun of Colorado	1101 E Lincoln Ave		80524	(800) 558 5262	
Colorado	Littleton	A Knitted Peace Inc	5654-C South Prince St		80120	(303) 730 0366	
Connecticut	Mystic	Mystic River Yarns	14 Holmes Street		06355	(860)536-4305	
Connecticut	Woodbridge	The Yarn Barn	1666 Litchfield Tpk		06525	(203)389-5117	
Delaware	Bethany Beach	Sea Needles	780 Garfield Parkway		19930	(302)539-0574	
Florida	Belleair Bluffs	Flying Needles	2933 W Bay Drive		33770	727-581-8691	
Florida	Coral Gables	The Knitting Garden	2716 Ponce De Leon Blvd		33134	(305)774-1060	
Florida	Sarasota	A Good Yarn (Rowan At)	7668 South Tamiami Trail		34231	941-487-7914	
Florida	Tampa	Knit 'N' Knibble	4027 S. Dale Mabry Hwy		33611	(813)837-5648	www.knitnknibble.com
Georgia	Atlanta	Knitch LLC (Rowan At)	1044 N. Highland Ave		30307	(404)745-9276	www.shopknitch.com
Georgia	Macon	Creative Yarns	134 Speer Ave		31204	(478)746-5648	
Georgia	Peachtree City	Sugarfoot Yarns	100 N Peachtree Parkway		30269	(770)487-9001	
Georgia	Roswell	Cast On Cottage	Coleman Village, 860 Marietta Hwy		30075	(770) 998-3483	www.castoncottage.com
Georgia	Woodstock	The Whole Nine Yarns	8226 Main Street		30188	(678) 494-5242	
Illinois	Chicago	Knitting Workshop	2115 N. Damen Ave		60647	(773) 278-3004	
Illinois	Downers Grove	Knitche Inc (Rowan At)	5150-B Main St		60515	(630) 852-5648	
Illinois	Geneva	Wool and Company	23 South 3rd St		60134	(630)232-2305	
Illinois	Glen Ellyn	String Theory Yarn Co.	477 North Main St		60137	(630)469-6085	
Illinois	Northbrook	Three Bags Full(Rowan At)	1927 Cherry lane		60062	(847) 291-9933	
Indiana	Indianapolis	Knit Stop (Rowan At)	3941 East 82nd Street		46240	(317) 595-5648	www.knit-stop.com
Indiana	Bremen	Broad Ripple Knits	3794 E Third Rd		46506	(317)255-0540	
Indiana	Indianapolis	Mass Avenue Knit Shop	862 Virginia Avenue		46203	317-638-1833	
Indiana	Newburgh	The Village Knitter(Rowan At)	8A West Jennings St.		47630	(812) 842-2360	
Iowa	West Des Moines	Knitted Together	7450 Bridgewood Blvd, ste 225		50266	(515) 222-9276	
Kansas	Lawrence	The Yarn Barn (Rowan At)	930 Mass Ave		66044	(800) 468-0035	www.YarnBarn-ks.com
Kentucky	Bowling Green	Crafty Hands	2910 Scottsville Road		42104	(270)846-4865	
Kentucky	Lexington	Magpie	513 East High Street		40502	(859)455-7437	
Kentucky	Louisville	Sophie's Fine Yarn Shoppe	10482 Shelbyville Rd		40223	(502)244-4927	
Kentucky	Lousville	The Knit Nook (Rowan At)	1140 Bardstown Rd., Ste. B		40204	(502)452-1919	
Maine	Freeport	Grace Robinson & Co (Rowan At)	208 US Rte 1, Ste 1		04032	(207) 865-6110	www.yarnandneedlepoint.com
Maryland	Baltimore	Woolworks (Rowan At)	6117 Falls Rd		21209	(410) 377-2060	
Maryland	Bethesda	Knit & Stitch = Bliss (Rowan At)	4706 Bethesda Ave		20814	(301)652-8688	www.knitandstitch.com
Massachusetts	Boston	Windsor Button (Rowan At)	35 Temple Place		02111	(617) 482-4969	
Massachusetts	Brookline Village	A Good Yarn	4 Station Street		02445	(617) 731 4900	
Massachusetts	Canton	Sheep Street Yarn Shop	535 Washington Street		02021	(781) 830-5648	
Massachusetts	Lenox	Colorful Stitches (Rowan At)	48 Main St		01240	(800) 413-6111	www.colorful-stitches.com
Massachusetts	Lexington	Wild & Woolly Studio (Rowan At)	7A Meriam St		02420	(781) 861-7717	
Massachusetts	Northampton	Webs (Rowan At)	75 Service Center Road		01060	(413)584-2225	www.yarn.com
Massachusetts	Salem	Seed Stitch Fine Yarn	21 Front Street		01970	(978)744-5557	
Massachusetts	Sudbury	Knit Purl (Rowan At)	730 Boston Post Rd		01776	(978) 443-5648	
Michigan	Ada	Clever Ewe	590 Ada Drive, SE		49301	(616) 682-1545	
Michigan	Ann Arbor	Knit a Round Yarn Shop	2663 Plymouth Rd		48105	(734) 998-3771	
Michigan	Berkley	Have you any Wool	3455 Robina Ave		48072	(248)541-9665	
Michigan	Birmingham	The Knitting Room	251 East Merrill St		48009	(248) 540-3623	www.knittingroom.com
Michigan	Holland	Lizzie Anns Wool Co (Rowan At)	54 East 8th St		49423	(616) 392-2035	
Michigan	Macomb	Craft Lady Trio Co	15401 Hall Road, Crosswinds Corner		48044	(586) 566-8008	
Michigan	Northville	Center Street Knits	111 N Center St		48167	(248)349-6700	
Michigan	Royal Oak	Ewe-nique Knits	515 South Lafayette Ave		48067	(248) 584-3001	
Michigan	Traverse City	Lost art Yarn Shoppe	123 E Front Street		49684	(231)941-1263	
Michigan	Traverse City	Yarn Quest	819 S. Garfield Ave		49686	(231) 929-4277	
Minnesota	Baxter	Among the Pines	15670 Edgewood Drive#130		56425	(218) 828-6364	
Minnesota	Coon Rapids	All About Yarn	455 99th Ave NW, Ste 180		55433	(763) 785-4900	
Minnesota	Maple Grove	Amazing Threads	11262 86th Ave		55369	(763) 391-7700	
Minnesota	Minneapolis	Linden Hills Yarn	2720 W. 43rd St		55410	(612) 929-1255	www.lindenhillsyarn.com
Minnesota	Minneapolis	Needlework Unlimited (Rowan At)	4420 Drew Ave S		55410	(612) 925-2454	www.needleworkunlimited.com
Minnesota	Stillwater	Darn Knit Anyway	423 South Main Street		55082	(612)963-9056	
Minnesota	St Paul	The Yarnery KMK Crafts (Rowan At)	840 Grand Ave		55105	(651) 222-5793	www.yarnery.com
Minnesota	White Bear Lake	A Sheepy Yarn Shoppe (Rowan At)	2185 Third St		55110	(800) 480-5462	www.sheepyyarnmn.com
Montana	Missoula	Loopy, LLC	115 W Front St		59802	(406)543-0560	
Nebraska	Omaha	Personal Threads Boutique (Rowan At)	8600 Cass		68114	(402) 391-7733	www.personalthreads.com
Nebraska	Omaha	String of Purls	8721 Shamrock Rd		68114	(402)393-5648	
Nevada	Reno	Jimmy Beans Wool (Rowan At)	5000 Smithridge Dr, #A11		89502	(775) 827-9276	www.jimmybeanswool.com
New Jersey	Basking Ridge	Angelfire Studio	403 King George Road		07920	(908) 604-4294	
New Jersey	Basking Ridge	Down Cellar	25 South Finley Ave		07920	(908) 766-2300	
New Jersey	Haddonfield	Woolplay	22 N. Haddon Ave		08033	856 428 0110	
New Jersey	Hoboken	Patricia's Yarns	107 4th St		07030	(201) 217-9276	
New Jersey	Madison	The Blue Purl	92 Green Ave		07940	(973)377-5648	
New Jersey	Martinsville	A Yarn for All Seasons	1944 Washington Valley Rd		08836	(732) 560-1111	
New Jersey	Montclair	Modern Yarn	182 Glenridge Ave		07042	(973) 509-9276	
New Jersey	Pennington	The Woolly Lamb (Rowan At)	7 Tree Farm Rd, Unit 103		08534	609-730-9800	
New Jersey	Princeton	Pins & Needles	8 Chamber St		08542	(609) 921-9075	
New Jersey	Westfield	Knit A Bit	66 Elm St, suite 2		07090	(908) 301-0053	www.knit-a-bit.com

State	City	Shop	Address	Zip	Phone	Website
New Mexico	Santa Fe	Tutto, Santa Fe	218 Galisteo St	87501	(877) 603-6725	www.tuttosantafe.com
New York	East Rochester	The Village Yarn & Fiber	350 West Commercial St	14445	(585)586-5470	
New York	Ithaca	Knitting Etc	2255 North Triphammer Rd	14850	(607) 277-1164	
New York	Katonah	Katonah Yarn Co	120 Bedford Rd	10536	(914) 977-3145	
New York	New York City	Annie & Co	1325 Madison Ave	10128	(212) 289-2944	
New York	**New York City**	**Knitty City (Rowan At)**	**208 W 79th Street**	**10024**	**(212) 787-5896**	
New York	New York City	Purl	137 Sullivan St	10012	(212) 420-8796	www.purlsoho.com
New York	Sayville	Rumpelstiltskin	22 Main Street	11782	(631)750-1790	
New York	Scarsdale	Sticks & Strings	45 Spencer Pl.,	10583	(914) 723-5478	
North Carolina	**Chapel Hill**	**Yarns Etc (Rowan At)**	**99 S Elliott Rd, Ste 2**	**27514**	**(919) 928-8810**	
North Carolina	**Raleigh**	**Great Yarns (Rowan At)**	**1208 Ridge Rd**	**27607**	**(919)832-3599**	
North Carolina	Wilmington	The Quarter at Oleander	5725 Oleander Drive, #B2	28403	(910)392-0020	
North Dakota	Fargo	Prairie Yarns	2615 South University	58103	(701) 280-1478	
Ohio	Cleveland	Fine Points	12620 Larchmere Blvd	44120	(216) 229-6644	www.shopfinepoints.com
Ohio	**Columbus**	**Knitter's Mercantile (Rowan At)**	**214 Graceland Blvd**	**43214**	**(614) 888-8551**	**www.knittersmercantile.com**
Ohio	Dublin	Temptations	35 South High Street	43017	(614) 734-0618	
Ohio	Hamilton	Lambikins Hideaway	217 South B Street	45013	(513) 895-5648	
Ohio	Lakewood	River Colors Studio	1387 Sloane Ave	44107	(216)228-9276	
Ohio	**Pickerington**	**Yarn Market (Rowan At)**	**12936 Stonecreek Dr, unit D**	**43147**	**(888) 996-9276**	**www.yarnmarket.com**
Ohio	Uniontown	My Sister's Yarn Shop	3477 Massillon Road	44685	(330)896-7040	
Oklahoma	Tulsa	Loops	2042 Utica Sq	74114	(918) 742-9276	www.loopsknitting.com
Oregon	**Ashland**	**The Web-Sters (Rowan At)**	**11 North Main St**	**97520**	**(800) 482-9801**	**www.yarnatwebsters.com**
Oregon	Beaverton	For Yarn Sake	11679 SW Beaverton	97005	(503)469-9500	
Oregon	McMinnville	Boersma's Knitting Center	203 NE 3rd Street	97128	503-472-4611	
Oregon	Portland	Close Knit	2140 NE Alberta St	97211	(503)288-4568	
Oregon	Portland	Knit Purl	1101 SW Alder	97205	(503) 227-2999	www.knit-purl.com
Oregon	Portland	Knitting Bee	18305 NW West Union Rd	97229	(503)439-3316	
Oregon	Portland	Yarn Garden	1413 SE Hawthorne Blvd	97214	(503) 239-7950	www.yarngarden.net
Oregon	Sisters	Stitchin' Post	311 West Cascade St	97759	(541) 549-6061	www.stitchinpost.com
Pennsylvania	Allentown	Conversational Threads	4113 Huckleberry Road	18104	(610)421-8889	
Pennsylvania	Chambersburg	Yarn Basket	150 Falling Spring Rd	17202	(717) 263-3236	
Pennsylvania	Doylestown	Forever Yarn	15 W Oakland Ave	18901	215) 348-5648	
Pennsylvania	Mcmurray	Bloomin Yarns	3323 Washington Rd, Ste 102	15317	(724) 942-1025	
Pennsylvania	New Hope	Twist Knitting & Spinning	6220 Lower York Road	18938	(215) 862-8075	
Pennsylvania	**Newtown Square**	**Slip Knot (Rowan At)**	**3719 W Chester Pike**	**19073**	**(610) 359-9070**	
Pennsylvania	Philadelphia	Rosie's Yarn Cellar	2017 Locust Street	19103	(215) 977-9276	
Pennsylvania	Pittsburgh	Knit One	2721 Murray Ave	15217	412-421-6666	
Pennsylvania	**Sewickley**	**Yarns Unlimited (Rowan At)**	**435 Beaver St**	**15143**	**(412) 741-8894**	**www.yarnsunlimitedpa.com**
Rhode Island	**Tiverton**	**Sakonnet Purls (Rowan At)**	**3988 Main Rd**	**02878**	**(888) 624-9902**	**www.letsknit.com**
South Carolina	Hilton Head Island	The Courtyard	32 Palmetto Bay Rd, Ste 10A	29928	(843) 842 5614	
South Dakota	Sioux Falls	Athena Fibers	3915 South Hawthorne Ave	57105	(605) 271 0741	
Tennessee	Brentwood	Threaded Bliss Yarn	127 Franklin Rd #170	37027	(615) 370 8717	
Tennessee	Nashville	Textile Fabric store	2717 Franklin Road	37204	(615)297-5346	
Texas	**Austin**	**Hill Country Weavers (Rowan At)**	**1701 South Congress**	**78704**	**(512) 707 7396**	**www.hillcountryweavers.com**
Texas	Austin	Yarnbow	1607 Ranch Rd, 620 North,Ste 800	78734	(512) 535 2332	www.yarnbow.com
Texas	Beaumont	Strings and Things	885 Evergreen Lane	77706	(409)225-5185	
Texas	Dallas	The Shabby Sheep	2110 Boll Street	75204	(214)953-0331	
Texas	**Houston**	**Yarns 2 Ewe Inc (Rowan At)**	**518 Shepherd Dr**	**77007**	**(713) 880 5648**	**www.yarns2ewe.com**
Vermont	Norwich	Northern Nights Yarn Shop	289 Main Street	05055	(802) 649 2000	
Virginia	Blacksburg	Mosaic Yarns	880 University City Blvd	24060	(540)961-4462	
Virginia	Charlottesville	It's A Stitch	188 Zan Road	22901	(434)973-0331	
Virginia	Charlottesville	The Needle Lady	114 E Main St	22902	(434) 296 4625	
Virginia	**Richmond**	**Lettuce Knit (Rowan At)**	**3030 Stony Point Rd**	**23235**	**(804) 323 5777**	
Virginia	Richmond	The Yarn Lounge	3003 West Cary St,	23221	(804) 340 2880	
Virginia	Vienna	Uniquities	421-D Church St NE	22180	(703) 242 0520	
Virginia	Williamsburg	Knitting Sisters	1915 Pocahontas Trail, ste B1	23185	(757) 258 5005	
Washington	**Bainbridge Island**	**Churchmouse Yarn & Teas (Rowan At)**	**118 Madrone Lane**	**98110**	**(206) 780 2686**	
Washington	Mount Vernon	Wildfibers	706 South First St	98273	(360)336-5202	
Washington	Preston	Yarn Country	30540 SE 84th St, Unit 4	98050	(425) 818 8096	www.yarncountry.com
Washington	Seattle	Little Knits	3221 California Ave SW	98116	(206)935-4072	
Washington	**Seattle**	**The Weaving Works (Rowan At)**	**4717 Brooklyn Ave, N.E.**	**98105**	**(888) 524 1221**	**www.weavingworks.com**
Washington	Seattle	Tricoter	3121 East Madison St	98112	(206) 328 6505	www.tricoter.com
Wisconsin	**Appleton**	**Iris Fine Yarns (Rowan At)**	**132 E. Wisconsin Ave**	**54911**	**(920) 954 9001**	
Wisconsin	Madison	The Knitting Tree	2614 Monroe St	53711	(608)238-0121	
Wisconsin	**Milwaukee**	**Ruhuma's (Rowan At)**	**420 E Silver Spring Dr**	**53217**	**(888) 669 4726**	**www.ruhamas.com**
Wisconsin	Sturgeon Bay	Spin LLC	108 South Madison Ave	54235	(920) 746 7746	

UNITED KINGDOM

'ROWAN AT ....' stockists carry a large range of Rowan Yarns.

Avon	Brislington	**Get Knitted (Rowan At)**	**39 @ Brislington, Brislington Hill**	sales@getknitted.com	**BS4 5BE**	**0117 3005211**	**www.getknitted.com**
Avon	Bristol	**John Lewis (Rowan At)**	**Cribbs Causeway**		**BS12 5TP**	**0117 959 1100**	
Bedfordshire	Leighton Buzzard	Nutmeg Needlecrafts	1-4 Peacock Mews		LU7 1JH	01525 376456	
Berkshire	Newbury	Calico Dress Fabrics	6 Inch's Yard	Sandra@calicodressfabrics.com	RG14 5DP	01635 38919	www.calicodressfabrics.com
Berkshire	**Reading**	**John Lewis (Rowan At)**	**Broad Street**		**RG7 4AH**	**01189 575955**	
Buckinghamshire	**Milton Keynes**	**John Lewis (Rowan At)**	**Central Milton Keynes**		**MK1 1NN**	**01908 679171**	
Buckinghamshire	Great Missenden	Rainbow Silks	85 High Street	caroline@rainbowsilks.co.uk	HP16 0AL	01494 862111	www.rainbowsilks.co.uk
Buckinghamshire	Buckingham	The Nimble Thimble	9 Bridge Street	sales@nimble-thimble.co.uk	MK18 1EL	01280 822236	www.nimble-thimble.co.uk
Cambridgeshire	**Cambridge**	**John Lewis (Rowan At)**	**10 Downing Street**		**CB2 3DS**	**01223 361292**	
Cambridgeshire	**Peterborough**	**John Lewis (Rowan At)**	**Queensgate Centre**		**PE1 1NL**	**01733 344644**	
Cheshire	**Knutsford**	**Fibre and Clay (Rowan At)**	**11-13 Minshull Street**	info@fibreandclay.co.uk	**WA16 6HG**	**01565 652035**	**www.fibreandclay.co.uk**
Cheshire	**Cheadle**	**John Lewis (Rowan At)**	**Wilmslow Road**		**SK9 3RN**	**0161 491 4914**	
Cheshire	Nantwich	Homemade	3 Mill Street	lizzydrippingsales@btopenworld.com	CW5 5ST	01270 625318	
Cheshire	**Chester**	**Stash (Rowan At)**	**Unit 48, Evan's Business Park, Minerva Ave**	stash@celticove.com	**CH1 4QL**	**01244 389310**	**www.celticove.com**
Cheshire	Northwich	Thimble Town	Blakemere Craft Centre	thimbletown@hotmail.com	CW8 2EB	01606 883133	
Co Durham	Barnard Castle	Button and Bowes	3 The Bank		DL12 8PH	01833 631133	
Co. Fermanagh	Enniskillen	Boston Quay Craft Shop	Down Street		BT74 7DU	028 6632 3837	
Cornwall	Wadebridge	ArtyCrafts	41 Molesworth Street	artycrafts@btconnect.com	PL27 7DH	01208 812274	
Cornwall	Penzance	Iriss	66 Chapel Street	rowan@iriss.co.uk	TR18 4AD	01736 366568	www.rowan-at-iriss.co.uk
Cornwall	Launceston	The Cornwall Yarn Shop	1 Madford Lane	info@thecornwallyarnshop.co.uk	PL15 9EB	01566 779930	www.thecornwallyarnshop.co.uk
Cornwall	**Truro**	**Truro Fabrics (Rowan At)**	**Lemon Quay**	info@trurofabrics.co.uk	**TR1 2LW**	**01872 222130**	**www.trurofabrics.com**
Cumbria	Penrith	Indigo	Unit 15 Devonshire Arcade	carolyn@indigoknits.co.uk	CA11 7SX	01768 899917	www.indigoknits.co.uk
Cumbria	Whitehaven	The Knitting & Sewing Centre	28 Duke Street		CA28 7EU	01946 63091	
Cumbria	Kendal	Williams Wools	3 Kirkland	adrienne@williamswools.co.uk	LA9 5AU	01539 724300	
Derbyshire	Matlock	The Compleat Knit	22 Firs Parade	ann@patchworkdirect.com	DE4 3AS	01629 593700	www.patchworkdirect.com
Derbyshire	Derby	Threads of Life	67 Borough St, Castle Donington	info@threadsoflife.co.uk	DE74 2LB	01332 811597	www.threadsoflife.co.uk
Devon	Totnes	Creative Crafts & Needlework	18 High Street		TQ9 5RY	01803 866002	www.creative-crafts-needlework.co.uk

Devon	**Exeter**	**Inspirations (Rowan At)**	**5 Central Station Buildings, Queen Street**		**EX4 3SB**	**01392 435115**	
Devon	Tavistock	Knitting Korner	9 Pepper Street		PH9 0BD	01822 617410	
Devon	Shaldon	Lana Pura	49 Fore Street	enquiries@lanapura.com	TQ14 0EA	01626 873615	www.lanapura.com
Devon	**Bovey Tracy**	**Spin A Yarn (Rowan At)**	**26 Fore Street**	**info@spinayarndevon.co.uk**	**TQ13 9AD**	**01626 836203**	**www.spinayarndevon.co.uk**
Devon	Plymouth	The Pin Tin	17 Wilton Street	andie.thepintin@yahoo.co.uk	PL1 5LT	01752 313931	www.thepintin.co.uk
Devon	Modbury	Wild Goose Antiques	34 Church Street	wildgooseantiques@tiscali.co.uk	PL21 0QR	01548 830715	
Dorset	Bournemouth	Carly's Crafts	Shop 1, 1a Cardigan Road, Winton	michelek1964@hotmail.com	BH9 1BJ	01202 512106	
Dorset	**Sturminster Newton**	**Hansons Fabrics (Rowan At)**	**Station Road**		**DT10 1BD**	**01258 472698**	
Dorset	Christchurch	Honora	69 High Street	support@knittingyarns.co.uk	BH23 1AS	01202 486000	www.knittingyarns.co.uk
Dorset	Wimbourne	The Walnut Tree	1 West Borough		BH21 1NF	01202 840722	
Dorset	**Swanage**	**The Wool & Craft Shop (Rowan At)**	**17 Station Road**	**sales@craftywoolshop.co.uk**	**BH19 1AB**	**01929 422814**	**www.craftywoolshop.co.uk**
East Sussex	**Brighton**	**C & H Fabrics (Rowan At)**	**179 Western Road,**		**BN1 2BA**	**01273 321959**	**www.candh.co.uk**
East Sussex	Eastbourne	C & H Fabrics	82/86 Terminus Road		BN21 3LX	01323 410428	www.candh.co.uk
East Sussex	**Forest Row**	**Village Crafts (Rowan At)**	**The Square**	**shop@village-crafts.co.uk**	**RH18 5ES**	**01342 823238**	**www.village-crafts.co.uk**
East Yorkshire	**Pocklington**	**Poppy's (Rowan At)**	**20 Market Place**	**info@craftypoppycanknit.com**	**YO42 2AR**	**01759 303120**	**www.craftypoppycanknit.com**
Essex	**Chelmsford**	**Franklins (Rowan At)**	**219 Moulsham St**		**CM2 0LR**	**01245 346300**	
Essex	**Colchester**	**Franklins (Rowan At)**	**13/15 St Botolphs St**		**CO2 7DU**	**01206 563955**	
Essex	Brentwood	We Three	16 Crown Street		CM14 4BA	01277 221709	
Gloucestershire	Cricklade	Creative Crafts & Needlework	89a High Street	info@crickladecrafts.co.uk	SN6 6DF	01793 750604	www.crickladecrafts.co.uk
Greater London	Herne Hill	Sharp Designs	226 Croxted Road		SE24 9DJ	020 8674 4382	
Greater Manchester	**Manchester**	**John Lewis (Rowan At)**	**Peel Avenue**	**The Trafford Centre**	**M17 8JL**	**0161 491 4040**	
Greater Manchester	**Didsbury**	**Sew In of Didsbury (Rowan At)**	**741 Wilmslow Road**	**enquiries@knitting-and-needlework.co.uk**	**M20 0RN**	**0161 445 5861**	**www.knitting-and-needlecraft.co.uk**
Greater Manchester	**Marple**	**Sew In of Marple (Rowan At)**	**46 Market Street**	**enquiries@knitting-and-needlework.co.uk**	**M17 8JL**	**0161 427 2529**	**www.knitting-and-needlecraft.co.uk**
Hampshire	Winchester	C & H Fabrics	8 High St		SO23 9JX	01962 843355	www.candh.co.uk
Hampshire	**Southampton**	**John Lewis (Rowan At)**	**West Quay Shopping Centre**		**SO15 1GY**	**0238 021 6400**	
Hampshire	Liss	Liss Wools	2 Station Road	hilary@lisswools.co.uk	GU33 7DT	01730 893941	www.lisswools.co.uk
Hampshire	Basingstoke	Pack Lane Wool Shop	171 Pack Lane, Kempshott	sales@packlanewool.co.uk	RG22 5HN	01256 462590	www.packlanewool.co.uk
Hampshire	Southampton	Rowan At John Lewis	West Quay Shopping Centre		SO15 1GY	0238 021 6400	
Hampshire	Lee-On-The-Solent	Sandcastle Yarns	176 Portsmouth Road	info@sandcastleyarns.co.uk	PO13 9AJ	02392 358808	www.sandcastleyarns.co.uk
Hampshire	Alton	The Knitting Habit	8 Market Street		GU34 1HA	01420 541977	
Hampshire	Southsea	The Yarn Barn Ltd	173 Eastney Road	info@theyarnbarnltd.co.uk	PO4 8EA	023 9275 2555	www.theyarnbarnltd.co.uk
Herefordshire	Hay-on-Wye	Bedecked.co.uk	5 Castle Street	thegirls@bedecked.co.uk,	HR3 5DF	01497 822769	www.bedecked.co.uk
Herefordshire	Hereford	Doughty's	5 Capuchin Road, Church Street	sales@doughtysonline.co.uk	HR1 2LR	01432 267542	www.doughtysonline.co.uk
Hertfordshire	St Albans	Alison's Wool Shop	63 Hatfield Road		AL1 4JE	01727 833738	
Hertfordshire	**Watford**	**John Lewis (Rowan At)**	**The Harlequin, High St**		**WD2 8HL**	**01923 244266**	
Hertfordshire	**Welwyn Garden City**	**John Lewis (Rowan At)**	**Bridge Road**		**AL8 6TP**	**01707 323456**	
Hertfordshire	Bushey	Mavis	44 High Street		WD23 3HL	0208 950 5445	www.mavis-crafts.com
Hertfordshire	Boreham Wood	The Wool Shop	29 Shenley Road		WD6 1EB	0208 9052499	
Isle of Man	Onchan	Joan's Wools & Crafts	5B & 6B Village Walk	joans_wools_crafts@manx.net	IM3 4EA	01624 626009	
Kent	**Canterbury**	**C & H Fabrics (Rowan At)**	**2 St George's Street**		**CT1 2SR**	**01227 459760**	**www.candh.co.uk**
Kent	Maidstone	C & H Fabrics	68 Week Street		ME14 1RJ	01622 762060	www.candh.co.uk
Kent	**Tunbridge Wells**	**C & H Fabrics (Rowan At)**	**113/115 Mount Pleasant**		**TN1 1QS**	**01892 522618**	**www.candh.co.uk**
Kent	**Greenhithe**	**John Lewis (Rowan At)**	**Bluewater**		**DA9 9SA**	**01322 624123**	
Lancashire	Chorley	& Sew What	247 Eaves Lane	info@sewwhat.gb.com	PR6 0AG	01257 267438	www.sewwhat.gb.com
Lancashire	Preston	Bow Peep	136 Liverpool Road (next to the Red Lion), Longton		PR4 5AU	01772 614508	
Lancashire	Ramsbottom	Clark Craft Products	Empire Works, Railway Street, Bury		BL0 9AS	01706 826479	www.clarkcraft.co.uk
Lancashire	Accrington	Sheila's Wool Shop	284 Union Road, Oswaldtwistle	sheila'swoolshop@aol.com	BB5 3JB	01254 875525	www.sheilaswoolshop.com
Lancashire	**Barnoldswick**	**Whichcrafts? (Rowan At)**	**29 Church St**	**crafts@whichcrafts.co.uk**	**BB18 5UR**	**01282 851003**	**www.whichcrafts.co.uk**
Lancashire	Oldham	Yarn Barn	16 Milnrow Road, Shaw	info@yarnbarnshaw.co.uk	OL2 8EQ	01706 843538	www.yarnbarnshaw.co.uk
Lancashire	Thornton	Yarns of Lancashire Ltd	Unit 15, Marsh Mill Village, Fleetwood Road	yarns@tiscali.co.uk	FY5 4JZ	01253 822922	
Leicestershire	**Leicester**	**John Lewis (Rowan At)**	**2 Bath House Lane**	**Highcross**	**LE1 4SA**	**0116 242 5777**	
Leicestershire	Leicester	Mary Clare	4 Shaftesbury Road		LE3 0QN	0116 255 1866	
Leicestershire	Loughborough	Quorn Country Crafts	18 Churchgate	quorncountrycrafts@hotmail.com	LE11 1UD	01509 211604	www.quorncountrycrafts.com
London	Central London	All the Fun of the Fair	Unit 2, 8 Kingly Court, Off Carnaby Street	buzzstokes@btinternet.com	W1B 5PW	0207 287 2303	www.allthefunofthefair.biz
London	Chiswick	Creations	29 Turnham Green Terrace		W4 1RS	020 8747 9697	
London	Barnes	Creations	79 Church Road		SW13 9HH	020 8563 2970	
London	Chingford	JJ Wool & Crafts	89 Station Road	jjwoolandcrafts@yahoo.co.uk	E4 9RH	0208 523 7172	www.jjwoolandcrafts.co.uk
London	**Central London**	**John Lewis (Rowan At)**	**Oxford Street**		**W1**	**020 7629 7711**	
London	**North London**	**John Lewis (Rowan At)**	**Brent Cross Shopping Centre**		**NW4**	**020 8202 6535**	
London	Finsbury Park	Lenarow	169 Blackstock Road	michael@lenarow.co.uk	N4 2JS	020 7359 1274	www.lenarow.co.uk
London	**Central London**	**Liberty (Rowan At)**	**Regent St**		**W1**	**020 7734 1234**	
London	Islington	Loop	41 Cross Street	info@loop.gb.com	N1 2BB	0207 288 1160	www.loop.gb.com
London	**Central London**	**Peter Jones (Rowan At)**	**Sloane Square**		**SW1**	**0207 881 6364**	
Merseyside	**Liverpool**	**John Lewis (Rowan At)**	**70 South John Street**		**L1 8BJ**	**0151 709 7070**	
Merseyside	Liverpool	Purlesque	The Bluecoat, School Lane	purlesque@gmail.com	L1 3BX		
Merseyside	St Helens	The Knitting Centre	9 Westfield Street		WA10 1QA	01744 23993	
Middlesex	Twickenham	Mrs Moon	41 Crown Road, St Margarets	info@mrsmoon.co.uk	TW1 3EJ	020 8744 1190	www.mrsmoon.co.uk
Monmouthshire	Monmouth	Cotton Angel	2 Church Street	info@thecottonangel.com	NP25 3BU	01600 713548	www.thecottonangel.com
Norfolk	Sheringham	Creative Crafts	47 Station Road	info@creative-crafts.co.uk,	NR26 8RG	01263 823153	www.creative-crafts.co.uk
Norfolk	Diss	Diss Wool & Craft Shop	2 Cobbs Yard, St Nicholas Street	sales@disswoolandcrafts.com	IP22 4LB	01379 650640	www.disswoolandcrafts.com
Norfolk	**Norwich**	**John Lewis (Rowan At)**	**All Saints Green**		**NR1 3LX**	**01603 660021**	
Norfolk	Dereham	Knitwits	1 Glencoe Court, Cherry Tree Car Park	knitwits.dereham@googlemail.com	NR19 2AX	01362 652961	www.knitwitsdereham.co.uk
North Yorkshire	Filey	Beachcomber	35 Belle Vue St		YO14 9HV	01723 514434	
North Yorkshire	Clapham	Beckside Yarn & Needlecraft	Church Avenue	info@becksideyarns.co.uk	LA2 8EA	01524 251122	www.beckside yarns.co.uk
North Yorkshire	Whitby	Bobbins	Wesley Hall, Church Street	bobbins@globalnet.co.uk	YO22 4DE	01947 600585	www.bobbins.co.uk
North Yorkshire	York	Craft Basics	9 Gillygate		YO31 7EA	01904 652840	
North Yorkshire	**Embsay**	**Embsay Crafts (Rowan At)**	**Embsay Mills**	**enquiries@embsaycrafts.com**	**BD23 6QF**	**01756 700946**	**www.embsaycrafts.com**
North Yorkshire	York	Poppy's	11 Colliergate	info@craftypoppycanknit.com	YO1 8BP	01904 270927	www.craftypoppycanknit.com
Northamptonshire	Weedon	Crafts & Quilts	Unit 5 The Barn, Heart of the Shires Shop Village	tintindowton@aol.com	NN7 4LB	01327 349276	
Northamptonshire	Northampton	House of Fraser	37 Newland Walk, Grosvenor Centre		NN1 2EP	0870 607 2835	
Northamptonshire	Rushden	Manfield Crafts	24 Griffiths Street	enquiries@manfieldcrafts.com	NN10 0RL	01933 314920	www.manfieldcrafts.com
Northern Ireland	Co Antrim	The Glen Gallery	48 Fenagh Road, Cullybackey		BT43 5PH	0282 588 0354	
Northumberland	Alnwick	Pavi Yarns	42 Royal Oak Gardens	info@paviyarns.com	NE66 2DA	01665 606062	www.paviyarns.com
Northumberland	Berwick upon Tweed	The Needleworks Ltd	54 Hide Hill	kp1612@btinternet.com	TD15 1AB	01890 819030	
Nottinghamshire	**Nottingham**	**John Lewis (Rowan At)**	**Victoria Centre**		**NG1 3QA**	**0115 941 8282**	
Nottinghamshire	Southwell	The Little Wool Shop	18 Queen Street	mac8142@aol.com	NG25 0AA	01636 814198	www.thelittlewoolshop.co.uk
Nottinghamshire	**Beeston**	**Yarns (Rowan At)**	**55 Chilwell Road**	**info@yarn-in-notts.co.uk**	**NG9 1EN**	**0115 925 3606**	**www.yarn-in-notts.co.uk**
Oxfordshire	Burford	Burford Needlecraft	150 High Street	info@needlework.co.uk	OX18 4QU	01993 822136	www.needlework.co.uk
Oxfordshire	Abingdon	Masons	39 Stert Street	sales@masonsneedlecraft.co.uk	OX14 3JF	01235 520107	www.masonsneedlecraft.co.uk
Oxfordshire	Oxford	Port Meadow Designs	104 Walton Street		OX2 6EB	01865 311008	
Scotland	**Edinburgh**	**Jenners (Rowan At)**	**48 Princes Street**		**EH2 2YJ**	**0131 225 2442**	
Scotland	**Aberdeen**	**John Lewis (Rowan At)**	**George Street**		**AB9 1BT**	**01224 625000**	
Scotland	**Edinburgh**	**John Lewis (Rowan At)**	**St James Centre**		**EH1 3SP**	**0131 556 9121**	
Scotland	**Glasgow**	**John Lewis (Rowan At)**	**Buchanan Galleries**		**G4 0BZ**	**0141 353 6677**	
Scotland	Glasgow	Mandors	13 Renfrew Street	fabric@mandors.co.uk	G3 6ST	0141 332 7716	www.mandors.co.uk
Scotland	**Edinburgh**	**McAree Bros (Rowan At)**	**19 Howe Street**	**sales@mcadirect.com**	**EH3 6TE**	**0131 558 1747**	**www.mcadirect.com**
Scotland	**Stirling**	**McAree Bros (Rowan At)**	**55-59 King Street**	**sales@mcadirect.com**	**FK8 1DR**	**01786 465646**	www.mcadirect.com
Scotland	Gourock	Once A Sheep	60 Kempock Street	info@onceasheep.com	PA19 1ND	01475 648089	www.onceasheep.co.uk
Scotland	**Castle Douglas**	**Outback Yarns (Art 2 Go) (Rowan At)**	**130-132 King Street**	**sarahmckie@btinternet.com**	**DG7 1LU**	**01556 504900**	**www.outbackyarns.com**
Scotland	Hamilton	Stitching Time	14 Haddon Street	getit@stitchingtime.co.uk	ML3 7HX	01698 424025	
Scotland	**Aberdeen**	**The Wool Shed (Rowan At)**	**Ryehill, Oyne**	**info@thewoolshed.co.uk**	**AB52 6QS**	**01464 851539**	**www.thewoolshed.co.uk,**
Scotland	Fife	Twist Fibre Craft Studio	88 High Street, Newburgh	enquiries@twistfibrecraft.co.uk	KY14 6AQ	01337 842843	www.twistfibrecraft.co.uk
Scotland	Berkwickshire	Woolfish	Northfield Farm, St Abbs	louise@woolfish.co.uk	TD14 5QF	01890 771133	www.woolfish.co.uk
Scotland	Aberdeen	Wool for Ewe	83-85 Rosemount Place	info@woolforewe.co.uk	AB25 2YE	01224 643738	
Shropshire	Telford	House of Fraser	244-250 New Row, Town Centre		TF3 4BS	0870 607 2838	
Shropshire	Much Wenlock	Ippikin	59 The High Street	info@ippikin.com	TF13 6AE	01952 728371	www.ippikin.com

County	Town	Shop	Address	Email	Postcode	Phone	Website
Shropshire	Ludlow	The Wool Shop (Rowan At)	13 Broad Street		SY8 1NG	01584 872988	
Somerset	Taunton	Hayes Wools Ltd	150 East Reach		TA1 3HT	01823 284768	
Somerset	Minehead	Jana Henrie	High Street, Porlock	info@janahenrie.com	TA24 8SP	01643 862058	www.janahenrie.com
Somerset	Frome	Marmalade Yarns	11 Catherine Hill	CatrionaandMaxine@marmaladeyarns.co.uk	BA11 1BZ	01373 473557	www.marmaladeyarns.co.uk
Somerset	Clevedon	The Spinning Weal	63 Hill Road	mail@spinningweal.com	BS21 7NZ	01275 876000	www.spinningweal.com
South Yorkshire	Sheffield	John Lewis (Rowan At)	Barkers Pool		S1 1EP	0114 2768511	
Staffordshire	Newcastle under Lyme	K2Tog (Rowan At)	97 High Street, Wolstanton	sales@cucumberpatch.com	ST5 0EP	01782 862332	www.cucumberpatch.co.uk
Staffordshire	Lichfield	The Knitting Corner (Rowan At)	Unit 3, Curborough Hall Farm, Watery Lane	theknittingcorner@btinternet.com	WS13 8ES	01543 415837	
Suffolk	Woodbridge	Anjays Fabrics	11 Gobbitts Yard		IP12 1DD	01394 387593	
Suffolk	Bungay	Knit and Yarn	3 Upper Olland Street	gillybell@knitandyarn.co.uk	NR35 1BD	01986 895400	www.knitandyarn.co.uk
Suffolk	Hadleigh	Threadneedle Fabrics	28 High Street		IP7 5AP	01473 824040	
Suffolk	Bury St Edmunds	Wibbling Wools	24b Angel Hill	lynz@wibblingwools.co.uk	IP33 1UZ	01284 749555	www.wibblingwools.co.uk
Surrey	Guildford	C & H Fabrics	6 Tunsgate Square		GU1 3QZ	01483 301380	www.candh.co.uk
Surrey	Camberley	House of Fraser	45-51 Park Street		GU15 3PG	08701 607230	
Surrey	Kingston	John Lewis (Rowan At)	Wood Street		KT1 1TE	020 8547 3000	
Surrey	Carshalton Beaches	Maxime Wools	68 Banstead Road		SM5 3NL	020 8661 5625	www.maximewools.co.uk
Surrey	Guildford	Pandora (Rowan At)	196 High Street	sales@stitch1knit1.com	GU1 3HZ	01483 572558	www.stitch1knit1.com
Surrey	Caterham on the Hill	The Yarn House	27 High Street	sales@theyarnhouse.co.uk	CR3 5UE	01883 345220	www.theyarnhouse.co.uk
Teeside	Guisborough	Leven Crafts	7-9 Chaloner Mews, Chaloner Street	info@levencrafts.co.uk	TS14 6SA	01287 610207	www.levencrafts.co.uk
The Wirrall	Brimstage	Voirrey Embroidery Centre	Brimstage Hall	mail@voirrey.com	CH63 6JA	0151 342 3514,	www.voirrey.com
Tyne & Wear	Newcastle upon Tyne	John Lewis (Rowan At)	Eldon Square		NE99 1AB	0191 232 5000	
Tyne & Wear	Whitley Bay	Ring a Rosie (Rowan At)	272/274 Whitley Bay	loweringarosie@aol.com	NE26 2TG	0191 252 8874	www.ringarosie.co.uk
Tyne & Wear	Newcastle upon Tyne	The Knit Studio	Blackfriars	annemakepeace@btopenworld.com	NE1 4XN	07540 277764	
Wales	Conwy	Ar-y-Gweill	8 Heol Yr Orsaf, Llanrwst		LL26 0EP	01492 641149	
Wales	Aberystwyth	Clare's Wools	13 Great Darkgate Street	webenquiries@clarewools.co.uk	SA23 1DE	01970 617786	www.clarewools.co.uk
Wales	Whitland	Colourway (Rowan At)	Market Street	shop@colourway.co.uk	SA34 0AJ	01994 241333	www.colourway.co.uk
Wales	Anglesey	Copperfield, Four Mile	Bridge Road Valley		LL65 4HB	01407 740982	
Wales	Monmouth	Cotton Angel	2 Church Street	info@thecottonangel.com	NP25 3BU	01600 713548	www.thecottonangel.com
Wales	Fishguard	Jane's of Fishguard	14 High Street		SA65 9AR	01348 874443	www.janes-fishguard.co.uk
Wales	Cardiff	John Lewis (Rowan At)	The Hayes		CF10 1EG	029 2053 6000	
Wales	Port Talbot	W T Hopkins (Port Talbot) Ltd.	110 Fairways, Sandfields	williamhopkins@btconnect.com	SA12 7HR	01639 889244	
Wales	Penarth	Yarn & Yarns	22 Cornerswell Road		CF64 2UZ	02920 712097	
Warwickshire	Shipston on Stour	Shipston on Stour Needlecraft (Rowan At)	24/26 Sheep Street	info@needlework.co.uk	CV36 4AF	01608 661616	www.needlework.co.uk
Warwickshire	Warwick	Warwick Wools	17 Market Place		CV34 4SA	01926 492853	www.warwickwools.co.uk
West Midlands	Coventry	Busy Fingers	29 City Arcade		CV1 3HX	02476 559644	
West Midlands	Solihull	House of Fraser	Warwick Road		B91 3DU	0870 607 2836	
West Midlands	Sutton Coldfield	House of Fraser	132-138 The Parade, Gracechurch Centre		B72 1PB	0870 607 2837	
West Midlands	Wolverhampton	House of Fraser (Rowan At)	71-78 Victoria Street		WV1 3PQ	01902 422311	
West Midlands	Solihull	John Lewis (Rowan At)	Touchwood		B90 4SH	0121 704 1121	
West Midlands	Coventry	Mrs T's (Rowan At)	55 Winsford Avenue, Allesley Park	mrstcoventry@btinternet.com	CV5 9JG	02476 713105	
West Sussex	Chichester	C & H Fabrics	33/34 North Street		PO19 1LX.	01243 783300	www.candh.co.uk
West Sussex	Shoreham by Sea	Shoreham Knitting (Rowan At)	19 East Street	sales@englishyarns.co.uk	BN43 5ZE	01273 461029	www.englishyarns.co.uk
West Yorkshire	Nr Hebden Bridge	Attica (Rowan At)	Unit 2, Brier Hey Business Park, Mytholmroyd	info@attica-yarns.co.uk	HX7 5PF	01422 884885	www.attica-yarns.co.uk
West Yorkshire	Leeds	Baa Ram Ewe	87 Otley Road, Headingley	info@baaramewe.co.uk	LS6 3PS	0113 278 1788	www.baaramewe.co.uk
West Yorkshire	Ilkley	Create (Rowan At)	Victorian Arcade, South Hawkworth St.	info@createcafe.co.uk	LS29 9DY	01943 817788	www.createcafe.co.uk
West Yorkshire	Holmfirth	Up Country (Rowan At)	78 Huddersfield Road	info@upcountry.co.uk	HD9 3AZ	01484 687803	www.upcountry.co.uk
Wiltshire	Trowbridge	Fabric Magic	7 Wicker Hill		BA14 8JS	01225 768833	
Wiltshire	Calne	Handi Wools	3 Oxford Road		SN11 8AA	01249 812081	
Worcestershire	Evesham	Cotswold Needlecraft	Evesham Country Park	info@cotswoldneedlecraft.co.uk	WR11 4TP	01386 761217	www.cotswoldneedlecraft.co.uk
Worcestershire	Worcester	House of Fraser	Crowngate		WR1 3LD	0870 607 2840	
Worcestershire	Malvern	The Knitting Parlour (Rowan At)	12 Graham Road	info@theknittingparlour.co.uk	WR14 2HN	01684 892079	www.theknittingparlour.co.uk
Worcestershire	Broadway	Wool in Broadway	2 Cotswold Court, The Green	pat.davies2@ntlworld.com	WR12 7AA	01386 853779	www.woolinbroadway.com

ROWAN INTERNET STOCKISTS

All Rowan Internet stockists offer secure online shopping facilities of a wide selection of Rowan products. ★ denotes retail store and internet

AUSTRALIA
www.sunspun.com.au — Sun Spun
www.woolshack.com — Wool Shack

FRANCE
www.leslaines.com — Les Lains
www.bleudetoiles.com — Bleu de Toiles
www.laine-et-co.fr — Laine and co
www.bouillon-de-couture.fr — Bouillon de Conture
www.laine-fil-et-blablabla.com
www.millemilliersdemailles.fr

GERMANY
www.wolleundesign.de — Wolle Design

JAPAN
www.rowan-jaeger.com

KOREA
www.myknit.com — My Knit

SWEDEN
www.wincentgarner.se — Wincentgarner

UK
www.colourway.co.uk — Colourway
www.cucumberpatch.com — Cucumber Patch
www.englishyarns.co.uk — English Yarns
www.upcountry.co.uk — Up Country
www.celticove.com — Stash
www.thewoolshed.co.uk — The Wool Shed
www.theknittingparlour.co.uk — The Knitting Parlour
www.kangaroo.uk.com — Kangaroo
www.laughinghens.com — Laughing Hens
www.getknitted.com — Get Knitted
www.craftywoolshop.co.uk — Crafty Wool Shop
www.almondhouse.co.uk — Almond House

www.lanapura.com — Lana Pura
www.jannettesrareyarns.co.uk — Jannette's Rare Yarns
www.mcadirect.com — McA Direct
www.knitsinthecity.co.uk — Knits in the City
www.serenityknitting.co.uk — Serenity Knitting
www.greatbritishyarns.co.uk — Great British Yarns
www.ethknits.co.uk — Peachey Ethknits
www.whichcrafts.co.uk — Whichcrafts?
www.mrsmacs.co.uk — Mrs Macs
www.attica-yarns.co.uk — Attica
www.wightyarns.webeden.co.uk — Wight Yarns
www.hulucrafts.co.uk — Hulu
www.createwithwool.co.uk — Create With Wool
www.fivevalleydesigns.com — Five Valley Designs
www.sandcastleyarns.co.uk — Sandcastle Yarns
www.artofyarn.co.uk — Art of Yarn

USA
www.colorful-stitches.com — Colorful Stitches
www.jimmybeanswool.com — Jimmy Beans Wool
www.royalyarns.com — Royal Yarns
www.yarnmarket.com — Yarn Market
www.letsknit.com — Sakonnet Purls
www.hamptonknittingyarn.com — Hampton Knitting Yarn
www.yarnatwebsters.com — Yarn at Websters

FABRICS - UK
www.antiqueangel.co.uk — Antique Angel Ltd
www.quilterscloth.co.uk — Quilters Cloth
www.saintsandpinners.co.uk — Saints and Pinners
www.greatbritishyarns.co.uk — Great British Yarns
www.gonetoearth.co.uk — Gone To Earth
www.tikkilondon.com — Tikki Limited
www.fabricsplus.co.uk — Fabrics Plus

ROWAN YARNS, GREEN LANE MILL, HOLMFIRTH, WEST YORKSHIRE, ENGLAND TEL: +44 (0)1484 681881

THE DESIGN GALLERY

ILLUSION

FANTASY
Purelife Organic Cotton 4 ply
Marie Wallin
Pattern page 147
Main image page 4, 6 & 7

BEGUILE
Kidsilk Haze
Fine Milk Cotton
Lisa Richardson
Pattern page 146
Main image page 8 & 9

MIRAGE
Kidsilk Haze
Marie Wallin
Pattern page 116
Main image page 10 & 11

FANCY
Kidsilk Haze
Erika Knight
Pattern page 99
Main image page 12

ILLUSION WRAP
Purelife Organic Cotton 4 ply
Marie Wallin
Pattern page 150
Main image page 13

ALLURE
Purelife Organic Cotton 4 ply
Lisa Richardson
Pattern page 106
Main image page 14 & 15

WONDER
Fine Milk Cotton
Martin Storey
Pattern page 108
Main image page 16 & 17

DAYDREAM
Purelife Organic Cotton 4 ply
Marie Wallin
Pattern page 101
Main image page 18 & 19

SUMMER ESSENTIALS

GENTIAN
Siena 4 ply
Grace Melville
Pattern page 123
Main image page 32 & 34

FOXTAIL
Cotton Glacé
Martin Storey
Pattern page 100
Main image page 35

CLEAVERS
Lenpur™ Linen
Erika Knight
Pattern page 124
Main image page 36 & 37

CICELY
Cotton Glacé
Grace Melville
Pattern page 127
Main image page 38

LOBELIA
Cotton Glacé
Sarah Dallas
Pattern page 134
Main image page 39

TEASEL
Lenpur™ Linen
Sarah Hatton
Pattern page 104
Main image page 40 & 41

HONESTY
Siena 4 ply
Marie Wallin
Pattern page 133
Main image page 42 & 43

HELLEBORE
Cotton Glacé
Martin Storey
Pattern page 113
Main image page 44 & 45

HOMESPUN

FULFILL
Purelife Revive
Lisa Richardson
Pattern page 139
Main image page 66

WHOLESOME
Denim & Pima Cotton DK
Jennie Atkinson
Pattern page 152
Main image page 68 & 69

HOME
Denim
Martin Storey
Pattern page 121
Main image page 70 & 71

ALLAY
Pima Cotton DK
Lisa Richardson
Pattern page 136
Main image page 72 & 73

SOOTHE
Lenpur™ Linen
Marie Wallin
Pattern page 137
Main image page 74 & 75

COMFORT
Pima Cotton DK
Erika Knight
Pattern page 110
Main image page 76

TEASE
Denim
Grace Melville
Pattern page 142
Main image page 77

POISE
Pima Cotton DK
Sarah Hatton
Pattern page 128
Main image page 78 & 79